Hitler was my Friend

Hitler's personal photographer, Heinrich Hoffman, assists in compiling evidence against late Führer's henchmen.

Hitler was my Friend

Translated by
Lt. Col R.H. Stevens

FRONTLINE BOOKS

Hitler was my Friend

This edition published in 2011 by Frontline Books,
an imprint of
Pen & Sword Books Limited,
47 Church Street, Barnsley, S. Yorkshire, S70 2AS
www.frontline-books.com

Email info@frontline-books.com or write to us at the above
address.

ISBN: 978-1-84832-608-8

Publishing History
Hitler was my Friend was first published by Burke Publishing
Company Ltd, London, in 1955. This edition has a new
introduction by Roger Moorhouse.

CIP data records for this title are available from the
British Library

Typeset by Mac Style, Beverley, UK
Printed and bound by CPI Group (UK) Ltd, Croydon, CR0 4YY

Contents

Preface

MY IMMEDIATE REACTION on reading the manuscript of Heinrich Hoffmann's *Hitler was my Friend* was a feeling of satisfaction that, though it features him so prominently in its title, this was not 'just another book on Hitler', about whom so much of both fact and nonsense has already been written, but the autobiography of a man, remarkable in both character and experience, already established long before Hitler was ever heard of, as one of the foremost photographers of his age: and one who merits interest in his own right and richly rewards the interest we accord him.

A man who has achieved so outstanding a success in his own profession must, I felt, be both ripe in experience and interesting in his reminiscences; a man who enjoyed Hitler's friendship and complete confidence for twenty-five years, and by so doing incurred the implacable and jealous hatred of the other Nazi leaders – and still survived – must possess both wit and resource; a man who, on the threshold of old age, suffers such violent reversals of fortune – from riches to penury, from security and comfort to the stark rigours of gaol – and still faces life with undiminished zest and vigour, must possess both character and courage to a high degree; and finally, a man who, on interrogation, was so swiftly and unconditionally released by our American allies cannot, obviously, be a criminal or, indeed, a bad sort of chap at all.

I was myself not ignorant of the Nazis and their ways. As a staff officer on special intelligence duties I had fenced with them and delved into their activities and secrets; as a prisoner in the hands of the Gestapo I had indulged in a desperate battle of wits, and had acquired a thorough insight into their methods of interrogation; and as an inmate for more than five years of Sachsenhausen and Dachau concentration camps, I had had more than a taste of their treatment of prisoners; and so, when I was invited to go to Munich and discuss the translation with Professor Hoffmann, I accepted with alacrity.

The figure I met was that of a short, comfortably tubby little man. Crowned by a shock of iron-grey hair was a strong and purposeful face, marked with the unmistakable stamp of suffering, which was belied by a pair of bright, merry and quickly twinkling eyes. The hand stretched out in greeting to me was small, tapering and beautifully moulded – the hand of an artist. Round the corners of a firm but sensitive mouth the lines drawn by bitter experience struggled in vain for mastery with a smile of irrepressible and bubbling good humour. His speech and gestures were rapid and expressive, and all his movements had the engaging swift pertness of a bird.

The plea of no interest or participation in politics is an apologia that we have recently heard *ad nauseam* from so many Germans, that we are rightly inclined to treat it with extreme scepticism. But my contact with this genial, happy-go-lucky *bon viveur,* this essentially bohemian, artistic Heinrich Hoffmann quickly convinced me that in his case, at least, the statement was completely true; and I cannot but feel that the reader, when he reaches the end of this book, will share my conviction.

I spent some weeks in constant daily company with Hoffmann, and in that time an impulsive, spontaneous creature, such as he is, will draw a picture of himself, crystal clear for anyone with eyes to look and ears to listen. He is a typical bohemian, grandiloquent in phrase and gesture, generous, unpractical, perhaps not always strictly accurate, but a born raconteur; in many ways a child, yet withal a shrewd judge of men; and whatever else might be said of him, he would never do a shabby thing, and he is steadfast in his loyalties.

To say of anyone so close to the Nazi throne that he hated injustice is to invite incredulity and derision. But Heinrich Hoffmann did hate injustice, and he hated cruelty. Whenever he came into personal contact with some case of stupid injustice or senseless cruelty he boldly called – not upon the Führer and Reichskanzler, but on his friend, Adolf Hitler, to rectify it; many a man incarcerated by a ruthless Gestapo was released as a result of his intervention – and a mass of grateful letters bears eloquent witness to the fact. 'You know, Colonel, this book of mine is a bit of a patchwork,' Hoffmann assured me in, for him, quite earnest tones, when we came to the end of our labours. 'A patchwork of reminiscence and impression; of events in which I took part and of people who played leading roles in them and whom I knew intimately. But it does not claim to make any particular contribution to history.'

In this I am inclined to think he is being overmodest. The responsible historian, with archives and records at his disposal, strives to give an accurate and factual account of events, to add perhaps to the sum total of our historical knowledge and, with comment justified by his profound research, to submit explanations and perhaps some new light for acceptance or rejection by his readers.

In this sense, admittedly, Hoffmann makes 'no particular contribution'. He confines himself to purely personal aspects, and while the earlier portion of his memoirs, from the peace and security of the opening years of the century through the turmoil of the first war and its aftermath, make lively, interesting and entertaining reading, it is, in the nature of things, on his uniquely intimate association with Hitler, from the earliest beginnings of the Nazi Party to its final annihilation, that our interest is primarily concentrated.

As colour and the deft addition of highlights to a portrait

bring life, warmth and reality to what is otherwise merely an academically correct drawing, so Hoffmann's personal descriptions – the atmosphere in the Führer's personal entourage, the vanity and jealousy of Ribbentrop, the keen intelligence and scathing sarcasm of Goebbels, the ruthless brutality of Bormann, the verbal snapshots of leading international statesmen, Hitler, the man – his shyness and austerity, his devotion to art, his attitude towards, and his influence over, women – all these things add highlights to the bare findings of historical research, and by so doing do, surely, make a contribution, and quite a fascinating contribution, if not to history itself, then at least to our better comprehension of it.

R.H. STEVENS

Mr. & Mrs. Leon Alderman
1272 Mapleview Street S.E.
Grand Rapids, MI 49508

Introduction

HISTORY HAS NOT been kind to Heinrich Hoffmann. At best, Hitler's former 'court' photographer is viewed as a genial buffoon; a 'useful idiot' whose artistic talents were exploited for Hitler's benefit. At worst, he is seen as an active and convinced acolyte; an aider and abettor of the 20th Century's most infamous dictator.

Whatever the precise degree of his complicity, Hoffmann's importance to the history of the Third Reich is incontrovertible. From their first meeting, in the sweaty, seething beerhalls of post-First World War Munich, Hoffmann and Hitler forged a personal friendship and professional alliance that would prove highly beneficial to both. Hitler secured the services of a photographer of considerable talent and ingenuity, whilst Hoffmann would, in time, hold a highly lucrative, virtual monopoly over pictures of the Nazi leader. And, though Hitler was far from being an ingenue in matters of public image and propaganda, it was Hoffmann who was chiefly responsible for converting his ideas into celluloid and print.

It was Hoffmann, therefore, more than any other, who shaped Hitler's public image and charted the rise of the Third Reich. Hoffmann's pictures of the Führer were sold worldwide, used for newspapers, magazines, postcards, placards and posters, even postage stamps. His pictures were ubiquitous: adored in countless German homes, just as they were often vilified abroad.

His published works alone – richly illustrated, coffee-table volumes – tell the story of the Third Reich as it presented itself to its own people. One series, for instance, shows the evolution and propagation of Hitler's image; *Hitler wie ihn keiner kennt*, "Hitler as Nobody knows him" (1935), *Hitler abseits vom Alltag* "Hitler off-duty" (1937) or *Das Antlitz des Führers*, "The Face of the Führer" (1939). Another, charts the expansion of Hitler's Reich; *Hitler baut Grossdeutschland*, "Hitler builds Greater Germany" (1938), *Hitler befreit Sudetenland*, "Hitler liberates the Sudetenland" (1938) or *Mit Hitler in Polen*, "With Hitler in Poland" (1939). In this way, Hoffmann provided the primary visual record for an entire generation of Germans.

Hoffmann's influence was not restricted to the realms of art and propaganda, however. Unusually amongst the leading cadre of the Third Reich, Hoffmann was older than Hitler, and as an established professional in his own right, was arguably more independent of the Führer than most of his fellows. Uniquely perhaps, he came closest amongst them – as the title of this memoir claims – to genuinely claiming Hitler as a friend. And this was a friendship that would have a number of not insignificant consequences. Firstly, it was through Hoffmann that Hitler came into contact with Dr Theodor Morell, who would later – and infamously – become his personal physician. Secondly, Hitler's mistress and later spouse, Eva Braun, first met Hitler when she was a humble assistant in Hoffmann's photographic studio in Munich.

Given this significance, it is perhaps understandable that Hoffmann should have suffered from the righteous indignation of his (and his master's) enemies in the immediate post-war years. Yet, it is more surprising that he continues to inspire opprobrium, with many apparently mistaking the messenger for the message. In his excellent study of the Nazi aesthetic, for instance, Frederic Spotts unfairly describes him as "a cretin and an alcoholic".[1] Hoffmann's significance as a photographer, it appears, is still overshadowed by his close connection to Hitler.

Leaving aside the odious political context in which he worked, it should be obvious that Hoffmann was actually one of the most important photographers of the 20th century. No other photographer in history landed the scoop that he did: intimate and exclusive access to a major head of state – and importantly, the chance to work with a subject who knew very well how to 'work' the camera, and paid painstaking attention to the cultivation of his public image.

Importantly, once handed that scoop, Hoffmann had the technological and artistic wherewithal to make the most of the opportunity. Rather than some Nazi upstart or placeman, he was already an established photographer by the time he first met Hitler in the aftermath of World War One. He had initially served an apprenticeship in the studio of his father, who had been court photographer to the Bavarian Royal family. He also photographed the Russian Imperial family and worked in Switzerland and under the renowned E. O. Hoppé in England, before returning to Munich to set up a studio in his own right in 1909. It would be Hoffmann who would take the iconic picture of the crowd celebrating the outbreak of World War One on the Odeonsplatz in 1914, in which a young Adolf Hitler was subsequently discovered.[2] Hoffmann, therefore, was a talented and accomplished photographer already long before the world heard the name of his most famous patron.

Hoffmann should also be counted as a pioneer of modern photo-journalism. Using the newly-developed Leica 35mm camera, he was amongst the first to take photography out of the stilted surroundings of the studio and into the real world beyond. Though he is perhaps synonymous with the rather more formal, posed portraits of Adolf Hitler and many of the other senior figures of the Third Reich, a glance at other pictures in his oeuvre quickly reveal that behind the propagandist there was a photographer of considerable talent and artistic merit.

The resulting body of photographs is arguably the most complete and comprehensive record of a wartime leader and his court, amounting – at Hoffmann's own estimate - to over two million images. Nothing on a similar scale emerged from any of Hitler's rivals. Hitler would be one of the most photographed men in history, and it was invariably Hoffmann who was behind the camera. If one can recall an image of Hitler – used at any time during the last 80 or so years – the chances are that it was taken by Heinrich Hoffmann.

Those images, tellingly, are still widely used today, even by those who deride the man who took them. With few exceptions, almost every one of the countless volumes dedicated to the subject of Hitler and the Third Reich every year, carries at least one Hoffmann image on its pages. A brief search of "Adolf Hitler" images available on the internet merely confirms this ubiquity. Yet, strangely, the name of Hoffmann rarely appears. Accused of profiteering after the war, Heinrich Hoffmann was stripped of his possessions and his archive was dispersed, with much of it finding its way either to the US National Archive in Washington, or later to the Bavarian State Archive in Munich. Hoffmann, therefore, is perhaps the world's most famous, unknown photographer.

When this memoir was first published, in the mid-1950s, Hoffmann was nearly 70 years of age and was approaching the end of his life. He was, in many ways, a broken man; the empire that he had created under the Third Reich – one in which he remarkably had earned a royalty even for stamps which bore his images of Hitler – had been smashed. Branded as a 'major offender' by the victorious Allies, he was subjected to a seemingly interminable round of interrogations, interviews and internments, in which he was only succoured by the attentions of his wife, Erna. When he was finally released in 1950, he was penniless.

Yet, for all that, the tone of his memoir is generally an upbeat one. The garrulous purveyor of anecdotes, so beloved of Hitler, comes across well and, incongruously perhaps, he is a genial guide through the period. His portrayal of Hitler – with whom he spent so many hours and days in often intimate contact – gives an illuminating glimpse of the dictator's personal appeal and charisma.

But, aside from this proximity to Hitler, Hoffmann was also a remarkable eye-witness to salient moments in the history of the Third Reich and its leader. One is accustomed, perhaps, to photographers recording events through the lens of their camera, but Hoffmann's reminiscences are often just as revealing. When Hitler withdrew into himself after the death of Geli Raubal in 1931, for instance, it was Hoffmann who coaxed him back from the depths of despair. When Hitler was appointed Chancellor in 1933, Hoffmann was waiting in an ante-room and was the first to congratulate Germany's new, rather over-excited, leader. And, when the Nazi-Soviet Pact was agreed in 1939, Hoffmann was one of those who were sent to Moscow to record the event for posterity. His presence at moments such as these make him a fascinating and vitally important source for the historian and the layman alike.

Of course, there is precious little sense of *mea culpa* in Hoffmann's account. Though he does not address the issue directly, one must infer that he did not feel that he had done anything for which he had to apologise. On the contrary, indeed, his is a rather self-serving, glossed version of events, in which even his least edifying chapter – that of his dubious involvement in Hitler's acquisition of artworks – is presented in a rather chirpy, harmless tone.

The view that Hoffmann gives is generally a rosy one; of lunches with the Führer and his entourage; of the cultural battles at home, rather than the real battles abroad. It is very much life seen from the perspective of the blinkered, cosseted inner circle of the Third Reich, with no hint of the darkness, corruption and horror that the regime propagated elsewhere. Indeed, when Hoffmann bemoans his fate after 1945 – being shunted from one prison or internment camp to another, with little prospect of release – one is tempted to juxtapose his experience with those of many of his countrymen and others who had languished in the prisons of the Nazi Regime. He fails to make the connection himself, of course, but the irony of his predicament is patently obvious.

Politically, Hoffmann *was* ambiguous. In these pages he claims that he was uninterested in politics *per se* and never sought or accepted high office within the Nazi regime, preferring the status of the privileged outsider. This is largely convincing; Hoffmann does not come across as a political animal, and it seems clear that his relationship with Hitler was one that was born primarily out of a personal, rather than an ideological affinity. But a few points serve to contradict his claims to political ignorance, not least his closeness to the Nazi ideologue (and Hitler's former mentor) Dietrich Eckart, and the fact that his membership of the Nazi Party actually predated Hitler's own. It may be, of course, that Hoffmann was indeed apolitical, and that he was simply an inhabitant of a highly Nazified milieu, but the question of his political motivations is one that the critical reader might like to bear in mind.

Despite, or perhaps because of, such unanswered questions, this is a fascinating memoir from a man whose importance in the wider history of the Third Reich, whilst undeniable, has traditionally been overlooked. Like many of the other books in the series – by Hitler's secretary Christa Schroeder, his valet Heinz Linge, or his driver Erich Kempka – Hoffmann's memoir affords us an illuminating view of Hitler as he was seen by those who were closest to him. But it also provides something more – it invites us to muse on the vexed question of whether art in the service of evil can still be good.

© Roger Moorhouse 2011

Notes

1. Frederic Spotts, *Hitler and the Power of Aesthetics*, (London, 2002), p. 173.
2. There is an as yet unproven suspicion that Hitler's presence in the picture might have been faked by Hoffmann's studio. See, for instance, Sven Felix Kellerhoff, "Berühmtes Hitler-Foto möglicherweise gefälscht". In: *Die Welt Online*, 14. October, 2010.

Chapter 1

My Camera and the Kaiser

'HITLER'S PHOTOGRAPHER'. Those two words will probably suffice to recall me to the minds of those who are sufficiently interested to ask themselves – who is this Heinrich Hoffmann?

By profession I have always been a photographer, and by inclination a passionate devotee of the arts, a publisher of art journals and a devout, if modest, wielder of pencil and brush. I served my professional apprenticeship in the well-established studio of my father, and in my turn became a master-craftsman in my art. In the course of years, kings and princes, great artists, singers, writers, politicians and men and women famous in all walks of life paused before my camera for those few seconds that were all I required to perpetuate the person and the occasion.

It was purely in the course of those professional activities that I first came into contact with Adolf Hitler – a chance assignment from which sprang a deep and lasting friendship, a friendship that had nothing to do with politics, of which I knew little and cared less, or with self-interest, for at the time I was by far the more solidly established of the two of us; but one that flashed into being at the contact of two impulsive natures, and was based partly on a mutual devotion to art and partly, perhaps, on the attraction of opposites – the austere, teetotal, non-smoking Hitler on the one hand, and the happy-go-lucky, bohemian *bon viveur,* Heinrich Hoffmann on the other.

But equally it was a friendship that kept me, throughout the most violent, turbulent and chaotic years in the history of the world, closely at the side of the man who was the central figure in them. With Hitler, the Führer and Chancellor of the Third Reich, I have but little concern; but Adolf Hitler, the man, was my friend, from the time of his earliest beginnings to the day of his death. He returned my friendship and gave me his complete confidence; he looms large in the tale of my life.

It was in 1897 that I entered the family business as an apprentice. Over the studio shared in common by my father and my uncle in the Jesuitenplatz in Regensburg hung proudly a pompous shield, bearing the proud inscription –

HEINRICH HOFFMANN, COURT PHOTOGRAPHER
His Majesty, the King of Bavaria
His Royal Highness, the Grand Duke of Hesse
His Royal Highness, Duke Thomas of Genoa,
Prince of Savoy

This shield had been a fairly costly investment, for in order to obtain permission to use the title, one had had to make a pretty solid payment to the Court Marshal's Office. But my father and uncle lost no opportunity of pointing out with pride that they had not bought, but had earned the titles; and indeed they had photographed many of the members of the Wittelsbach royal family, as well as the Grand Duke von Hessen und bei Rhein, the Duke of Genoa and many other princes. In recognition of their meritorious performances in the art of photography they had been presented by the Prince Regent, Luitpold of Bavaria, with a handsome gold tie-pin, with a large L in brilliants, as a mark of his particular appreciation, and every Sunday there was always a voluble argument between the two partners as to whose turn it was to wear the royal pin!

When I started work, my most urgent task was to look after the head- and arm-rests that, in those days of long exposures, were used as supports for our illustrious clients and to guard them against the dangers of a stiff neck. In addition it was my duty to dust all those other props that were thought essential in every self-respecting studio. There was, for instance, a boat with all its sails set – a giant broken egg, into which naked babies were popped, giving the impression that the new citizen of the world had not been delivered by stork, but had been well and truly hatched, and many other monstrosities.

Our studio itself was designed in the Makart style, after the house of the once famous Viennese painter, Hans Makart, whose imposing picture, *The Entry of Charles V into Antwerp,* brought him such fame. When this picture was first exhibited in Vienna it aroused the greatest possible excitement. Indeed, among its naked hetairae many a husband of Viennese society thought he recognised his wife, who had obviously posed for the artist and had been faithfully and completely perpetuated for all time; and a crop of suicides and divorces had been the result.

In those days I simply loathed Makart, because the copies of his bouquets, which hung in profusion on our walls, his gilded vases stuccoed with rice and his picture frames were one and all quite exceptional as receptacles for dust.

One Sunday afternoon, just as I was about to close the studio, a man came in.

'I want my photo taken!' he declared abruptly.

With suitable expressions of regret I told him that there was no one available who could fulfil his wish.

'Well – you're here! You take me!'

I declined. 'I'm sorry,' I said, 'but I'm afraid I'm not competent.' The man, however, was not to be denied and assumed a threatening attitude; and so I took my decision, trembling and protesting all the time that I could not guarantee a good picture. Taking not the slightest notice of me, the man went into the dressing room and from his suitcase took out a new suit of clothes.

Having packed his discarded clothes into the suitcase, he assumed his pose. I disappeared beneath the black cloth, focused the camera and with a thumping heart stammered the conventional, 'Now – smile and look pleasant, please!'

The man stood as expressionless as a memorial statue. When the sitting was over, my forceful client departed, leaving his suitcase behind him and saying that he'd pick it up later, when he called for the photographs. The photograph turned out to be a very good one. With pride I showed it to my father and uncle. But the client never returned, either to collect his photograph or to retrieve his belongings.

Weeks later, we opened the suitcase and found that, in addition to the old suit, it contained a purse full of gold coins and an air gun. The police established the fact that the money and the suitcase had belonged to a peasant woman who had been found murdered in the vicinity of Regensburg. Later it was further established that the murderer had enticed his victim to come out of her cottage by imitating the cries of agitated hens! But of more interest to the police than this find was the photograph I had taken. It appeared on the 'WANTED' notice boards of all police stations, and so my first photograph was a great sensation.

My apprenticeship ended in 1900, but I was to have remained in the family business until I attained my majority. I myself, however, was anxious to be off; and so at the age of sixteen, I found myself working for Hugo Thiele, Court Photographer to the Grand Duke von Hessen, in Darmstadt, and to me it was most interesting to be allowed to help with the photographing of members of the Grand Ducal family, who frequently patronised my employer.

About this time the Artists' Colony founded by the Grand Duke was opened on the Mathildenhöhe. This exhibition, which opened up new vistas in both architecture and art, was a great success and had a marked effect throughout Germany, not only on art, but also on photography. It was from Darmstadt that the revolutionary movement started to get rid of the old baronial hall drop-curtain, the palms, the battlements and all the other monstrosities and fustian that cluttered up the photographer's studio, and instead, with natural lighting and in natural surroundings, to give an entirely new look to photographic portraiture. Weimer, another leading photographer of Darmstadt, was the first to cast aside all these old impedimenta and to strive to replace the artificiality of the posed portrait with an easy, natural picture. Whenever he could, he always preferred to photograph his clients in their own homes, surrounded by their own belongings, at ease in an atmosphere that was familiar to them, rather than have them come to his studio.

When, as often happened, we were commanded to the Grand Ducal Palace to take photographs, there was always great excitement. The Grand Ducal court, thanks to the close family ties that bound it to all the most powerful princely houses of Europe, enjoyed at that time an importance out of all proportion to the size of the State. Of the three sisters of the reigning duke, Ernst Ludwig, all of whom I saw when they were being photographed during various visits to their brother, one had married Prince Henry of Prussia, the second had married into the Russian Royal Family, while the third, Princess Victoria Elizabeth, had become the wife of Prince Louis of Battenberg, who later became the Marquess of Milford Haven.

I was at the time profoundly impressed by the air of tragic melancholy that hovered over the great ladies from Russia, like an omen of the terrible fate that was later to destroy them. The Tsarina was always shy and aloof in the presence of strangers, and she always seemed to be relieved when the business of taking photographs was completed. Her much more beautiful sister, the Princess Sergei, was more gracious and natural. I heard later that after her husband had been murdered, she visited the murderer in his Moscow cell and with truly divine patience tried to find out the motive for the crime; and that finally, like a true angel of mercy, she had forgiven him.

It was axiomatic that our illustrious clients should not be

incommoded in any way, and we did our utmost to speed up the process as much as possible. Any delay in placing the camera in position, any long drawn-out correction of the pose called forth a sharp reprimand and an urge to swifter dexterity. The Grand Ducal family tired easily and was inclined to be impatient.

A dark room had been fitted up in the Palace, and plates were developed as soon as they had been exposed. In this way, in the event of any failure, the photo could swiftly be taken again. The developing was part of my duties, and on one occasion during a visit of the Princess Sergei, I was hastening into the dark-room, when a gentleman who was unknown to me asked if he might come with me, as he was very interested in the process of developing.

Cordially I invited him to accompany me. While at work, I asked him whether he thought it would be possible for me to catch a glimpse of the Grand Duke? My interest, I explained, was heightened by the fact that our family studio bore the proud title 'Heinrich Hoffmann, Court Photographer to the Grand Duke Ernst Ludwig von Hessen und bei Rhein', but that, although I had been in the Palace often enough, I had so far never seen him.

'Furthermore,' I continued, 'I am really one of the Grand Duke's subjects, for my father was born in Darmstadt and served in the White Dragoons.'

'I think it might be arranged,' smiled my visitor, and as we left the darkroom together he thanked me and pressed a handsome tip into my hand. I was intrigued, and I asked a servant who the gentleman was.

It was none other than the Grand Duke himself, and he had presented me with a thaler with his portrait on it!

I was anxious to obtain practical experience in as many branches of photographic art as possible, and so, in 1901 I thought the time had come to move on, and I went to Heidelberg, to work for Langbein, the University photographer. Langbein made a speciality of photographing the *Mensur* – the famous students' duels, and my part therein was the tinting-in of the student corps' caps and sashes.

In those days the students ruled the roost in Heidelberg, and His Majesty the Student reigned supreme – in our studio as everywhere else in the town. Many an old gentleman, I am sure, has one of those *Mensur* photographs, which we took with such pains and care, still hanging above his desk. Each individual participant, and sometimes specific groups of participants, had to be photographed separately in the studio. Then each figure had to be cut out most carefully and pasted on to the photograph of the empty Duelling Hall, which formed the background. Finally this composite picture had to be re-photographed and the net result gave a vivid impression of a furious duel in full progress. To achieve correct perspective, any figures standing in the background had to be reduced to the appropriate size, and Langbein certainly possessed exceptional skill and produced most realistic and life like results.

In 1902 I was on the move again – this time to Frankfurt, to work in the Theobald studio, the speciality of which was soldiers' portraits. The 'military photographer' was not considered to rank among the artists of his profession, but I consoled myself with the thought that in order to master everything one had to try one's hand at anything.

The studio was situated exactly opposite the barracks. Our great day was Sunday, and on that day the sons of Mars used to pour in to have the glamour of their 'review order' perpetuated in a photograph. Soldiers are tricky clients. They were up in arms at the slightest inaccuracy, and the minutest little crease in a uniform roused their ire. We had to watch every little thing like hawks. Tinted photographs were very popular, and these enabled me to earn a little 'on the side'. The price for tinting a photograph was one mark; those who merely wished for a gaily-coloured lanyard paid fifty pfennigs, while those who desired the sprouting of their incipient moustaches to be emphasised a charge of thirty pfennigs was made. Half of what I earned from this sideline I had to give to my employer; and the other half he regularly took off me at cards in the evenings.

When I started work for Theobald, I wanted to reform the art of military photography. Usually, the young warriors stood in what is called the 'at-ease' position, with a fixed and glassy stare directed on the camera, as if they were momentarily expecting a stream of Sergeant-Major's incivilities to emerge from it. My motto was: Let us abandon the 'memorial' type of picture and have instead a more informal pose and a 'smile, please' expression. But my attempt was a dismal failure. I got one soldier to put one knee negligently on the edge of a chair, and the result was quite shattering – the Army, it appeared, enlisted soldiers with one wooden leg!

I did not stay long with Theobald, for I only wanted to gain some experience of his type of work and had no intention of specialising in it, and early in 1903 I took up my next post, with Thomas Voigt, the famous Imperial Court Photographer, in his studio in Homburg. This, of course, was a very different type of work; Homburg, one of the most elegant and fashionable spas in Germany, was the playground of the British, of Russian grand dukes, princes, multi-millionaires and the high and mighty from all over the world. The international tennis tournaments were always interesting, for among the Upper Ten Thousand it was considered to be 'the thing' to be seen at them; and in the vicinity of the tennis courts I used to reap a rich harvest.

Among the many eccentric dignitaries with whom I came in contact in Homburg was Chulalongkorn, the King of Siam. Of his portraits he always ordered almost life-sized enlargements, most artistically tinted. These gigantic pictures had then to be packed in zinc-lined crates and sent to Siam. Without the flicker of an eyelid His Majesty paid the bill for 27,000 gold marks that we presented to him.

Of a somewhat unique character was my meeting with the Russian Grand Duke, Michael Michaelovitch. I was commanded to take his photograph, but, alas, I did not succeed in preserving it for posterity. As a matter of fact, His Imperial Highness was so imperially drunk, that the photo simply 'slipped off the plate,' as we say professionally. I took over a dozen pictures – and in the darkroom the distressing results of my labours became abundantly clear!

Taking photographs of the Kaiser afforded me my greatest thrills. On 5th November 1903, my chief was commanded to go and take photographs of the Kaiser on the occasion of his historic meeting with Tsar Nicholas of Russia at the old Schloss in Wiesbaden. Herr Voigt had got everything ready in the castle and had stationed me in the corridor to give warning of the Kaiser's approach; and there I waited and waited.

August personages always keep one waiting. At first one does not know how to pass the time, and then, when they do arrive, things can't happen fast enough. The Highest and the All-Highest in the land are graciously pleased to be damnably impatient!

At long last I saw a figure approaching along the dim corridor; all I could distinguish was the beard and the vertically turned-up moustache, the typical Kaiser Wilhelm II, known colloquially as the 'I've done it!' But as he drew nearer, the man, I saw, was in mufti – a morning coat, so, obviously it was not the Kaiser. It was, in fact, Haby, his personal hairdresser who, by introducing the moustache net, had helped to make the Kaiser Wilhelm moustache so popular throughout the country.

At last the Kaiser arrived, and what followed was a regular fancy dress ball! Wilhelm II, Honorary Colonel of innumerable foreign regiments, wished to be photographed in the current uniforms of all of them! And so, in a whirlwind – out of one uniform and into another; a colonel of Russian Guards, a British colonel, a colonel of the Royal Hungarian Hussars – Horse, Foot and Guns succeeded each other in bewildering array; of them all, the Hungarian Hussar with its gold-braided Attila was the most striking, and later the photo was destined to become extremely popular.

On another occasion, when the Kaiser was staying for a while at Schloss Friedrichsruh near Homburg, I found out that he had accepted an invitation to visit Herr Marx, the sub-prefect of the district, whom he esteemed highly. That, I thought, would make a fine photograph, and I found out exact details of time and place of the visit. In front of Herr Marx's villa I installed my camera on some scaffolding and sighted it carefully on a point that the Kaiser would be bound to pass as he left the villa. In front of me, a number of army veterans in frock coats and toppers and with gaily-coloured sashes across their chests had taken up their stand. In spite of their well-nourished rotundity they did their best to stand as erect as ramrods, though the effort was not in all cases successful.

Above this glistening roof of toppers stood my camera, fixedly aimed at the selected spot, with me beside it, perched on a rung of the scaffolding, gazing over the sea of heads and holding the rubber ball, ready to release the shutter. All I had to do was to wait and then I'd get him.

'Here comes the Kaiser!'

A rousing roar of hurrahs greeted his arrival. Enthusiastically the veterans hurled their toppers into the air in loyal acclaim of their War Lord. And I? All I did was to photograph a cloud of toppers flying through the air! By the time they – and the excitement – had subsided, there was no further sign of the Kaiser – either in the flesh or on my plates!

Some time later, I had better luck. When the Kaiser inspected the Saalburg, an old Roman castle that had been reconstructed at his instigation, with his royal uncle, King Edward VII of England, I took a series of photographs, which were published in the leading newspapers throughout the world. Among them was one showing the Kaiser and his sisters standing with their royal guest beside the latter's Daimler, the luxuriousness and elegance of which had astonished all Germany. This was just about the time when Edward threw over his arrogant nephew in favour of the renowned *Entente Cordiale* with France.

For three years I stayed with Voigt, working in Homburg

during the season and in his Frankfurt studios during the winter. Then I moved on to Switzerland, where for a while I joined forces with the well-known photographer Camillo Ruf in Zurich.

Ruf was one of the most distinguished photographers of his time. I enjoyed working with him immensely. But by this time I was longing to set up shop on my own, and Ruf helped me towards the realisation of my ambitions by putting me in sole charge of two small, subsidiary studios, where I was able to potter and experiment to my heart's content.

From Switzerland I returned to Munich. In spite of the serious and undivided attention I had hitherto given to learning my profession, the desire to become an artist still burned fiercely in my heart. But this my father categorically refused even to consider, and he allowed me to pursue my studies of art and painting only in so far as they had a direct bearing on my profession as a photographer.

In this way I studied drawing under Professor Knirr of Munich, attended lectures on anatomy by Professor Mollier at Munich University and worked for a while in Paris under the tutelage of Reutlinger, the famous photographer of the fashionable world and of beautiful women.

It was for me a year of unfettered joy, but after this interlude as a carefree art student, I had, alas, to return to my own profession.

For a long while I had harboured the wish to get to know England, and in 1907, supported by first-class testimonials and by my practical experience, I plucked up courage to hop across the Channel, obsessed with the optimistic idea that England was just waiting for me to come.

The resumé of my qualifications, which I had had written for me in English, was invariably handed back to me with a few kind words, which for the most part I did not understand, but whose meaning was not difficult to gather from the deprecating smile that accompanied them. My attainments were greeted with respect, but no one had anything to offer me. My money began to dwindle alarmingly, and in this crisis, as so often happened in my life, a pure chance came to my assistance.

One day, I received from Professor Emmerich, the founder of the Munich Institute for Photographic Instruction and Research, a letter of introduction to England's most famous photographer, E.O. Hoppé. This master of the photographic art received me like an old friend of the family; I was at once invited to the traditional tea-party, and there I made the acquaintance of a number of prominent artists and photographers.

As the guests were leaving, Hoppé asked me to stay on, so that we might get down to business at once.

"What is your financial position? How much can you afford to pay?' asked Hoppé as an opening gambit.

I'm afraid I did not look over-intelligent when faced with these questions. Pay? Here I was, with accepted professional knowledge, not a few notable attainments to my credit, and backed by the best possible references – and I was being asked to pay to be allowed to work! Somewhat taken aback, I made a clear exposition of my position.

'Unfortunately, I cannot afford to practise photography as a hobby,' I said. 'It is the way I earn my daily bread. Even so, I am much more capable than you, perhaps, suppose!'

Hoppé thought for a moment.

'Look here,' he said, 'you come and work with me for a few days, and then we'll see what can be done.'

It so happened that in the course of the next few days I had to go to the Franco-British Exhibition, to take photos of the Colonial Section. Scarcely had I started work, than a shattering explosion shook the very hall in which I found myself. I snatched up my camera and rushed out into the open into the midst of an appalling panic. What on earth had happened? A captive balloon, one of the side-shows, had exploded and crashed. The dead lay mingled with the wounded, bloody, groaning and writhing on the ground; the smoking, still burning remains of the balloon made a sinister background, and, setting up my camera, I swiftly took pictures of the disaster.

The pictures were good and caused a sensation. By chance I had beaten all my competitors by miles. Hoppé's pictures – my pictures, really – were printed in all the leading newspapers in England and abroad, and the *Daily Mirror* put one on the front page. My employer netted a tidy sum in fees, and my own share was by no means to be despised. This success of mine made a great impression on Hoppé; he gave me a permanent job, and very soon I was working as a photo-reporter, and it was in this way that the exploding balloon gave the initial impetus to my subsequent activities as a reporter with a camera.

Hoppé's speciality was portraiture, and at this he was a master. He was a master, too, of the oil and rubber pressure technique, and while I was with him I learnt a great deal. One of his ventures was the production of a volume, entitled *Men of the XX Century*, and to me he entrusted the task of photographing well-known British personalities; and in fulfilling my task I obtained an *entrée* into circles that otherwise would have remained closed to me.

All sorts of famous people, whose names were on everybody's lips, faced my camera, and it was not very long before I attained a definite style of my own, which earned the approval even of the Royal Photographic Society. I had one picture accepted for the very exclusive Annual Exhibition, and in 1908 another of my pictures was published in Snoden Ward's *Photographs of the Year,* 1908 – a carefully chosen selection of the best photographs of the year.

Shortly after this Hoppé went abroad for a visit of several months' duration, and I had no option but to try and stand on my own feet. That, in a city like London, is no easy task. I set up shop in the Uxbridge Road and engaged models whom I photographed for advertisements in the illustrated press for books and posters. Most of my income at the time, however, came from cash prizes. I entered for a great number of competitions, and was lucky enough to find my name many times in the list of prize winners.

Day and night I scratched my head over how I could infuse some life into my business. At last, I had an idea. From *Who's Who* I selected all the famous men who, in the course of the year, would celebrate birthdays of an exact number of decades. These I visited personally, saying that I wanted their photograph for the illustrated papers. Human vanity is very strong, and almost without exception and with great alacrity they allowed themselves to be taken. Naturally, I sent each of them a complimentary copy, and as the photographs really were good, I received quite a solid number of orders for further copies on payment. Business now prospered steadily, and very soon I had accumulated sufficient means to think of setting up an establishment of my own in Germany.

In 1909 I returned to Munich. I had enjoyed my sojourn in England immensely, but – there's no place like home.

Early in 1910 I took a lease of a studio at 33 Schellingstrasse. I had set up shop as a specialist in male portraiture, but if any lady came and expressed a desire to be photographed, I naturally obliged.

In the early spring of the same year a young woman walked into my studio. 'I have heard so much about your artistic prowess, Herr Hoffmann,' she said with a charming smile, 'and I want you, please, to make a very special portrait of me for a friend abroad.'

She was a lovely girl, tall, fair and slim, with the lissom grace and radiant colouring of youth and perfect health – a picture to entrance the eye of any artist.

I have always been a creature of impulse; and seldom have I ever had to regret it. As far as I was concerned, it was love at first sight. This lovely creature, I thought – or no one else in the whole wide world!

My first portrait of her was a good one, though to my enraptured eye, it was but a sorry counterfeit. But Lelly was pleased with it. To my infinite delight I found that she was fond of photography, and she seemed to take a real interest in the art and technique of it. She formed the habit of popping in and asking me for tips and guidance. In my agitated state of mind, goodness alone knows what sort of arrant nonsense I babbled in the way of professional instruction; but she seemed quite contented, and that was all that really mattered. Gradually it dawned on me – though I hardly dared believe it was true – that the art and science of photography were not the only objects of her interests. Could she …?

A few enchanted months slipped quickly by, adorned with the simple delights of those who are young and in love, and early in 1911 we were married. I was still pretty poor, and there was no money for a honeymoon. The ceremony took place in the morning, and a few hours later we were standing side by side, hard at work in my studio. My wife's interest in photography was no feminine wile, and she was of great assistance to me in our early days, and was, too, a perfect model for many of the cover illustrations I made for the press.

The added incentive seemed to bring me luck, and little by little both my business and my reputation began to grow. One day in the autumn of 1911 I received a message saying that Fürstenheim, the Editor-in-Chief of the *Münchner Illustrierte Zeitung,* wanted to see me urgently.

'Caruso,' he said, 'has just arrived in Munich, and as sure as my name's Fürstenheim, you'll get a princely fee from me if you can get me a photograph of him. I want it for the front page.'

I immediately hastened off to the Hotel Continental, where Caruso was staying, and within a few minutes was granted audience – not, indeed, by Caruso himself, but by his impresario, Ledner, to whom I made my wishes known, adding that the *Münchner Illustrierte* wished to publish the photograph on the front page.

The impresario listened attentively and then, with an apologetic expression, explained that Caruso was not allowed to pose for photographs.

'All photographic rights,' he said, 'have been acquired by an American agency. But if it's just a photo you want, why, help yourself – there are plenty to choose from.'

This offer I declined with thanks. I was not interested in photos taken by other people.

'But surely,' I objected, 'Caruso, being a public figure, must find it very difficult to avoid being photographed?'

'Oh, there's nothing to prevent you from taking a snap of him in the street,' replied Ledner. 'The contract is confined to studio portraits. You might get one of him leaving the hotel.'

When, approximately, I asked was that likely to be? And I was told that Caruso had been invited to lunch with Thomas Knorr, the co-founder and proprietor of the *Münster Neueste Nachrichten,* at that time the leading newspaper in South Germany.

In front of the hotel a whole crowd of my fellow photographers had already taken up their positions, their cameras already mounted and trained on the hotel entrance. 'If I join that crowd,' thought I, 'it's goodbye to my "princely fee"! Every one of these chaps will rush off and offer a photo of sorts to Fürstenheim. I must do something better than that.' I thought for a moment, and then I had a brilliant idea.

Off I went to Thomas Knorr's house, a palace of a place in the Brienerstrasse, furnished with the most exquisite taste and one of the centres of the cultural life of the Bavarian capital. A venerable and dignified retainer, every inch of him bristling with unapproachability and reserve, received me.

'I must speak to Herr Knorr very urgently,' said I.

'May I enquire in what connection?'

'Please just mention the password *La Bohème,*' I answered unconcernedly. (*Bohème* was the opera with which Caruso was opening his appearance in Munich.) Silently the servant disappeared. A short pause and he was back.

'Herr Knorr says will you kindly come in.'

When I found myself face to face with the greatest newspaper proprietor in all Bavaria, I clutched desperately at my courage.

'Impertinence,' I whispered to myself, 'please don't desert me now!'

'How did you know that Caruso was coming here?' asked Knorr with interest.

'That, I'm afraid, I am not at liberty to disclose,' I answered with a significant smile. 'I can, however, tell you that I have been directed to take a photograph of Caruso in this setting' – which was more or less true, for I had after all been commissioned to do something of the sort.

'Aha! I see! by Caruso himself, you mean,' exclaimed Herr Knorr. The old proverb that silence is golden flashed through my mind. I said nothing, and Knorr took my silence to indicate acquiescence. He was obviously very pleased that Caruso wished to be photographed in the Knorr establishment, side by side with his host. For myself, I quite frankly started to sweat! If only it came off!

At last Caruso arrived, accompanied by his impresario. I advanced on Herr Ledner and greeted him effusively as an old friend. Admittedly he seemed to be somewhat astonished, firstly at seeing me there at all and secondly because I had perhaps overplayed the old-friend-act a little. Caruso, on the other hand, appeared to assume that I had been engaged for the occasion by Herr Knorr.

Everything went marvellously. The two of them posed, and I took several photographs. Then I left the house as quickly as I could. In great excitement I developed the plates and to my joy found that they were excellent.

Fürstenheim beamed when I placed the prints on his desk. These portraits made a great name for me. I sent the proofs, of course, to Caruso, 'on approval', at the Hotel Atlantik in Hamburg, and he, too, was delighted with them and ordered quite a goodly number, which I sent him, accompanied by an appropriately massive bill!

When Caruso returned to Munich in 1919, he presented me

with a signed caricature, drawn by himself – although he had long since paid his bill.

In the course of his career, every press photographer probably finds that some picture or other of his creates a sensation, caused not by the merit of the picture itself, but simply as the result of the caption attached to it. At the time of the notorious Zabern affair, a perfectly harmless snap that I took of Kaiser Wilhelm II caused an international furore, simply because of the caption that the press added to it.

Early in 1913 there occurred in the little town of Zabern certain events that developed into an international incident. A very young and inexperienced lieutenant in the local military School of Instruction declared that there were 'a hell of a lot of "Wobblers" in Zabern and district'. Wobblers was a particularly virulent term of local abuse, used to denote the more unreliable elements among the frontier population of Alsace.

The population, as may well be imagined, was very indignant, the press fanned the flames, and in a moment relations between the civilians and the Corps of Officers became acutely strained. Some youths shouted a string of abuse at an officer in the street. The incident, of itself of quite minor significance, resulted in military measures that caused great excitement throughout the Reich. Troops marched in with arms loaded, machine-guns were placed in position, and by roll of drum the inhabitants were ordered to vacate the streets and squares, otherwise fire would be opened.

On Monday, 1st December, the Chancellor of the Reich, von Bethmann-Hollweg, and the Minister for War, von Falkenhayn, reported to the Kaiser, who at the time was staying in Donaueschingen. As it happened, I, too, was in Donaueschingen on a commission for the periodical *Die Woche,* to take some snaps of the Kaiser, who had accepted an invitation to shoot with Prince Egon zu Fürstenberg.

The conference on the Zabern affair between the Kaiser and his ministers was to take place in the complete isolation of the park of Schloss Donaueschingen; with the tacit acquiescence of the Prince, however, but with strict injunctions not to let myself be seen by anyone, I had been allowed to slip into the park, and was standing behind a tree, waiting for the Kaiser's arrival.

At last His Majesty appeared, accompanied by von Bethmann-Hollweg. For some time he remained in lively conversation with his ministers and with General Deimling, the local Commander, and a few other officers stood respectfully at a distance. Just as the Kaiser left the Chancellor and turned towards one of the officers of the nearby group, I snapped him, in such a manner as not to include the group of officers on the plate.

The next day, when I sorted out the prints destined for the press, I found one snap among them which, I thought, might give rise to misconceptions. I put it carefully aside, to make sure that it should not get mixed up with the press photos.

A few days later I chanced to glance at *L'Illustration,* the most famous of the French periodicals – and I could hardly believe my eyes. There before me was the photo I had put to one side and under it the sensational caption:

'THE KAISER TAKES BRUSQUE LEAVE OF HIS CHANCELLOR, AFTER DIVERGENCIES OF OPINION OVER THE ZABERN AFFAIR !'

Through a breach of confidence on the part of one of my assistants, *L'Illustration* had got hold of the picture, and had added to it this highly tendentious caption.

My affairs continued to flourish in a modest way, and my wife and I were happy in the bonds that tied us and the work we shared so eagerly together. A monarchy, of course, affords an interesting and very lucrative opportunity for the press photographer, and I had my share of good fortune. But I was more devoted to the arts than to politics or Society, and in the artistic field my contacts were numerous indeed, and at one time or another all the famous stars of theatre and music – Bruno Walther, the conductor, Richard Strauss and many others – posed before my camera.

On 3rd February 1912, our daughter, Henriette, was born and added joy and contentment to our lives, which continued blissfully ignorant, thank Heaven, of the years of turmoil, bloodshed and disaster that were stalking, grimly, towards us.

For me, as for millions of others in the world, the bombshell of the Sarajevo assassination blew my private life to smithereens.

On the evening of the assassination, as I was sitting in the well-known cabaret run by Papa Benz in Munich, I received a message saying that a violent riot had broken out in a popular café in the middle of the city. I jumped into a taxi and went home for my camera. When I got to the Karlstor, I saw the results of misguided enthusiasm. The famous Café Fahrig was completely destroyed! Furniture, glass, crockery had all been smashed to bits, and a crowd was gathering bricks from a nearby building site and hurling them through the plate-glass windows.

I clambered through the hole of one of the gaping windows and took my photos. By the time I came out, the police were already on the spot, breaking up the excited crowd. One policeman came up to me and said he must confiscate my plates. I handed him the plate-case without demur, for I had already taken the precaution of handing the other case, containing my snaps, to a friend. I then asked one of the demonstrators what the trouble was all about. 'The Bandmaster,' he told me with great indignation, 'refused to play *The Watch on the Rhine.*'

A few days later I received a telegram: 'Your appointment as war photographer sanctioned report metz intelligence section 22 Genstaff.'

In 1914 there were only seven war photographers in the whole Reich, and from Bavaria I was the only one.

My appointment was made at my 'own expense and responsibility', and I was sent to the Western Front to join the III Bavarian Army Corps. The title 'war photographer' was a bit of a misnomer, for I had received permission to take photographs only on the lines of communication, and it was only on very rare occasions that some senior officer was good enough to take me up to the front line with him.

In spite of these restrictions, the photos we took were very highly prized both behind the front and abroad.

One particular photograph I took was of considerable historic interest. In the Preysing Palace in Munich I had the opportunity of taking the Irish independence leader, Roger Casement, just before his departure for Ireland. Casement was being backed by Germany and had been given the task of returning to Ireland and stirring up a rebellion there. He was betrayed, arrested by the British as he landed, tried as a spy and shot.

After about seven months of war the 'Photographic and Film Office' was formed, and we assumed a more military status; we were enlisted as soldiers, and we became subject to Military Law and discipline. I myself was sent to No. 298 Flying Group, where my duties consisted in developing and classifying the aerial reconnaissance photos – not, admittedly, a very warlike occupation, but a very important one.

At the end of October, 1918, I was posted to a unit in Schleissheim, where a new unit was to be formed and sent to the front. But it never got there, for on 8th November, on instructions from the Ministry of War, we were given leave to attend, if we so wished, an open-air mass political meeting.

I myself used the leave not to attend the mass meeting, but to hasten home and change out of uniform into mufti, and I ran straight into the revolution in the making.

Headquarters of the revolution were installed in the Maetheser – a typical example of the fact that on such occasions, Munich shows a marked preference for its beercellars! The next day the revolution was proclaimed in the Bavarian parliament by the Soldiers' and Workers' Council.

Early on the morning of 9th November, sporting a home-made red armband and with my camera in my hand, I was out and about. With some difficulty I succeeded in getting into the parliament building. Here was a chance to take a look at our new masters, and at the same time I obtained the first photographs ever taken of the newly-formed Soldiers' and Workers' Council. My red armband had been most useful.

Work as a press photographer had become most interesting, but also rather dangerous. In a very short time, I had caught all the leading personalities with my camera, and my photo of the new Bavarian Prime Minister, Eisner – the first of its kind to be taken – appeared in all the periodicals at home and abroad.

On 21st April 1919, Count Arco shot Eisner. This fateful shot led to revolt by the Radicals, which ended in their victory and the proclamation of the Soldiers' and Workers' Republic.

Munich was in an uproar, and the streets were full of shouting, gesticulating men. Once more I donned my red armband and, with my camera, wandered through the streets intent on photographing a bit of history in the making. Work was at a complete standstill; no trams were running. The Executive Council of the Soldiers' and Workers' Council had called for a general strike. The Bavarian Parliament had fled to Bamberg.

But on this day of complete strike, I, at least, had my hands full. The mass of demonstrators surged through the Ludwig-strasse; Egelhofer, the Commander-in-Chief of the Red Army and at the same time the Town Commandant of Munich, stood in a lorry opposite the Ludwigskirche and took the salute as the gigantic columns filed past.

I photographed furiously, anywhere and everywhere, and plate after plate disappeared into my pockets. Engrossed in my work, I half-heard a 'Look out for that photographer' from one of the organisers, but the significance of the remark passed me by.

Suddenly, rough hands seized me, and I found myself standing between two Red Army soldiers, rifles in hand and their belts festooned with hand grenades. To the applause of the crowd I was marched off. I was taken before the Deputy Commandant, who was in a small room seated at a desk, with his back towards me. Some anxious moments followed, during which the man took not the slightest notice of me. Then at last he turned.

I could hardly believe my eyes. 'Why, Good Lord,' I thought to myself, 'that's Alois, my old apprentice!'

He, too, recognised me at once. 'Egelhofer must have made some mistake,' he said, turning to the soldiers. 'Why, that's Herr Hoffmann, a very good friend of mine.' He turned to me. 'Egelhofer,' he continued apologetically, 'of course, doesn't know that you were the straightest boss I ever had!'

My camera was returned to me, and from the Deputy Commandant I received a written pass, authorising me to take photographs when and where I liked.

My permit removed all obstacles from my path. I was the officially authorised photographer of the Soldiers' and Workers' Republic! A mass of most interesting pictures was swiftly added to my archives; but not all of them, alas, have survived.

One man was still missing from my collection of photos of the leaders of the revolution, the Red Town Commandant, Egelhofer himself.

Egelhofer was from the Munich suburbs, and almost overnight he had found himself appointed Commander-in-Chief of the Red Army and Town Commandant of Munich. With my red armband as my guardian, I set off for the lion's den in the Ettstrasse, where he had set up his office in Police Headquarters. In the ante-room, I wrote a brief note, in which I assured the Commandant that it would constitute a deplorable gap in the completeness of my historic archives if one of the most important personalities remained missing.

A few minutes passed, and then the door opened, and there stood Egelhofer himself, four-square in the doorway. He gave me an appraising look, and then: 'You've come just in time, you 'ave; I've been waitin' for yer.'

Now what? That might mean that he was friendly and willing, but it might equally well mean the reverse. My doubts were soon settled.

'Orl right – you take me jest where I am,' he continued, closing the door of the Holy of Holies behind us. 'But I tell yer one thing, Mister, if anyone else sees the picktcher, I'll bloomin' well shoot yer!'

What he wanted, he said, was a picture about the size of a passport photograph, and that as quick as I could make it; and if ever a copy of it found its way into Police Headquarters files, then Gawd 'elp me!

Egelhofer sat himself in a swivel-chair and posed. Swiftly I took the necessary snaps, and then, laying aside the spectacles that he had put on for the photograph, he turned to his bodyguard and ordered them to accompany me and not to let me out of their sight until the plates had been developed and the prints made. 'And take the plates off 'im, so's 'e carn't send no copy to die noospapers,' he finished sharply.

With my heavily armed escort I returned to my studio. Here they watched my every movement with alert suspicion, and any idea of a little sleight of hand with one of the prints had to be abandoned. I went back and personally delivered plates and prints to Egelhofer and tried at the same time to persuade him to change his mind. He would not dream of it, but he offered me money instead; and when I assured him that it was honour enough for me to have been privileged to photograph him, he suddenly opened a drawer of his desk, took out a photo of himself as a sailor and handed it to me!

'There y'are – you can publish that one,' he said kindly. 'But these 'ere' – pointing to my recent efforts – 'no bloody fear!' And with that I had to be disappointedly content.

A few weeks later the Republic collapsed. Egelhofer was shot dead in the Residenzstrasse, and on his body was found a passport under another name. The photograph in it was the one I had taken of him – Egelhofer in spectacles, things he otherwise never wore!

On 21st April the news spread like wildfire through the whole of Munich that at the last moment and just as they were about to be set free, the hostages who had been held in the Luitpold School had been shot by the Reds. Consternation among the citizens struggled with indignant anger for supremacy. A band of determined men disarmed the Red Guard posted on the Residence, and very shortly afterwards the first units of the army of liberation marched in from all sides, to be greeted with relief and enthusiasm.

In the middle of the night, someone rang my front door bell. It was Alois, no longer looking like the victorious revolutionary of a few days ago. His desire was obvious, and I kept my word. I hid him and his intellectual colleague, Hermann Sachs, the American, in my own house.

Many years later, my secretary said that an SA-man who refused to give his name wanted to see me. I told her to bring him in, and there, smartly turned out in SA uniform, stood Alois, the one time Deputy Commandant and former photographer's apprentice!

With the entry of the Government troops, conditions in Munich rapidly returned to normal, and, under the title of *A Year of Revolution in Bavaria*, I published a book of photographs, which had a great success.

Once more I was extremely busy. Munich in 1920 was just one long series of demonstrations, marches and mass meetings, and wherever they took place, there was I with my faithful camera. On one occasion I attended a district meeting of the local Citizens' Army. Among other speakers was one Adolf Hitler. I saw no reason for wasting a plate on this nonentity, who was only enunciating the same old political demands as the rest of them. I did not pay much attention to what he did say – I was a press photographer, not a reporter.

These political events, or rather, the photographs I took of them, coupled with the success of my publication, brought me in a great deal of money. Very few photographers had had the hardihood to stand in the midst of the demonstrators and often in a hail of bullets to take snaps; my photos, therefore, were in many ways unique, and consequently they fetched high prices.

Money piled up in the till. The bank notes betrayed me. Their nominal values, admittedly remained unaltered, but their purchasing power dwindled rapidly from one day to the next. That I had managed to keep my head above water at all was thanks to the business I did with foreign newspapers.

I sold my studio for seventy thousand marks (theoretically £3,500), and at the time I thought I had got a terrific price for it. But when the first half was paid to me, all I could buy with it was a second-hand reflex camera; and by the time I got the second half, it did not quite suffice for the purchase of half a dozen eggs!

Rather in desperation I turned to the film industry, and with two other enthusiasts, we formed a company and made a film, in which we employed actors well-known to Munich audiences. The structure of the film was built around the grotesque-comic rather on the lines of the American burlesque. In it a hairdresser discovers a hair restorer of immense potency. Bald men acquire in no time the manes affected by artists, the beardless are transformed into Barbarossas in a flash, but then one of the apprentices plays the fool with the preparation with the most grotesquely frightful consequences.

This was our first, last and only film. I and my associates were thankful to get out of the business with only a black eye!

Chapter 2

Wanted – A Photograph of Hitler

OR THE NEXT eighteen months or so we lived a precarious, hand-to-mouth existence but, although I had joined the Nazi Party in April, 1920, with Membership Card No. 427 (for at that time its programme seemed to offer the only possible solution to the chaotic problems with which my country was overwhelmed) it was not until I received a telegram:

Send immediately photo adolf hitler offer hundred dollars

that I came into personal contact with Hitler.

This telegram, from a well-known American photographic agency, reached me in Munich on 30th October 1922, and I was amazed at the handsomeness of the offer. For a photo of Ebert, the President of the Republic, the usual price was five dollars; for other prominent people one got much the same amount, and yet for the comparatively unknown Hitler they were ready to pay an exorbitant fee like that!

A hundred dollars! What a fee! Dietrich Eckart's the chap, I thought to myself; he must put me in touch with Hitler.

I expressed my astonishment to Dietrich Eckart, editor-in-chief of the *Völkischer Beobachter* and a good friend of mine who happened to be with me at the time. Eckart was also an intimate friend of Hitler, whose political movement he was financing with the proceeds drawn from his *Peer Gynt* translation and the theatrical royalties being received from Switzerland.

In his blunt dialect Eckart told me to forget it; Hitler, he said, would not allow anyone to photograph him.

'If anyone wants a photo of Hitler,' he said, speaking slowly but with great emphasis, 'he'll have to pay not a hundred or a thousand dollars, but thirty thousand dollars.' For a moment I thought my friend had taken leave of his senses. Hitler, I told him, was now in the public limelight and he had no copyright of his photograph. Any photographer was perfectly entitled to snap him without paying a farthing, for he had become a personality in public life. I didn't think, I added, that anyone could be found, who would be foolish enough to pay thirty thousand dollars.

I've taken photos of emperors and kings and famous people from all over the world,' I went on, 'and never have I been asked to pay anything. On the contrary, it is I who have always been paid – even by Caruso, to whom no photographer ever submitted a bill. And even you must admit that Caruso is a bit better known than Hitler!'

Eckart listened attentively to me, and then quietly and soberly he began to explain. Hitler, he said, had good reasons for refusing to be photographed; it was one of his many moves in the game of political chess he was playing, and the effect of his camera-shyness was quite sensational. Everybody was hearing and reading about him, but nobody had ever seen a picture of him. People were most curious and intrigued, and that was why they flocked to his meetings. They came out of curiosity; but they left as enrolled members of the movement. For Hitler, he said, had that gift of making every single member of an audience feel that he himself was being personally addressed. By this time Eckart was well away on his favourite theme, and the 'Hitler gramophone record', as our friends called it, was in full swing. 'You say no one would be such a fool as to offer thirty thousand

42

dollars for a photo of Hitler; well, let me tell you he has already turned down an offer for twenty thousand.'

To me it seemed incredible that any man should fail to jump at such an offer. But, countered Eckart, that only showed how little I understood Hitler. He was standing out for thirty thousand dollars for a picture that would be a photographic rarity, so that he could further expand the corps, already in process of formation, which was responsible for security and order at his meetings; and thirty thousand, after all, was no great sum to pay for a photograph that would carry exclusive copyrights throughout the whole world.

Eckart pointed to the Munich magazine, *Simplissimus,* which was anything but friendly towards Hitler, but which nevertheless was rendering him a valuable service from the propaganda point of view. Under the caption: 'What does Hitler look like?' it was publishing a series of caricatures with which it claimed to answer its own question.

All this gave me furiously to think. If I could 'shoot' Hitler, then nobody could challenge my claim to the twenty thousand dollars offered. Well, nothing is impossible. My professional zeal was aroused, and determination took possession of my thick Bavarian pate, which, it seems, is just about as thick as Herr Hitler's Austrian skull!

Eckart promised to keep quiet about my proposed photographic coup, but Hitler, he warned me, knew all the tricks of the trade.

My studio at 50 Schellingstrasse was exactly opposite the Müller Printing Press, in which Hitler's newspaper, the *Völkischer Beobachter,* was printed, and Hitler in a very old green Selve car was a frequent visitor there. I started to keep watch. The fever of the chase gripped me, and day after day, hour after hour I waited.

Then, a bare week after my talk with Eckart, I suddenly spied the eagerly awaited car, drawn up outside the publisher's office. Was Hitler in the editor's office? I had to make sure. Nothing simpler, I thought to myself, and into the offices of the *Völkischer*

Beobachter I marched, to enquire whether my friend Eckart was there. As I entered the editor's room, I saw Hitler writing at a desk. It was he, all right. I had already seen him once or twice, and I could have picked him out of hundreds, if only on account of his characteristic little moustache, the trench coat and the riding crop that he invariably carried, as a sort of talisman, and which now lay on the desk beside him. He turned towards me, and I asked him whether Eckart was in.

'No,' answered Hitler. 'I'm waiting for him, too.'

Thanking him, I said I'd come back later.

Swiftly I ran back to my studio and got my camera, a big 13 × 18 Nettel. Back in the street I kept my eyes glued on the green Selve. As a car it wasn't much to look at; it was already pretty ancient, and the seaweed stuffing with which it was upholstered was sprouting out of the back seat. A cart pulled up immediately behind it, and the horse, mistaking it for hay, pulled out a goodly mouthful of the upholstery. He quickly found, however, that it was by no means to his taste, and he sneezed and snorted violently in his efforts to clear his nose of the pungent dust with which the seaweed was plentifully impregnated. Meanwhile, the chauffeur, thoroughly bored, sat at his wheel and saw nothing of what was going on behind him. To get into conversation with the fellow, I unsportingly 'denounced' the unfortunate horse.

'Hi there! You – Mister! That old horse behind you is making a grand meal off your back seat!'

The chauffeur turned and fired a volley of incivilities in the best and broadest Bavarian at the horse's owner; but I, as I had hoped, had won favour in his eyes. After a friendly little chat, he smilingly agreed (for a consideration) not to hurry too much, when the time came for him to depart.

Hour after hour passed. Again and again I examined my camera to make sure that all was in order, and the process did something towards curbing my impatience and making the time pass. Having to wait has always been a thing that quickly destroyed the best of humours for me. Then – at last – Hitler came out, accompanied by three others. The time for action had come.

Click! The shutter snapped. Got it, by jove! The next moment I found my wrists gripped by pretty rough hands. The escorting three had flung themselves upon me! One of them grabbed me by the throat, and a furious struggle ensued for possession of the camera, which I was determined not to surrender at any cost.

But the odds were too great. In sullen rage I watched the men take out the plate and expose it to the light. My snapshot was ruined.

'This,' I shouted, 'is an unwarranted restriction of the liberty of the individual, a gross interference with the legitimate prosecution of my profession!'

Vouchsafing not a word in reply, the three men turned back to the slowly moving car, in which Hitler was already seated, and jumped in.

With my tie awry and my camera ruined I stood there, and Adolf Hitler just smiled at me.

What a flop!

It isn't easy to earn twenty thousand dollars. What had Dietrich Eckart said? Something about Hitler knowing all the tricks of the trade? Too true; those three men of his must have had quite a lot of practice in dealing with unwelcome photographers!

After this ignominious failure, to obtain a photo of Hitler became an obsession with me. Months passed; then one day I ran into my friend, Hermann Esser, a member of Hitler's inner circle, who told me that he was about to get married.

I must certainly give this chap a wedding present, I thought. But what? After a moment's reflection, I said to Esser that rather than give him a third dinner service or cake-stand number five, my present would be to provide the wedding breakfast. I would put up such a feast in my own house in the Schnorrstrasse, I said, that even Lucullus himself would find no cause for complaint.

Obviously delighted by my offer, Esser then told me that Drexler, the founder of the German Labour Party, from which the NSDAP subsequently sprang, and Hitler himself had promised to attend the wedding as witnesses.

Adolf Hitler! Now or never! I thought. In my own home, surely, I should succeed in getting the longed-for snap! Hitler, so Eckart had told me, was at the time very partial to cakes and sweetmeats of all sorts. I ordered the wedding cake from a confectioner of my acquaintance who, I knew, was an ardent Hitlerite, and he promised to produce a real masterpiece of his art. With a twinkle in his eye this master of his profession said that he would produce also a real surprise.

When Hitler arrived with the other wedding guests he at once recognised me as the 'Thwarted photographer'. 'I am really very sorry that you were so rudely disturbed while taking your picture,' he said, apologetically, 'and I hope today that I shall certainly have the opportunity of giving you a more detailed explanation of the circumstances.'

I did my best to pass the whole thing off on a jocular note, and I assured him that in my profession one had to be ready to put up with little incidents of that kind; and from his expression I could see that he really was grateful to me for harbouring no malice and for treating the whole thing as a joke.

'Herr Hoffmann, it would really have been most painful for me if the memory of your bad luck had soured your good humour today and ruined this festive party.'

The breakfast went with a swing. Although Hitler never touched alcohol, he was in complete harmony with the spirit of the gathering and showed himself to be a charming and witty conversationalist. When he was asked to make a speech, he refused, however.

'I must have a crowd when I speak,' he declared. 'In a small, intimate circle I never know what to say. I should only disappoint you all, and that is a thing I should hate to do. As a speaker either at a family gathering or a funeral, I'm no use at all.'

After the meal came coffee and the wedding cake, a superb edifice well nigh two feet high – and the great surprise was out! In the middle of the cake was an effigy of Adolf Hitler, made of marzipan and surrounded by sugar roses! With mixed feelings I looked across at him. What, I wondered, would Hitler's reaction be to this sugary tribute?

From his expression I could gather nothing. With blank mien he gazed at the very indifferent reproduction, in which the tiny moustache alone bore a vague resemblance to the original. I did my best to shield the confectioner. He had meant well, I said, and bad workmanship could always be forgiven if it were carried out with a good heart. Hitler smiled understandingly. 'Look here, we can't possibly cut the man up and eat him before his very eyes,' whispered Esser. I got out of the dilemma as best I could. 'Please help yourselves,' I said airily, waving an inviting hand towards the cake, at the side of which lay a great knife.

Gingerly and with great care guest after guest sliced himself a small morsel, taking great pains to avoid defacing the effigy.

After coffee seemed to me to be a good time to get into closer contact with Hitler and to turn to the subject of photography; and under cover of the general conversation, our withdrawal to my office passed unnoticed.

With obvious interest Hitler examined the medals and diplomas that my prowess as a photographer had earned for me – the gold medal for progress in the art of photography, awarded to me by the South German Photographic Association; the King Gustav of Sweden gold medal, won at the Malmo exhibition; the Great Silver Medal of Bugra, the Leipzig and other awards, and so on.

On my bookshelves were numerous works on painting, and before them Hitler came to a surprised halt.

'I was quite determined to become a painter, and at one time I was a pupil of Professor Heinrich Knirr's Academy,' I explained. 'Unfortunately, my father had other ideas and insisted that I should adopt the profession of photography and thus equip myself to take over the family business. "Better a good photographer than a bad artist," was my old man's dictum.'

'To me, too, the career of a painter has been denied,' replied Hitler with a rueful smile.

For some time we discussed art, and as Hitler became more and more engrossed, I summed up the courage to give another turn to the conversation.

'Dietrich Eckart recently explained to me the reasons for your camera-shyness,' I said, 'and to a certain degree, I can well appreciate them. But to turn down an offer of twenty thousand dollars, that seems to me to be inconceivable.'

'On principle,' he retorted with emphasis. 'I never accept offers; I make demands. They're carefully thought-out demands, mark you. Don't forget that the world is a very big place. When you think out what it means to a newspaper concern to obtain exclusive rights to publish my photographs in thousands of newspapers all over the world, you will realise that my demand for thirty thousand dollars is mere chicken-feed. Anyone who accepts an offer without further ado simply "loses face", as the Chinese say.'

His voice assumed a slightly contemptuous tone. 'Just look at our present-day politicians,' he continued. 'They live in a state of perpetual compromise, and one of these days they'll come to a bad end as a result. Mark my words – I'll haul all those bargain-hunting, pact-making gentlemen clean off the political stage. I'll …'

Hitler's voice rose as if he were on a platform. The hum of conversation that we could hear from the neighbouring room ceased abruptly; the wedding guests thought that Hitler and I were quarrelling, and for me, too, this sudden outburst was rather embarrassing. He must have noticed that I was ill at ease, for he, too, stopped shouting and after a while continued in a quiet, matter-of-fact manner.

'When I shall permit myself to be photographed I cannot say; but this much I can promise you, Herr Hoffmann – when I do so, you will be allowed to take the first photos.' Hitler stretched out his hand and I grasped it.

'But I must ask you,' he added, 'to refrain from now on from trying to take any snaps without my permission.'

At that moment a messenger came in and handed me a print and a photographic plate. Unobtrusively I had set up my camera in a suitable place and had taken Hitler's photo.

All this I explained to him, adding that my assistant had had orders to develop the plate at once.

Hitler looked first at the print and then at me, quizzically.

I held the plate up to the light. 'Yes – this is the negative, all right. See for yourself,' I said.

'Somewhat under-exposed,' said Hitler.

'But good enough for a perfect print; or rather – it would have been good enough.' With these words I smashed the plate on the edge of the table. Hitler looked at me with astonishment.

'A bargain is a bargain,' I assured him. 'And until you ask me to do so, I will photograph you no more.'

'Herr Hoffmann, I like you! May I come often and see you?' There was a ring of complete sincerity in his voice, and I replied heartily that I should always be most pleased to welcome him as my guest. Hitler kept his word, and from that day he became a frequent visitor to my house.

Both my wife and myself were at once conscious of the personal magnetism of the man and the absolute sincerity of his outlook; and while for the scatterbrained me it was the man himself, his charming manners, his modest mien, his happy enjoyment of the simple pleasures and perhaps most of all his passionate attachment to, and appreciation of, the arts that counted most, my more serious-minded wife was also fired with enthusiasm for his political theories and plans, and very quickly she became an ardent supporter of the Party.

In the nineteen twenties, the coffee-house played an important role in the daily life of Adolf Hitler – a habit for which his long sojourn in Vienna, where life and business revolves round the cafés, is probably responsible.

In Munich there were three cafés of which he was a regular *habitué* – the Café Weichand, next door to the Volkstheater, the Carlton Tea Rooms, the rendezvous of the élite in the Briennerstrasse, and the Café Heck in the Galerienstrasse, the meeting-place of the solid Munich citizenry.

Of these, his favourite was the Café Heck, and in a secluded corner of its long and narrow room he had his reserved table. Here, in the furthermost corner on the right, he could sit, with no one behind him, and see the whole café – a state of affairs that he regarded as important from the security point of view, and his table became quite a social centre in miniature.

He revelled in the artistic atmosphere. It had been the great ambition of his life to become an artist – an ambition that he sternly sacrificed to his conviction that he had a mission and that his political plans, if only he could bring them to fruition, would be the salvation of his country; and for that no sacrifice was too great. It was, then, an oasis, a blessed relief, to get away for a while from the political turmoil and to enjoy the company of a man whose mode of life he so envied and would so dearly have shared, a man, he felt, who welcomed him for himself alone; and it was with great delight that he, a somewhat lonely man in terms of personal human relationship, accepted my frequent invitations to visit our modest, but withal very comfortable home, with its goodly collection of fine paintings, many of them gifts from my artist friends, its carefree bohemian atmosphere and the artistic circles that frequented it.

In those first early years of my friendship with Hitler, my wife, ardent supporter of the Party's politics though she had become, was inclined to resent the dislocation of the happy and prosperous life we had been leading; our daughter was emerging from the kindergarten stage, and our little son, Heinrich, who was born in 1916, was fast approaching the age when a father's constant presence and companionship could play a decisive role in the moulding of his character. But it was, I think, less the plain fact of this dislocation than the apparent inconsistency of it which irritated her. Had I been a fanatical adherent of the Cause, she could well have understood it; as it was, she could not but feel that I was disrupting our home life, was perhaps jeopardising my career, simply to gratify the whim of boon companionship with one more kindred artistic spirit – of whom, God knows, I already had enough in the circle of our friends.

For my own part, well aware as I was of all this, I was inexorably drawn steadily closer to my friend; his feelings towards me were sincere, I knew, and I also realised how lonely he was, how desperately he relied on the outlet that this friendship in an entirely different world afforded him.

But my good wife was as tolerant as she was loyal, and though she failed to appreciate the significance of it all, she did not allow it in any way to disturb the affectionate harmony of our lives.

We had gathered around us a wide group of friends – painters, musicians, writers, actors, in which the artistic circle of Munich abounded, and these continued to constitute the hub of our social activities; we entertained – and were entertained – freely, but in an atmosphere of carefree camaraderie rather than on any pretentious and lavish scale.

In 1923 Hitler became very active. Every day the number of his adherents increased, and the movement began to be taken seriously – and to be feared.

One of the most prominent of the daily circle was Captain Röhm, who knew Hitler from the days when he had been an education officer in the Army and who addressed him with the familiar 'du'. Once one had accustomed oneself to the grim scars on his face, the heritage of a severe war wound, Röhm proved to be a pleasant and entertaining conversationalist.

At the time he was being heavily attacked by the leftish press on account of his unfortunate mode of life; this, however, carried no weight with Hitler.

'In a man like Röhm,' he said to me, 'who has lived so long in the tropics, a disease like this – for it is as a disease that I prefer to regard his habits – deserves special consideration. With his Army connections, Röhm is very valuable to the Party, and, as long as he remains discreet about things, his private life is of no interest to me; and I certainly should never think of reproaching him or of taking any action against him.'

Another prominent member of the circle, a man of strong personality, was Professor Stempfle, an ex-Jesuit priest. At first Hitler was suspicious of him and thought that he was a spy of the Church party; but gradually the Professor gained his full confidence, and, indeed, he it was who frequently counselled Hitler to be more moderate.

On 27th January 1923, I watched hundreds of SA-men parade on the Marsfeld, to receive from Hitler's hands four standards, which he himself had designed. After the parade the columns marched through the town. People looked askance at these men who, they knew, were completely devoted to Hitler, but no one dared to challenge them.

During the ensuing weeks feelings ran high, and it was obvious that a triangular trial of strength between the Bavarian Government, the Communists and Hitler could not long be delayed.

Throughout April there were persistent rumours that the Communist Party intended to transform their normal May Day demonstration into a *coup d'état* and to seize power. Hitler for his part was convinced that the Communists would first of all attack and destroy his own SA, and accordingly he quietly called into Munich as many of his SA adherents as he could muster from all over Bavaria. On 1st May the situation in the city was critical in the extreme. The Government had sanctioned the holding of the Red mass meeting and procession on the Theresienwiese, the famous square in the centre of Munich and venue of the well-known annual October Festival – but only on condition that the whole demonstration should confine itself within the prescribed square mile. Meanwhile, Hitler's SA units, well armed with rifles, light and heavy machine-guns (obtained, according to Röhm, from the Reichswehr) had assembled on the Oberwiesenfeld, the airfield on the immediate outskirts of the city, which rapidly assumed the appearance of a vast, armed camp.

In a very short time the Hitler army was on the march. The square mile of the Reds was completely surrounded, and all streets leading out of it were sealed off by armed detachments of SA men, their rifles much in prominence and their machine guns posted for instant action.

I myself was with Hitler all the time. He was carrying a steel helmet by its chin-strap, and though I tried to persuade him to put it on, he refused. What a grand snap that would have made! But never once in his life, not even during the war, did Hitler ever wear a steel helmet.

He confidently expected that the Reds would be provoked to violence; indeed, I am quite sure he hoped that they would, for, if they did, then he, with his well-armed, well-disciplined SA units would have routed them instantly and would then have been able to ignore the Government and seize power. Nothing, however, happened. Much to Hitler's disgust the Reds appeared to have appreciated the weakness of their position, and they studiously avoided any sort of provocative action. Hitler withdrew his forces and after a short series of manoeuvres outside the city, the units gradually dispersed. Though this day of tense crisis had ended on a note of complete anti-climax, it was not without its significance. As a preliminary trial of strength it had been instructive.

Throughout the summer and autumn I was with Hitler as he travelled up and down the country, recruiting, making speeches, organising Party branches and attending to the thousand and one problems with which a very rapidly expanding movement confronted him.

It was in Nuremberg, on the occasion of the 'Deutscher Tag', that I was 'scooped' and Hitler was compelled finally and irrevocably to abandon his dream of thirty thousand dollars for his first photographic sitting.

The members of the national units had marched on to parade, and Hitler was standing in the midst of their officers, when Pahl, a photographer of the Associated Press, calmly took advantage of a favourable opportunity and snapped him.

Before even Hitler's bodyguard could intervene, Pahl had disappeared into the crowd. He'd done it at last, and it was all up with any idea of the thirty thousand dollars.

Immediately after the success of Pahl's 'photo by assault', Hitler beckoned to me to come over to him. 'Hoffmann,' he said, 'tomorrow I'll come to your studio in Munich. The time has now come, and at last you shall take your photographs.'

At the end of October we returned to Munich and, on the afternoon of 8th November, Hitler and I were sitting, as we often used to do, in the little teashop in the Gärtnerplatz. It was a place to which he liked to go, when he wished to get away from his friends. We were talking about quite trivial matters, when suddenly Hitler expressed the wish to go and see his very intimate friend, Esser, who was in bed with jaundice. Off we accordingly went, and on arrival Hitler asked me to wait for a moment in the sitting room.

After a brief visit we left and drove to the Schellingstrasse, where the SA had its headquarters in the same house as the *Völkischer Beobachter.* Here we met Göring, who at that time was the senior commander of the SA. Under his arm he had a bulky package, which I later learned contained his steel helmet, with its Swastika, and a pistol. Once more Hitler drew Göring aside and spoke with him out of my hearing. What's all this mysteriousness about, thought I, and left them to it. Before I went I asked Hitler what he was doing that evening and he replied that he would be very busy on a very important job.

I went off to the Café Schelling-Salon, near my house, where Dietrich Eckart was waiting for me, and we settled down to our usual game of Tarock 'whist'. Little did either of us guess that at that very moment the preparations for the 9th November putsch were in process of being made. Even those who were to take part in the putsch did not know exactly what was expected of them.

I went blithely home, and just before I was going to turn in, my telephone rang. It was the confectioner who had made the famous Hitler wedding cake.

'The national revolution has been proclaimed from the Bürgerbräukeller,' he said. 'Hitler and Ludendorf have over-thrown Kahr's Socialist government. A new government has already been formed, and Kahr, Lossow and Seiser are in it.'

'Impossible!' I retorted disbelievingly. 'Why, I was with Hitler only two hours ago!'

'Well – a telegram to that effect is already being published in the *Münchner Neueste Nachrichten;* and SA men and the Oberland Union have already occupied all public buildings.'

Without further ado, I rushed out into the streets, which were almost empty, except for the marching columns of SA and Oberland Union units. But the social democrat *Münchner Post* newspaper office was besieged by hundreds, while those who had burst in were destroying the printing presses and other installa-tions.

Now for the first time I began to understand the whispered consultations with Esser and Göring. Later I found out that Hitler had visited Esser to tell him to organise a meeting in the Löwenbräukeller as a manoeuvre to distract attention from the happenings in the Bürgerbräukeller. But about the putsch itself, apparently, he did not say a word.

When I returned home about midnight, I found Esser waiting for me. As soon as his meeting in the Löwenbräukeller ended he had hastened off to the Bürgerbräukeller, there to gain a most depressing impression.

'It's all over – the putsch has collapsed!' he cried, springing from the armchair in which he had slumped.

'But – for God's sake! What putsch? What's happened? Begin at the beginning. I know nothing!'

Esser sat down again. 'You know, don't you,' he said, speaking a little more calmly, 'that the local volunteers had arranged a reunion for this evening in the Bürgerbräukeller and had invited members of the Government to attend it? Well, when everyone had arrived, Hitler suddenly seized possession of the hall with an SA Commando group. Firing his pistol through the roof to obtain silence and attention, he informed the astonished gathering that a new government had just been formed by Ludendorf and himself, and that Kahr himself and several others of the late Government had consented to join it.'

'And then?'

'Then Hitler and Ludendorf very foolishly let Kahr, Lossow and Seiser leave the reunion, and as soon as they were free these three of course took all steps necessary to inform the people that they had only joined Hitler under compulsion! Barbed wire has already been put round all government buildings, and most of the units of the Oberland Union are being contained in their barracks by regular troops,' Esser concluded.

Early on the morning of that memorable 9th November I was out with my camera. It was a dull day, and the light was very poor from the photographer's point of view. From the tower of the Rathaus the Swastika flag was flying, and below it National Socialist agitators were making speeches to an enthusiastic crowd, who, obviously, had no idea of latest developments.

I arrived just in time to see the socialist and communist councillors arrested, and very soon my supply of plates ran out. When someone told me that a discussion was at the moment in progress in the Bürgerbräukeller to decide whether it would be a good idea to try and gain the sympathy of the people by organising an unarmed march through the city, I hastened back home and got some more plates. I thought I would go back to the Bürgerbräukeller in about an hour's time.

But when I reached the Feldherrenhalle on my way back, I was told of the terrible *dénouement*. The small unarmed column had marched from the Bürgerbräukeller to the Feldherrenhalle, there to be met by a hail of bullets from a body of Government troops. By some miracle General Ludendorf, who was marching at the head of the column with Hitler, escaped injury. Hitler apparently had flung himself to the ground at the first salvo and had disappeared; but all that I was in time to see with my own eyes was the removal of sawdust, drenched with the blood of the fourteen victims, from the gutters of the street.

I had missed the chance of taking an historic photograph, for which later Hitler would have been particularly grateful.

Hitler, it seems, hurt his shoulder badly, and someone, most probably Christian Weber, succeeded in dragging him into safety. He then took refuge in Uffing, a little village in Upper Bavaria. Very quickly, however, he was found by the police, was arrested and sent to Landsberg fortress.

The artists in the Hitler movement planned to celebrate Christmas at the Blüte Café in the Blütestrasse with a *tableau viuant,* entitled: 'Adolf Hitler in prison'.

I was given the task of finding a suitable double for Hitler. As it happened I came across a man who bore a most striking resemblance to him. I asked him if he would take part in this *tableau vivant,* and he agreed to do so.

The great hall of the Blüte Café was filled with people. A reverent hush fell as the curtain went up and a prison cell became visible on the half-darkened stage. Behind the small, barred window, snowflakes could be seen falling. At a small table, his back to the audience, his face buried in his hands, sat a man. An invisible male choir sang *Stille Nacht, Heilige Nacht.*

As the strains of the last note died away, a tiny angel came into the cell, carrying an illuminated Christmas tree, which was placed gently on the table of the lonely man.

Slowly 'Hitler' turned until he was face to face with the audience. Many thought that it was indeed Hitler himself, and a half-sob went through the hall.

The lights went up, and all around me I saw men and women with moist eyes, handkerchiefs hastily disappearing. That same evening, the man who played Hitler joined the Party. His name was Achenbach – a name that later was to become very familiar to all Party members, for by profession he was a geneologist, and he it was who organised and ran the bureau for the investigation of Aryan racial purity.

On 26th February, 1924, Hitler was tried in court, which sat in the former Military Academy in the Blütenburgstrasse in Munich. *Chevaux-de-frise* and barbed wire barred all approaches, and a large number of police in green and blue uniforms examined the entry permits with keen scrutiny. Everybody was searched for hidden weapons, and it was obvious that the authorities feared an attempted rescue by Hitler's supporters and were taking no chances. I myself succeeded in getting into the hall, but was told that no photographs could be taken. I could, however, take just one group picture.

In spite of this strict injunction, I did, in fact, succeed in taking a photograph – with the 'Stirnschen' secret camera, which had been invented about the beginning of the century and of which one is to be seen in the photographic section of the Deutsches Museum. I had the apparatus concealed under my waistcoat, with its lens pushed into a buttonhole. Of the snaps I took, only one was any good, but that one sufficed.

The charge against him – that of high treason, was a serious one, punishable at law by 'death or any such lesser sentence as the Court may award'. But public sympathy was entirely on Hitler's side, and the mild sentence of six years' imprisonment came as a great relief to the excited masses.

I was lucky enough to be among those who succeeded in obtaining permission to visit Hitler in prison. Even so, there were endless formalities before I and the huge basket of fruit that I had brought for him and his fellow prisoners stood before him.

Hitler was obviously very popular with the prison officials for willing warders helped me to carry my heavy burden through the labyrinth of corridors and squares through which I had to pass. My camera, unfortunately, I had to leave in the guardroom, for photography was forbidden. It did not, however, matter very much, for I had managed to conceal another camera about me.

This I managed to pass surreptitiously to a confederate among the warders, who took a photo for me after we left the cell and handed back the camera to me before we left Landsberg.

After the arrest of Hitler, the Party had split into two factions. To the Greater Germany People's Commonwealth adhered Esser, Streicher, Dintner and Bouhler, while the leaders of the People's Block were Rosenberg, Strasser and Buttmann.

My conversation was of necessity brief and guarded.

'When you come out, Herr Hitler,' I asked, 'which of the two factions will you recognise?'

'Neither!' said Hitler decisively. 'When I come out I shall expect every one to rally to me, who realises that there can only be ONE leader; and if that is essential in the Party, it will be doubly so later in the State.'

Ten years later I recalled this visit, when Hitler, then already Chancellor of the Reich, and I went back to Landsberg to look at his cell. What a difference! All, from the Governor downwards to the warders, were sent for to receive Hitler's personal thanks for their considerate treatment while he was under their supervision. The cell itself had not changed at all. But on the table lay a copy of *Mein Kampf,* in the midst of a laurel wreath, and everywhere there were flowers in profusion.

Hitler posed beside the barred window. With a far-away look in his eyes he turned to me.

'Well, Hoffmann, now you can photograph me in my cell,' he said, 'without any fear of restriction.' Then, 'It was here,' he added, 'that I wrote *Mein Kampf,* not even prison bars can prevent epoch-making ideas from finding their way to the minds and hearts of the people.'

A few days before Christmas 1924, Adolf Müller, the proprietor of the Munich Publishing House, came to see me. 'Would you like to come on a little picnic with me,' he asked, 'to Landsberg' I understood, of course. He was going to visit Hitler.

To be on the safe side, I took my camera with me. One never knows one's luck.

I was surprised to see that Müller did not take his chauffeur with him, but drove his big Daimler-Benz himself. As we settled in the car, he told me that he was going to fetch Hitler! 'Very few people,' he added, 'know the exact date and time at which he will be released.' This, indeed, was a surprise!

But so tremendous and persistent had been the pressure of public opinion, that the Government had felt itself compelled to release him within a few short months.

'Once Hitler is back again,' said Müller, as we drove along, 'there will be a very different atmosphere. I am curious to see what Ludendorf will have to say. He certainly won't like having to step down again from the leadership!'

Müller was hard of hearing, and like all somewhat deaf people, he talked very loudly. 'In whose favour will Hitler decide, I wonder,' he said, musingly, 'the Greater Germany People's Commonwealth faction of the People's block?'

Very soon the big Daimler-Benz drew up outside Landsberg Fortress. I got out and prepared my camera. Then I heard a grinding noise – the gates were being opened. The historic moment, apparently, was upon us! But in reality, it was not! It was only the uniformed gatekeeper, who drew my attention to the fact that all photography was forbidden. I retorted that he was exceeding his authority, which did not stretch beyond the confines of the fortress itself; to which he replied quite calmly that if I ignored his warning, he would confiscate my camera. This was more than I was prepared to stand, and I demanded to see the Director. The Director was friendly, but quite firm. 'Instructions from the Government,' he said. 'Hitler is not to be photographed as he leaves the fortress.' And that was that.

Angrily I returned to the car. I have no luck with Hitler,' I yelled in Müller's ear. 'First of all he himself wouldn't let me photograph him, and now other people forbid it.'

And I told him of my interview with the Director.

At that moment Hitler came out through the gateway. With a terse greeting, he stepped swiftly into the car, and we drove off.

'I'm glad that you have come along,' he said, turning to me; 'now you can photograph me without let or hindrance.'

'I haven't noticed it,' I retorted, and I told him of my passage of arms with the fortress authorities. It seemed to me essential that a photograph to mark the occasion should be taken in Landsberg itself; and if that were not possible in front of the fortress, then I must take one elsewhere. I suggested that we stop by the old city gates, where we would still retain something of the fortress atmosphere. To this Hitler agreed, and I took several pictures.

The same day, I sent the photographs to all the various home and foreign newspapers, with the caption 'Adolf Hitler leaves Landsberg Fortress.' As I anticipated, the picture was published all over the world. But when I received my copies, I could not help laughing. Not a single newspaper had used my caption. Instead: 'The first step to freedom' – 'The Fortress Gate has opened' – 'On to new deeds' – 'Thoughtfully, Hitler stands in front of his prison – what will he do now?'

What Hitler actually did was to say to me: 'Get a move on, Hoffmann, or we'll have a crowd collecting; and anyway, it's bloody cold!'

We returned to the car, and I asked him what he intended to do next. 'I shall start again, from the beginning,' he said decisively. 'The first thing I want is office space. Do you know of anything in that line, Hoffmann?'

I told him that at 50 Schellingstrasse, there were thirteen empty rooms to let.

'That's fine!' he answered gleefully. 'I'll take twelve of them.' Hitler, among other things, was very superstitious.

When Hitler left Landsberg, he gave all the cash he possessed – 282 Reichsmarks – to his less fortunate fellow prisoners. He set up his Party headquarters in my former studio, and without a farthing in his pocket he started on the task of rebuilding the Party. At that time he was dependent on the help of Party members, who by their contributions made it possible to rent the twelve vacant rooms and furnish them.

One of his most ardent supporters, a wealthy member of a famous aristocratic family and the wife of a highly respected businessman, arranged a personal office for him and furnished it with furniture of her own, which for years had been in a depository. But the mothholes in the ancient upholstery worried him so much that he could never work there, and preferred to remain in his furnished room in the Thiersch-Strasse.

He transformed the only studio in the house in the Schelling-strasse into a memorial hall, in which the rescued colours and standards, including the 'blood standard', were hung; and he further intended to inscribe the names of the fallen on two big marble tablets. Before he could do so, however, the Barlow House in the Briennerstrasse was acquired and was given the name of 'The Brown House'.

Initially, in spite of the emphasis he laid on the 'Führer principle', Hitler appears to have been quite sincere in his intention to give a democratic foundation to the Party, and the preparation of a senatorial chamber, designed to accommodate thirty-nine senators, in the Brown House affords good proof of the sincerity of his intentions.

Towards the rebuilding of the Brown House every Party member subscribed his modest mite, and the subscriptions that poured in from all sides enabled Hitler to design and furnish the house according to his own taste. The Senate Hall was some 20 yards long and 15 yards wide; its chairs of red morocco leather were arranged in a horseshoe of two rows, and their mahogany backs were adorned with the crest of the sovereign eagle. On either side of the entrance stood two standards and two bronze tablets, bearing the names of those who lost their lives on 9th November 1923; and the chamber was further decorated with the busts of Bismarck and Dietrich Eckart, who, released from prison in a desperate state of health, had died at Christmas 1923,

When Edward VII visited the Kaiser and his sisters, his luxurious Daimler caused a sensation throughout Germany.

The Kaiser
fox-hunting
– not in the
best British
tradition!

THE ZABERN AFFAIR – 'The Kaiser takes brusque leave of his Chancellor.'

When I told Hitler of the vast Munich crowd I photographed on the declaration of war in 1914, he exclaimed, "I was in that crowd." After meticulous search, we picked him out.

World War I – Hitler in a dugout, with moustache and helmet.

Enrico Caruso – he did me the honour of paying for his photographs.

The first of the many – Hitler with Schaub, Schreck, Maurer and Schneider.

Hitler's first trial of strength with the Communists – 1st May, 1923.

The Hitler trial – 1924 – to which I took a camera concealed under my waistcoat.

I snap Hitler on his release from Landsberg prison.

In Landsberg prison – taken with a smuggled camera.

A portrait in SA Uniform – which Hitler never wore again.

My first portrait of Göring – dripping wet and arrayed for war.

With von Pfeffer; Hitler carries his familiar whip.

After his last visit to the President who died in July, 1934.

President Hindenburg with his grandchildren and Hitler.

I was asked not to publish this photograph as Hitler considered it *infra dig*. ['beneath one's dignity'] to be pictured thus attired.

I photograph Hitler as he rehearses, so that he could later "vet" gestures and expressions.

Hitler was sensitive about his appearance, and relied on my camera to check this before appearing in public.

The very first picture of the new Reich Chancellor at his desk.

In close discussion with Röhm.

Hitler's soldiers of the 1930s.

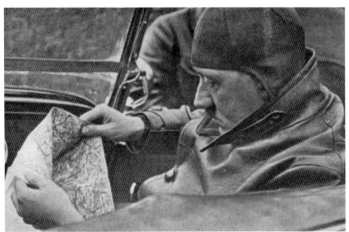

Hitler relaxes while checking his route on an election tour.

I snap Hitler leaving the church after Bormann's wedding.

Two typical watercolours by Hitler. Had he devoted himself to painting, Hitler would undoubtedly have earned a high place in contemporary art.

Hitler enjoys the joke as the Mercedes is revved up.

Under inspection – the Mercedes-Benz racing car built at Hitler's request.

With colleagues at the Hofbräuhaussaal, 1932.

Hitler becomes Reich Chancellor – with Göring he acknowledges the cheers of the crowd.

I snapped the Duke of Windsor in animated conversation with Dr Goebbels.

The Duke and Duchess of Windsor leaving after their visit to Obersalzberg.

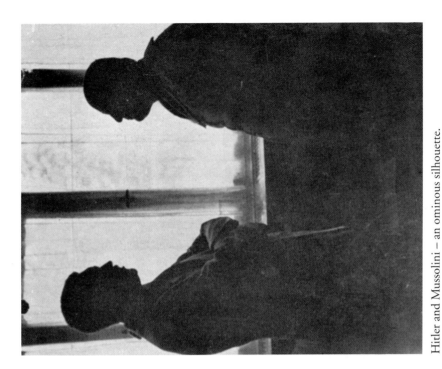

Hitler and Mussolini – an ominous silhouette.

An den Fuehrer und Reichskanzler.

Beim Verlassen Deutschlands danken die Herzogin
von Windsor und ich Ihnen aufrichtig fuer die grosse
Gastfreundschaft, die Sie uns gewaehrt haben und fuer
die vielen Moeglichkeiten, das zu sehen, was fuer das
Wohl der schaffenden Deutschen getan wird.

Wir nehmen einen tiefen Eindruck von unserer Reise
durch Deutschland mit und werden nie vergessen, mit
welcher Aufmerksamkeit wir von Ihren Beauftragten um-
geben worden sind, und eine wie herzliche Aufnahme wir
ueberall gefunden haben.

Besonders danken wir Ihnen fuer die schoenen
Stunden, die wir mit Ihnen auf dem Obersalzberg ver-
bracht haben.

EDWARD

23-X-37

The Duke of Windsor's letter of thanks to Hitler.

in Berchtesgaden. Double sentries of SA and SS formed a guard of honour outside the Senate Hall.

But no Senate ever met in the hall, and no Senate was ever constituted; later, the hall became the office of Hitler's deputy, Rudolf Hess.

Hitler succeeded in giving a marked and striking character to his Party. The gigantic Swastikas, the brown uniforms, the Colours and Standards in revolutionary red, the sparkling colours of his placards, the decoration of assembly rooms with bouquets of flowers and slogans printed on great strips of cloth – all these things were designed for propaganda purposes and had a great effect.

Another calculated piece of propaganda was the American format that he adopted for his newspaper, the *Völkischer Beobachter*. There was considerable criticism within the Party, which regarded this format as unusual for a German newspaper and unwieldy to handle. These views, however, did not influence Hitler, who was determined that the originality of his newspaper should burst the bonds of normal complacency. He himself designed the title-head of the paper, using the unusual Antiqua type, as a contrast to the block capitals used by the majority of other papers.

Apart altogether from my connection with Hitler, business prospered, and my life became anything but a sedentary one. I had earned a great deal of money – my book, *A Year of Revolution in Bavaria,* had alone brought me a gross profit of half a million marks – about £25,000 – but taxes and expenses took a good share and inflation swallowed the rest. But we survived and soon our fortunes began to revive. At first we had a small Opel, and then later a bigger Mercedes, and our household consisted of a cook, a maid and a chauffeur.

My activities as a press photographer meant that I was con-stantly on the move. I had already a room as a permanent *pied-à-terre* in the Kaiserhof Hotel in Berlin, and gradually the business began to assume almost the form of a miniature industry. One after another I opened subsidiary studios, in Berlin, in Vienna, in Frankfurt, in Paris, in The Hague, until finally I had no less than twelve studios and a hundred or more employees dotted all over Europe.

In 1928 a great disaster all but overwhelmed me. In that year Munich was swept by an epidemic of most virulent influenza, and to it my dear wife fell a victim and died. The sheet-anchor of my life had gone, and for a while I was completely adrift. But the responsibility of the children, the intensity of the historical events in which I was participating, and the sense of the utter unimportance of the individual that they inculcated, came, I think, greatly to my aid and set me steadily on my course again.

One rainy Sunday in 1932, Hitler and I were sitting, as we so often did, in the Café Heck. The foul weather had a depressing effect on us, and conversation languished; even Hitler could find nothing to say that might give rise to an animated discussion. He suggested going to the cinema and called for a newspaper; but he found nothing that he wanted to see and angrily threw the paper aside. Then, quite suddenly, he turned to his chauffeur. 'How long do you require,' he asked, 'to make the preparations necessary for a fortnight's journey?'

'I can have everything ready within an hour,' answered Schreck.

Hitler turned to me. 'Would you like to come with me?' he asked curtly. 'You'll certainly get some very interesting photographs! It's no use sitting still, doing nothing; I want power and I am determined to get it,' he continued, giving me some inkling of what was in his mind and of the object and purpose of the projected journey. 'The first thing to be done is to mobilise the financial world; when I've done that, I shall be in a position to extricate Germany from her present predicament.'

The next day we went to Weimar to see Sauckel, the Gauleiter of Thuringia, who arranged for Hitler to address the industrialists of Thuringia. A week later Hitler explained his programme to a meeting of the Industrial Association in Düsseldorf. His appeal met with immediate response. Sixty-five thousand marks made a good foundation; the first step towards the assumption of power had been taken.

And if it had not been raining on that Sunday in Munich, or if Hitler had found some film he wanted to see, who knows what might have happened!

Chapter 3

No Photographs Allowed

FOR WEEKS AT A TIME, when he was not travelling on an election campaign, Hitler, before he came to power, stayed in Berlin, where he took up his quarters in the Hotel Sans Souci in the Linkstrasse, a hotel much patronised by the landed gentry and by the German nationalists. It was here that he held all the political conferences.

I myself had a flat on the fourth floor of the Kaiserhof Hotel, and towards the turn of the year Hitler moved in and occupied the whole of the second floor. Here his days were filled with conferences and discussions with the leading personalities in politics, industry and the armed forces. Living cheek by jowl as we were, I was obviously well placed to see all that was going on and to draw my own conclusions. Sporadically, I saw a lot of Hitler, and very often he would make some terse but illuminating remark as he hastened by. But the whole political situation was very delicate, and I held my own counsel. In the afternoons, I would see Hitler taking tea in the main lounge of the hotel, and nearly all the ministers and secretaries of state of the future were invited, each in his turn, to take tea with him. I too, on the more informal occasions, was invited to join them. Goebbels was always present and kept a detailed diary of all conferences, on which he later based his book *From the Kaiserhof to the Chancellery of the Reich.*

In Berlin the rumour quickly went round that the future strong man of Germany had permanently reserved as his own the table in the corner of the big lounge in the Kaiserhof Hotel, and the great room, furnished in the imperial style and usually somewhat deserted, quickly became thronged every afternoon.

Hitler was very fond of the Kaiserhof. He found the soft music relaxing and soothing. Later, however, when he found out that some rapacious head waiter was reserving the tables in the vicinity of his own table for people who were prepared to pay a stiff price for the privilege, he abruptly ceased to take tea there.

Shortly before the end of January, I met him hurrying along the corridor to his apartments; catching me by the arm, he drew me along with him.

'Hoffmann,' he said softly but urgently. 'Today I am expecting a visit which I regard as a most excellent omen. On the instruction of Hindenburg himself, the Chief of his Presidential Chancellery is coming to see me!'

'*Donnerwetter! Das ist ja allerhand!*'

'Now – listen! this is serious, extremely important and extremely secret. No photos of any sort or kind and – *keep your mouth shut!*'

As a result of this meeting Hitler was able to assure the President a few days later, when they met, that he was in a position to meet all the objections and obstacles that Hindenburg's old friends were likely to raise with the politicians and the military authorities; and thus were laid the foundations on which the decision of 30th January was made.

'Come with me, Hoffmann, and don't forget your camera. I'm not quite sure, but I rather think you'll have the chance of perpetuating in pictures a moment of historical importance!' Thus said Hitler on 30th January in the vestibule of the Hotel Kaiserhof. 'But – keep your mouth shut!' he added, warningly.

'As I know no details, I'm not in any case in a position to say much,' I ventured.

'But you've got a pretty shrewd idea!' he retorted.

Together we drove to the President's Palace, where Hitler told me to wait in the ante-room till he sent for me. 'I'll let you know in good time when you're wanted,' he assured me, and with that he left me.

After a little while he emerged from the President's room, and I could see that he was very excited. Catching sight of me, he clapped his hand to his head. 'Good God!' he exclaimed angrily, 'I forgot all about you, Hoffmann! And now, I'm afraid, it's too late!'

We went out to the car and drove back to the hotel. If Hitler had forgotten all about me, I thought, he must certainly have been very excited.

Suddenly he turned to me. 'All's well,' he said. 'The old gentleman has signed it!'

Hitler was Chancellor of the German Reich! And I was one of the very first to congratulate him.

In those days of intense political tension, the Kaiserhof Hotel was a focal point of interest and was invariably besieged by a crowd hundreds strong; and on the fateful day of Hitler's nomination to the Chancellorship, the crowd, quite unconscious of what had just taken place, accorded him the usual ovation on his arrival. A few minutes later, the dramatic announcement was made. 'Adolf Hitler has been made Chancellor of the Reich!'

Once more I was lucky enough to be on the spot and once more I was here, there and everywhere, perpetuating with my camera the scenes of an historic occasion.

The jubilation was indescribable. Like lightning the news spread throughout the town, and in a matter of minutes the hotel was surrounded by a vast crowd of enthusiastic and cheering people. In the evening Hitler went to the Chancellery to take the salute at a torchlight procession, organised by Goebbels and executed by the SA, the SS and the Reichswehr. Goebbels had arranged a masterpiece, and this imposing and impressive manifestation of enthusiasm showed that he knew all that was to be known about propaganda. 'This little doctor,' said Hitler to me, 'is a magician. How on earth did he conjure up all these thousands of torches in the space of a few hours?'

One by one, Göring, Goebbels, Frick and Blomberg took their turn to stand beside Hitler at the little Chancellery window, at which there was no room for them to stand all together. For hours on end the procession continued and roar upon roar of hurrahs for the new Chancellor and his colleagues rent the air. It was a picture that made a profound impression on the foreign diplomats and press representatives, an impression that they faithfully passed on to the governments and press of their own countries.

At a window of the President's Palace, next door to the Chancellery, sat the grisled figure of the aged President Hindenburg and he, too, was greeted with cheers that were equally warm-hearted and rousing, and which, obviously, moved him deeply.

Hitler held Hindenburg in deep veneration. My father, my friend and my adviser, he used to call him.

For Hitler and his new Cabinet 'Full steam ahead' was the slogan of the days that immediately followed; and for me, too. There was no end to the things asking to be photographed – Hitler as Reich Chancellor, then each of the new ministers, the oath of allegiance by the officials of the old Reich and the Chancellery and so on and so on.

Then, it was my privilege to be the only person present when for the first time, Hitler spoke on the radio as Chancellor of the Reich to the German people and to the whole world. I was also permitted to take photographs during the course of this historic broadcast. His desire to see wireless become the hand-maiden of propaganda had been fulfilled. Although he himself never listened to radio programmes, he fully appreciated the importance of wireless in politics.

On one occasion, when General Schleicher was to make an important speech, Hitler refused to listen to the broadcast. 'I do not wish to allow myself to be influenced in any way,' he declared, 'and for that reason I refuse on principle to listen to any political broadcast.' This principle he adhered to very strictly, and he refused to listen even to the speeches broadcast by foreign statesmen.

The assumption of power also necessitated drastic changes in the conduct of my own affairs. Berlin had now become the centre of great political events, and to Berlin I therefore had to shift. At 10 Kochstrasse I founded 'Presse Illustration Hoffmann', and a little later opened my studio in the Bristol Hotel. Goebbels insisted that I should join the Ministry of Propaganda, but I rejected the offer with thanks. I had no desire for political office, and I was determined to remain just a businessman. My archives already contained the results of twenty-five years of labour and my duty, I felt, was to continue to build them up into a collection of true historic value.

In any case, in 1933 I had not the slightest intention of becoming a subordinate of any ministry or of taking orders from anybody. My friendship with Hitler was a purely personal relationship, and so, I was determined, it should remain.

It was my continued lack of interest in politics, in power or in position, my persistent refusal to accept any office under the Party and my sincere insistence on the purely personal aspect of our relationship that caused him to give not only his friendship but his full confidence to a man who, he well knew, had no personal axe to grind and who would talk frankly and freely to him to the best of his limited ability. Of one thing I am quite certain; our friendship would never have developed as it did had I accepted any post under the Party aegis, and it is, I think, significant of the value that he, too, placed on the personal aspect, that it was at his own express desire that I continued always to address him as 'Herr Hitler', and never as 'Herr Reichs-kanzler' or 'mein Führer'.

Immediately after the assumption of power Goebbels declared to the inner circle of Hitler's colleagues that, to conform to his new status, Hitler should in future be addressed as Herr Reichskanzler. I asked Hitler how he wished me to address him in future.

'For you, Hoffmann,' he said, placing his hand on my shoulder, 'I shall always remain plain Herr Hitler.'

Nor did this friendship have any direct influence on my work. I was, and remained, a press photographer, and I continued to sell my pictures abroad to any newspapers that would accept them, regardless of whether their politics were Left, Right or Centre. After 1933, of course, my work at home appeared exclusively in Nazi papers, for the Party had assumed complete control of the entire national press, and there were no other papers.

One of Goebbels' actions that was by no means unanimously approved, and which called forth the sharpest possible criticism in Party circles, was the famous book-bonfire in the Berlin Gendarmenmarkt.

I did not hesitate to tell Hitler quite frankly what I thought of it. 'Things like that,' I said, 'merely bring the Reich and the Party into disrepute, especially when they are carried out wholesale – and all they accomplish is to raise a few cheap cheers from the mob and rabble. Lots of the stuff burnt was certainly rubbish; but lots of it consisted of works of established international reputation. Why – even dictionaries were burnt, simply because they had been compiled by Jews!'

Nevertheless, Goebbels succeeded in getting his own way. 'The people must see for themselves,' he declared, 'that this is a real revolution, even though it has been a bloodless one.'

The burning of the books was a symbolic act. But the burning of the Reichstag was an act of vandalism that was destined to become a beacon!

Together with Hitler, I had accepted an invitation to dine with Goebbels in the Reichskanzlerplatz on the 26th February,

1933. In deference to Hitler, there were no meat courses. Apart from vegetarian dishes, there was, however, some fish; but when a large carp was offered to him Hitler refused it.

'I thought you ate fish, my Führer,' said Frau Goebbels. 'Fish isn't meat, you know.'

Hitler smiled somewhat sarcastically. 'I suppose then, that fish, in your opinion, dear lady, is a plant!' The telephone bell interrupted the somewhat frivolous conversation. Goebbels himself answered it, and I remember the conversation as well as if it had occurred yesterday.

'Goebbels here – who's that? Oh – hullo, Hanfstängl! What is it?… What!? I can't believe it! Half a minute – I'll hand you over to the Führer himself!'

'Hullo, Hanfstängl, what's up?… Oh, get along with you!' (Hitler seemed to be highly amused.) 'Are you seeing things – or have you had a drop too much whisky? What? You can see the flames from your room?'

Hitler turned to us. 'Hanfstängl says the Reichstag building is on fire. There appears to be no doubt about it.'

We looked out of the window, and the sky over the Tiergarten was in fact blood-red.

'It's the Communists!' suddenly shouted Hitler in a furious voice. He banged down the receiver. 'We'll have a showdown over this! I must go at once! Now I've got them!'

Together Hitler and Goebbels set off for the scene of the fire. I at once rang up my office and was told that one of my reporters was already on his way to the Reichstag; that sufficed. I assumed that every photographer in Berlin would have a rendezvous there, and so there was little to interest me, personally. I remained quietly where I was with Frau Goebbels and enjoyed my fish. Later I made my leisurely way to the Reichstag, and by the time I got there I saw that the fire brigades had already got the conflagration under control. Göring was interrogating a 'suspect', and Hitler was inside, inspecting the damage. 'Good riddance to that trashy old shack,' he said contemptuously to me.

At midnight I accompanied Hitler to the offices of the *Völkischer Beobachter.* The editorial offices were empty. The only leader-writer in the place was down in the proof room. When Hitler entered he was engaged in hastily writing an article on the fire for insertion on the 'local news' page. Hitler was furious.

'An occurrence like this must go on the front page,' he shouted angrily. 'Surely, your instinct as a journalist should make you realise that!'

The chief leader-writer was hauled out of bed and roundly cursed. 'I can only hope that you will show more sense of responsibility as a captain than you do as a leader-writer! Your article ought to be humming through the rotary presses now! All I can say is that it's a masterpiece of inefficiency!'

Hitler hurled his trench coat, his hat and crop on to a chair. Swiftly he went over to the desk and dashed off a leading article with a most provocative headline:

COMMUNISTS FIRE THE REICHSTAG

It was only in the early hours of the morning, after he had seen the first copies of the day's issue coming off the presses, that Hitler left the printing press. The next day, in its report featured prominently on the front page, the *Völkischer Beobachter* foretold decisive action against the Communists.

The Reichstag fire, as is well known, resulted in the dissolution of the KPD (the German Communist Party); its leaders were arrested and its headquarters, the Liebknechthaus, was confiscated.

A year later, in April 1934, I got married again. It was in December 1929, that I had met Erna Gorebke for the first time, in the café Osteria Bavaria, an artists' rendezvous in Munich, which shortly afterwards was to become famous as one of Hitler's favourite haunts. In Erna, the daughter of Adolf Gorebke, a leading operatic tenor of his time, and an equally well-known Viennese actress, I found a kindred spirit, a great lover of art and music, a bohemian, to whom the excitement and bustle of the theatre were the breath of life, and a person very much after my own heart. We kept in touch and saw each other as frequently as the somewhat feverish life I was leading permitted. Our friendship ripened with each meeting, and in 1934, Erna consented to become my wife.

She was less interested, if possible, in politics than even I was. 'Now, look you,' was one of the first things she said after our wedding, just because I'm now your wife, don't run away with the idea that you're going to make a National Socialist or a Party member of me; you're not!' And neither then nor later on did she take the slightest interest in politics or ever become a member of the Party.

To her, Hitler was the friend of her husband, and a man whose gracious manner she found both pleasing and attractive; she was happy in his company and was always ready to discuss art, music and the humanities with him; but she refused to have anything to do with his political activities. Our wedding reception was arranged for us by Hitler at his house in the Prinzregentenstrasse, but we were prevented from spending our honeymoon in Paris, as we had planned.

With the wives of leading Nazis my wife was as polite as convention demanded, but she made no attempt to become in any way intimate with any of them. The one exception to this was Professor Morell and his wife, who had always been great and intimate friends of us both.

We were, of course, invited to a large number of official functions, and here again Erna would do all that was required of her – but no more. Into the artistic circle of our friends in Munich, in which I, too, spent as much time as I could snatch, she slipped with joyful contentment. Her great interests were the theatre and classical music, but occasionally she would deign to accompany me to some musical comedy, which was much more in my line.

On 17th June, 1934, Erna and I went to Paris, on our postponed honeymoon. Werlin, the director of the Mercedes-Benz works, was waiting for me in the French capital, where I was to take photos of the record-breaking Mercedes-Benz car, which was to take part in the Grand Prix on 21st July.

The day before the race, just as we were leaving the theatre, we heard the excited shouts of the newspaper vendors. Crowds were rushing to buy the paper, on the front page of which was sensationally displayed:

'Attempted putsch in Germany defeated. Röhm and six other senior SA officers shot!'

By the light of a streetlamp we stood and read the staggering news. Röhm, one of Hitler's most trusted men, a traitor? I could not believe it – I knew him far too well. What could have happened?

Suddenly I remembered Hitler's last words to me as we were leaving for Paris: 'Well – if some damn silly foreign motor race seems more important to you than an event which will be unique in history – off you go!'

Very shortly before our departure, he had invited me to join him on a tour of inspection of the Arbeitsdienst's camps in the Rhineland, and had been somewhat put out by my refusal. Normally I regarded an invitation from Hitler as more or less an order, but on this occasion, the promise I had made to my wife prevailed, and to Paris we went instead.

As I stood there in the Paris street, the newspaper still in my hand, these last words of Hitler's came back to me. A unique event, he had said. Had he at the time already got details of the attempted putsch? Had Röhm really intended to brush Hitler aside? It said so in the paper. But it couldn't be true. Röhm's one idea, as I knew so well from my many talks with him, was to transform the SA into a huge voluntary army, such as no other nation possessed. In this he was at complete variance with Göring and Himmler, both of whom saw in him their most dreaded opponent, the man behind whom stood thousands of SA-men, who already regarded themselves as the armed forces of the country; and Röhm enjoyed the additional advantage that he was on far more intimate terms with Hitler than they were.

Whatever it was that took place behind the scenes will remain an eternal secret.

Our honeymoon came to an abrupt end, and we returned to Germany at once. I hastened to Hitler, who seemed deeply moved. 'Think of it, Hoffmann!' he said, gripping my arm and speaking with obvious emotion, 'these swine have also murdered my good Father Stempfle!'

Later, when I started to ask Hitler what had happened, he cut me short with an abrupt gesture. 'Not another word,' he said, commandingly; and so it has remained throughout all the years that followed.

It was shortly after that Goebbels directed that all employees of public photographic agencies were to wear a special armband. This easily visible badge, with its tin shield, was designed to prevent unauthorised persons from posing as press photographers. Goebbels approached me with the request that I, too, should wear this official badge; as I was a servant of neither the Party **nor** the State, he hoped in this way to gain some measure of authority over me. But I refused categorically to have anything to do with it. 'I am invariably with Hitler himself,' I told him bluntly, 'and I only photograph events at which he himself is present. Everybody knows me, with or without number or badge or anything else. All other occasions are covered by my four assistants, all of whom wear your badge. I am not Number XYZ – I am Heinrich Hoffmann.'

At Christmas I was helping my wife to decorate the tree, when a gigantic bouquet of roses for her and a small packet for me was delivered 'with the compliments of Dr Joseph Goebbels'. A present from Goebbels! What, I wondered, could that mean? I opened the packet with great curiosity, and there I found a flaming red armband, with a large 'Number 1' inscribed on its metal disc. 'My dear Professor,' said the accompanying letter, 'Allow me to wish you and your lady a happy Christmas and a prosperous New Year, both on my own behalf and on that of my wife. Convinced that the enclosed Badge of Honour No. 1

will give you, the senior and best known of our photographic reporters, great pleasure ...' I read no further. So the sly old fox thought he'd get me that way, did he? Well – he would be disappointed! I was really very angry, and I flung the gadget on to the Christmas tree. A few minutes later, Hitler arrived, to pay us his customary Christmas Eve visit. Christmas Day itself we always spent alone, and although I more than once invited him to join us, he always refused, saying: 'Christmas is a family fete; I will impose myself on no one.'

Before we sat down to our meal, we admired the table with the presents, which my wife was still in the process of decorating. Hitler tasted some of the home-made Christmas biscuits, and gave some to our dogs. Seeing an empty space, he fixed a glittering tinsel globe on the Christmas tree. Then he caught sight of the red armband. 'What on earth is that?' he asked in astonishment.

'That,' I replied, 'is Dr Goebbels' Christmas surprise for me!'

Indignation again mastered me, and in silence I handed him the covering letter.

'Come, come, Hoffmann,' said Hitler comfortingly. 'Don't let a little thing like that spoil your Christmas! I am your armband!'

After the assumption of power, Berlin, of course, became the centre of the Party's political activities, and statesmen from all over the world came there, hoping to visit Hitler. Among the many such who posed before my camera let me mention just a few: Jean Goy, the ex-President of French ex-Services Association; the Marquess of Lothian, Liberal; Lord Allen of Hurtwood, Labour; Simon and Eden. When Simon and Eden arrived, I was introduced to them, shook hands and exchanged a few friendly words with them; and on Hitler's instructions I took a number of pictures during the subsequent conversations. On 15th June 1935, I photographed a delegation of the British Legion, under the command of Major Featherstone Godley, in the Chancellery garden; on 16th February I took the American Under Secretary of State, William Phillips, and in the same month, Lord Londonderry and Colonel Lindbergh; there is a photo in my files of Lindbergh, the first conqueror of the ocean, standing with Göring beside a plane. Göring respected Lindbergh very greatly, and it was with great pride that he showed him his art collection.

Many of these distinguished visitors were old friends, and although, of course, I took no part in the conferences, they were all invariably kind enough to greet me with a pleasant word. I have particularly happy memories of William Phillips, the genial American Under Secretary of State, whose invariable greeting was something like: 'How are you, Herr Hoffmann? Grand to see you again. Going to take some more of those excellent photos of yours? Be a friend, and don't forget to send me some copies of 'em.'

And in the few cases where a newcomer stood before my camera Hitler always made a point of introducing me: 'You've heard of the great Hoffmann, of course! Well – here he is in person.'

The number of visitors from France was particularly great; between 1936 and 1938, among other prominent people, Hitler was visited by Labeyrie, the Governor of the Bank of France, Bastide, the Minister for Trade, and General Veuillemin, the Commander-in-Chief of the French Air Force. And in 1936, for the Olympic Games, even Lord Vansittart, who was anything but well disposed towards Germany, deigned to visit us.

A very special event was a visit from Lloyd George. I took a photograph of this very popular British statesman in Munich, as, accompanied by a guard of honour from the SS, he was in the act of laying a wreath on the memorial to the unknown soldier, standing before the War Museum, which has since been destroyed by bombing.

The next day he was Hitler's guest at Obersalzberg, and after they had had a long conversation, I was given the opportunity of taking more photos. Obviously impressed by Hitler, Lloyd

George took his leave. While I accompanied him to the cloak-room, I had the chance of exchanging a few words with him. I told him that some thirty years previously I had had the honour of photographing him on an estate in the vicinity of London. He remembered the occasion and seemed very pleased at my having mentioned it. When the aged gentleman left, he patted me on the shoulder and said: 'You can thank God that you have such a wonderful Führer.'

Hitler accompanied his departing guest to his car, and when he had gone, he could not hide his delight at the visit. 'For me,' he said, 'it has been a great honour to make the acquaintance of this renowned British statesman.' He repeated the phrase that he had coined in 1925: 'I do not wish to see a single pearl fall from the Imperial Crown of Britain. That would be an evil thing for Europe!'

The visit of the Duke of Windsor and his wife in 1937 aroused the interest of the entire world. For us, too, it was a sensation.

From the first moment of his arrival, the Duke made a most happy and friendly impression. Hitler and the ex-King of England had a long conversation alone together in the Great Hall, while the Duchess remained on the terrace, admiring the view and chatting to me.

In the charm of her engaging personality, I quite forgot to take in any details of her apparel; all I could recall was the impression of dignified harmony that the quiet elegance of her country clothes left upon me.

Hitler accompanied his guests in person to their car; and that evening round the fire, the Windsors, naturally, were the main topic of conversation.

'That would have been the man,' declared Hitler, 'with whose co-operation I could have realised my long cherished desire for an alliance with Britain.'

The impression seems to have been mutual, for shortly after-wards he received the following letter:

To The Führer and Chancellor of the German Reich.

On our departure from Germany, the Duchess and I take
the opportunity of expressing our sincere thanks both for the
hospitality which you were kind enough to extend to us, and for
the many opportunities you gave us to see all that is being done
for the well-being of the industrious German people.

Particularly do we wish to thank you for the delightful hours
which we spent with you at Obersalzberg.

EDWARD

In 1937, too, I had the great pleasure of revisiting England – for
the Coronation of His Majesty King George VI. Any description from my pen of that great and historic occasion would be
superfluous, and I shall confine myself to describing briefly my
own activities and those of the German Embassy, in which I
stayed as a guest.

For Ribbentrop and the Embassy the Coronation was an event
of the highest importance, and neither expense nor trouble were
spared, not only to prepare regal entertainment for the many
guests who were expected, but also to entertain them in a milieu
worthy of all that was best in the Third Reich. In this, Frau
Ribbentrop, a lady of impeccable artistic taste and knowledge,
made a most valuable contribution, and thanks to her exertions
an almost unique collection of German works of art was gathered
together and exhibited in the Embassy.

Whether Ribbentrop did not invite them, or whether
they were invited and did not attend, I do not know; but it
is an interesting fact that no leading members of the German
Government were among the Embassy guests, who were made
up almost entirely of eminent private individuals, mostly from
artistic circles.

I took some hundreds of photographs in colour, and I intended
to follow my usual practice on such great occasions and publish
the collection in book form. In this, however, I was thwarted

by the intense rivalries between the German Ministries for Propaganda and Foreign Affairs, each of which claimed the right to use my pictures and to issue a volume as an official Ministry publication. To this demand I refused resolutely to accede, and as a result, though many of my pictures appeared individually in the press, the collection, as such, was never published.

Chapter 4

Our Diplomatic Excursions

IT WAS NOT FOR the outside world alone, but also for his immediate entourage that Hitler was always preparing surprise packets. He was a master of the art of concealing his intentions, and he told no one of his plans, except those who were indispensable to the execution of them. And woe betide anyone who failed to keep the objurgation to silence imposed on him!

Nor was this habit restricted to official affairs; in private life he loved to spring surprises and see the astonished faces of the onlookers. A case in point was my nomination as Professor. On the occasion of the opening of the first exhibition in the Haus der Deutschen Kunst in 1937, Goebbels announced that the Führer had been pleased to make me a professor. I had no inkling of what was coming, and Hitler, apparently, had given Goebbels strict instructions not to tell me anything about it beforehand.

In 'this age of *faits accomplis*', as Hitler used to say, the various foreign secret services had a hard time of it. Whenever Hitler got up in the Reichstag and said that the time of surprises had now finally come to an end, one could be quite certain that something or other was cooking!

One day in March 1937, Hitler invited me to dine with him in the Chancellery.

'I don't think I can, Herr Hitler,' I said. 'Doctor Goebbels has already bidden me to attend some important press meeting in the Ministry of Propaganda.'

'Important meeting? Nonsense, my dear fellow. Don't you go to Goebbels' dull show – you come here instead, and believe me, you won't regret it!' Hitler's face had assumed that expression that, as I knew so well, meant that he was secretly enjoying a little joke of his own. This, I thought, is a tip straight from the horse's mouth, so I cut the press meeting and dined with Hitler instead.

The editors of the leading German newspapers and the press photographers for their part attended a conference in the Ministry of Propaganda.

'Gentlemen, the Führer has directed me to invite you here and to tell you of an impending action, which requires your co-operation,' Goebbels began, mysteriously. 'As it is the Führer's intention to present the German people himself with the *fait accompli,* it is essential that what I am about to tell you should remain strictly secret,' he continued, gazing round the circle of mystified editors and reporters. 'You will, I am sure, appreciate in principle the reasons which have impelled me to deny to you for this night all contact with the outside world, and to cause all the doors of this Ministry to be locked. The telephone exchange has been put out of action. Anyone who requires anything for the journey you are about to be invited to undertake has only to tell me, and the Ministry will take steps to procure his wants.'

A great deal of guessing was indulged in, but no one got anywhere near the truth. When the representatives of the press entered the waiting aircraft and took off, the flight direction was no more helpful and gave no clue. Even the pilot did not know where he was going! Only after a specific time of flight in a specific direction was he to open the sealed envelope containing his instructions and then act accordingly.

The next day I was in the Reichstag listening to Hitler's address, in which he dramatically told the House: 'As I speak to you, gentlemen, German troops are crossing the Rhine and re-taking possession of the occupied Rhineland!'

And indeed as the planes landed on the other side of the Rhine, the press was informed that German troops had crossed the river and were in process of occupying their old garrisons!

After the occupation of the Rhineland had been accomplished, Hitler said to me, 'For two nights before the move, I couldn't sleep a wink! Again and again I asked myself the same question: What will France do? Will she oppose the advance of my handful of battalions? I know what I would have done, if I'd been the French; I should have struck and I would not have allowed a single German soldier to cross the Rhine. The whole thing was possible only if the strictest secrecy were maintained. Goebbels did a good job of work; that we sprang a surprise on the world is thanks entirely to him!'

'In a few days' time, I'm going to Munich,' said Hitler to me in Berlin at the beginning of March 1938.

When we got there and were sitting, as usual, in the Café Heck, he suddenly turned to me and said: 'Hoffmann, I've got a small conference in Mühldorf. Would you like to come with me? I expect we shall be back in Munich by the evening, but just in case, you'd better take whatever you want for the night with you. But – above all – don't forget to bring your Leica!'

In Mühldorf, not far from the Austrian frontier, Hitler went straight to the village school, where he was received by a number of general officers. On the tables I noticed that large-scale General Staff maps had been spread out. Now what? Manoeuvres? At this time of the year? I had heard, of course, that troops had been concentrated on the frontier, in order to impress the gravity of the situation on the Austrian Government; but at the same time, I had also heard that the whole thing was a bluff.

When Hitler left the school, he was in high spirits. 'Gentlemen,' he said, 'how would you like to accompany me to Simbach? It's only a few miles away, and I would dearly like to have a look at my birthplace, Braunau, which is on the opposite bank of the inn.'

As we drove into Simbach, it was obvious that Hitler was expected. Flags and banners with slogans flew everywhere, and workmen were working furiously to complete the decorations of some of the streets and houses.

A roar of cheering greeted our arrival. Suddenly Hitler stood up in the car. He drew himself stiffly to attention. 'Now – over the bridge and into Braunau!' he ordered.

In the middle of the bridge, at the Austro-German frontier, a German officer stood waiting; little children in festive garb surrounded the car, offering their bouquets of flowers to the Führer. It was only then that we realised what the people of Simbach already knew – we were off to Austria! Hitler turned round and laughed joyously at our surprised faces. Another surprise packet had come off! Braunau was in a turmoil of excitement. And it was now for the first time that we heard that, hours before, the German troops had crossed the frontier and had everywhere been greeted with tremendous enthusiasm. We wondered where on earth the population had got hold of those masses of Swastika flags, photos of Hitler and slogan-bearing banners, all of which were forbidden in Austria, under pain of heavy penalty. Standing on the running board of the Führer's car, I started to record the enthusiasm of the crowd with my Leica. The camera does not lie, and the films prove conclusively that in 1938 the overwhelming majority of the Austrian population was in favour of Adolf Hitler and the Anschluss with Germany.

Hour after hour the cries of 'HEIL!' rang in our ears, and wherever the Führer's car stopped for an instant, enthusiasm rose to a tornado of cheers. Late in the afternoon we reached Linz, where Hitler had spent a part of his youth. Here we went to the Hotel Weinzinger, where the officials of the town and the leading Party members were already assembled to welcome us.

In a trice the whole picture altered. The 'private little

excursion,' as Hitler had called it, was over. The hotel became a headquarters.

The telephone rang ceaselessly. The Chancellor, Dr Seyss-Inquart, arrived from Vienna, to be received by Hitler with the words: 'For Austria I have to thank you!' And on the same evening Hitler spoke from the balcony of the Municipal Buildings to an excited and enthusiastic crowd; all Linz was there.

Conferences went on until the early hours of the morning, and even when he at last retired, Hitler did not go to bed, but had tea sent up to his room for us and the gentlemen from Vienna. Plans were discussed and details arranged for the annexation of Austria and the taking over of the government and administration. Hitler was in the highest spirits, for step by step the great dream of his boyhood – to play a leading part in the affairs of his fatherland – was being realised to an extent to which even he had never aspired.

Throughout the night, too, he kept in constant and close touch with Mussolini. The Duce, he thought, might well be looking towards the Brenner Pass with some misgiving, particularly as there were already rumours of liberation celebrations and bell-ringings in the South Tyrol. Hitler knew Mussolini's temperament, and he felt that only by keeping him fully and constantly informed of events as they occurred could he safeguard the Italian friendship that was so important to him.

The owner of the hotel had given him the room he and his wife normally occupied, and it was quite the best room in the hotel. But the floor was covered with all kinds of stuffed wild beasts, and Hitler stumbled two or three times over the head of a polar bear, while all the other heads with which the walls were festooned brought no joy to the Führer, who was a great opponent of blood sports of any kind.

Over the great double bed, handsomely bedecked with gilded angels, was a framed gravure of the well-known dancer, Joséphine Baker, while on the walls was a huge copy of a Rubens and a pastel copy of Astet's *Erblüht*, a woman's head in profile with long hair. Such was the room in which the final negotiations for the incorporation of Austria into the German Reich took place.

From Linz the triumphant march went on to Vienna. On the way we overtook a column on the march, which was under the command of Major Lacelle, a holder of the *Pour le Mérite* medal, who immediately came up to report to Hitler. He galloped up with drawn sword and planted himself just in front of the car. Then suddenly his horse shied, threw him and broke his arm.

This tragi-comic episode caused Hitler to make some terse remarks on the use of horses for military purposes. With modern progress, he said, something technically more reliable could surely be used!

All the enthusiasm we had so far met paled into insignificance when we reached Vienna. The city's whole two millions seemed to be jammed on the pavements, and the Hotel Imperial in the Ringstrasse was permanently surrounded by a vast crowd, shouting: 'We want the Führer!' and 'Back to the Homeland!' And again and again Hitler had to appear on the balcony and show himself to the shouting, gesticulating masses.

After the incorporation of Austria in March, 1938, we had another veritable invasion of foreign visitors. For the Munich conference I accompanied Hitler to Bad Godesberg to meet Chamberlain.

'No photos of the arrival, Hoffmann,' said Hitler, crisply. 'I'm told that the old gentleman dislikes being suddenly snapped with flashlights, and I am most anxious that he should be spared all inconvenience after his long journey.'

My photographs at the conference, however, which decided the fate of the Sudetenland and temporarily preserved world peace, together with those of Hitler, Mussolini, Chamberlain and Daladier, became known all over the world.

Equal interest was aroused by the photographs taken on the occasion of the signing of the Franco-German Treaty of Friendship in Paris in 1938.

In the same year, Beck, the Polish Foreign Minister, toured

Bavaria in a car placed at his disposal by Hitler and saw for himself all that was being accomplished in the new Germany. He was extremely impressed!

Among others who fell to my camera before the outbreak of war were Stojadinovich, the Premier of Yugoslavia, and Gömbös, the Hungarian Prime Minister. The latter I snapped at a shooting party in Erfurt, given by Göring and attended by Gömbös and Hitler, on the occasion of a big SA rally.

Every now and then, in the evening after some such conference and in the intimacy of his own circle, Hitler would express terse, off-the-record opinions of his recent visitors.

'Bloody butcher – and looks like it!' he exclaimed with reference to the Hungarian Premier, Gömbös, to whom he had taken a violent dislike solely because he was an ardent big game hunter! Daladier he regarded as a very sincere and honest man of the middle classes. The letter in which Daladier pleaded that war could bring but destruction, devastation, blood and tears to all and victory to none evoked a sympathetic echo in Hitler – but also the remark: 'That is well and good; but I fear that Destiny will pursue its own course.' Mussolini he liked, but his admiration for his many qualities did not blind him to the Duce's little weaknesses and foibles. 'Where Art is concerned, the man's a fathead!' he asserted; and from the moment he saw a photograph of Mussolini in bathing trunks he lost all respect for him as a statesman. The Balkan statesmen he usually referred to as 'the Balkan Bandits'; but Ataturk he admired greatly, and a bust of him by the famous sculptor Professor Thorak was one of his cherished possessions. Beck and Pilsudski, too, he regarded as eminent statesmen. He particularly respected the latter, and when Warsaw was occupied, he paid a visit to Pilsudski's former residence and placed a wreath in his death chamber. With the exception of Ambassador Henderson, of whom he said: 'He's a confirmed bluffer; but so am I – and the only difference between us is that he is a rotten bluffer and I'm a good one!' it was the British statesmen who commanded Hitler's greatest respect. Of the statesmanlike qualities of Eden and Simon as diplomats he always spoke warmly, but for him, the greatest statesman of them all was Lloyd George.

During the war, King Boris of Bulgaria was a frequent visitor at Führer-Headquarters, where his naturalness and charm made him very popular. I myself liked him particularly because he was always ready at any time to accede to my request to stand and pose for a photo; apart from that, whenever he paid us a visit he always presented those of us who were in the Führer's immediate entourage with a large box of very special cigarettes, with the King's effigy on them.

King Michael of Rumania and his mother, Paul, Prince Regent of Yugoslavia, Ali Cotinkaya, the Turkish Minister for Public Works, Cinzar Marcovic, the Yugoslav Foreign Minister, Caski, the Hungarian Premier and many others – all had their photographs taken by me or my assistants.

Each New Year the foreign ambassadors, with the Papal Nuncio as doyen of the diplomatic corps at their head, came in their magnificent full-dress uniforms to pay their respects to the Head of the German State, and never in my life have I ever photographed so much fervent friendship and hand-shaking as at these New Year receptions. Nobody, and certainly not photographer Heinrich Hoffmann, could have any doubt about the sincerity and enthusiasm of their assurances of friendly and peace-loving goodwill! Even Churchill himself wrote in an open letter in *The Times* in 1938:

'I have always said that if Great Britain were defeated in war I hoped we should find a Hitler to lead us back to our rightful position among the nations.'

'Hoffmann, I will give you a unique opportunity to take a photo!' The speaker was none other than Mussolini himself – and did I jump at the chance! It happened years before the war, during a visit to Rome my wife and I made with the German press men. In addition to the usual sightseeing, we were invited to visit the sports academy in the magnificent, marble-bedecked Forum Mussolini. Here Mussolini himself assumed charge.

When we entered the fencing hall, an instructor was already waiting for him, and I had the chance of taking snaps and my wife an excellent film of a unique and historical foil match, in which, of course, Mussolini was the victor. But, like the good showman that he was, he did more; he caused the fencing masks to be removed, and before my camera stood two 'unprotected' fighters! A truly sensational picture! Nor was that the end of it. On the way to the usual *rinfresco* we passed through a classroom of the Academy pupils; Mussolini sat down at one of the forms and banged the desk before him with both fists, and in good German there came ringing to my ears a line from the old student song – *Es war eine köstliche Zeit!*

Köstlich – cherished – it certainly was, both for his memories and for my camera! A dictator sitting on a form in school – that was certainly a new experience for me!

The Duce, like all his fellow-countrymen, was always a willing victim to my camera; he well knew that, in contrast to his 'very good friend, Hitler', he 'took well,' and he emphasised it by striking all sorts of poses, ranging from Julius Caesar's to the Napoleonic.

Yes – those two and their photographs! What astonishing contrasts! My mind goes back with professional pain to Hitler's visit to Venice in June 1934; in that photo, the German, badly dressed and ill-tempered, looked far more like a retainer of the Italian than a future Axis partner and, later, Lord of the Axis! At that time it almost seemed as if the personal and political failures of Hitler had transferred themselves to my photos. The series was a photographic triumph – for Mussolini!

How different was the picture at the time of Hitler's Italian 'honeymoon' in May 1938, and what very different pictures my camera took of it! Before it now stood two men of at least equal stature, and seldom have I taken such excellent photographs as those taken under the eternal blue sky in Rome, in Naples and in Florence. I later published a collection in a book entitled *With Hitler in Italy*, which came to be highly prized. In it the dictators can be seen on board battleships, visiting museums, being cheered by crowds, at festivals and all over the place – a symposium, in short, of the zenith of their friendly relations in all their glory.

Not for diplomats and courtiers alone was this journey somewhat tricky; Italy was a kingdom, and, notwithstanding his very thinly veiled expression of antipathy for the monarchical system, there was nothing that Hitler could do about it; if he had had his way, I should have re-touched my photographs and expunged king and queen, crown prince, court and all the rest of them!

As it was things turned out quite differently. The royal photographs, naturally, survived, but apart from that I was destined to have an entirely unexpected 'professional' talk with the first lady of Italy. I was staying with Hitler and his suite in the Quirinal, the old Roman castle of the House of Savoy, and when the Queen heard that I was among the party she requested Hitler to tell me to call on her, that she might 'ask my professional advice.' I soon found, however, that she had no need of it.

Queen Elena was a passionate and expert amateur photographer, and her really artistic studies, mostly of her very happy family life, aroused my genuine admiration. I am only sorry that I was unable to preserve in picture form this photographic rendezvous, under the title: 'A Queen with a Camera'.

In spite of his anti-royalist sympathies, Hitler was by no means impervious, during this Italian tour, to the fascination of southern feminine beauty and the exceptional wisdom that so often went with it. He was particularly attracted by Maria José, Crown Princess, on account of her having married Umberto.

Years later during the war her long conversations with Hitler in Germany, which decided the fate of her brother, King Leopold of Belgium, must undoubtedly be regarded as a great, if hard-won success for her; and the photographs that I took of them at the time give some inkling of the difficulties, both political and personal, which beset them and which finally brought them before my camera, sitting side-by-side at a tea table.

The Countess Ciano, Mussolini's favourite daughter, allowed herself a freedom of expression of opinion, which would have been permitted to no other foreign woman.

Hitler's greatest admiration, however, was for the Countess Eleanora Attolico, 'Italy's most beautiful representative', as he called the wife of the very wise Ambassador to Berlin. Her classical beauty and her personal charm, in contrast to the violent anti-Nazi attitude of her predecessor, Elizabetta Cerruti, made a tremendous appeal to Hitler and delighted his sense of the artistic.

Years later, speaking of this very exceptional woman, Hitler said: 'If all diplomats brought wives like that with them, they would certainly find success much easier to attain. It is a point to which the attention of our own gentlemen might well be invited. In future, I shall see to it that our overseas representatives follow this good example.'

I wish that the photographs of these happy days of a happy year had been the last I was to take of Mussolini; but I was destined, alas, to take also those fateful photos in September 1943, when he arrived at Führer-Headquarters from the Gran Sasso; and the photographs that I took of him and Hitler, standing among the ruins at Führer-Headquarters after the 20th July attempt, can be given but one title: The Twilight of the Gods.

No, indeed, these were anything but 'halcyon days', and the pictures I then took show it more plainly than could be expressed by any words.

Is there anything more impartial in the world than a camera? By this time I had had them all before my camera – emperors and kings, statesmen and diplomats, revolutionaries and popular leaders, and all had come willingly. The three dictators, Hitler, Mussolini and Stalin, had been caught by my magic eye and preserved for all time. All that was missing was the land of Velazquez and Goya, the land of the toreros and *Carmen*, and that, unfortunately, I have never seen. But I did meet General-issimo Franco and his son-in-law, Serrano Suñer, the Foreign Minister, in Hendaye-Irun on 23rd October 1940, and during the visit of the latter to Obersalzberg.

Nothing can plunge 'a photographer of history' into retro-spective reverie as the contemplation of his own pictures. In those days Hitler and Ribbentrop seemed to be building an empire that would last for all time and in which the Spaniards were to occupy but a very modest niche – and that only on condition that they came into the war. Today, the only survivors of that whole circle are Franco and his son-in-law; and to the students of history I recommend a careful study of the portraits of two foreign ministers: the Spaniard, cool, careful and calcu-lating ; the Italian, frivolous, vain and impulsive! The camera is indeed a mercilessly dispassionate judge! And when it looks at the visitors from the lands of oranges and lemons, nothing escapes it.

On 14th March, 1939, I was dining with Hitler. 'It was exactly a year ago today,' I remarked, 'that we marched into Vienna.'

For a while we chatted about the enthusiasm with which he had been greeted as a liberator on that day, and I told him how I went to a Viennese cabaret show, in which one of the comedians sang the amusing song: *Is that the lot – or is there any more to come?* 'Actually,' I went on, 'we answered his question pretty quickly, for only a very few months later came the Sudetenland.'

Hitler gave me a quick look, 'And more to come yet,' he said. 'Today I am expecting Hacha, and we have another historic day before us, of which the world as yet has no inkling.'

'Well! Is *that* the lot – or is there still more to come?' I asked with surprise. But before Hitler could answer, he was told that Hacha had arrived in the Reichs Chancellery; he rose swiftly and hastened out to greet his guest, and I followed him with my camera, ready to make records of the historic scene that was to be enacted.

On such occasions, the normal procedure was for a formal,

official photograph to be taken first. Hitler took up his pose, with his colleague beside him, and I snapped. Hitler usually asked his guests if they had any objection to further snaps being taken for publication in the press. Meanwhile, I got the camera ready again, for no guest had so far ever been known to object. Nor did Hacha, and, having taken a snap or two, I withdrew to a discreet distance, but remained in the room. A photographer must always be on hand, but he must not be too conspicuous or disturb the principals in any way. It is left entirely to his discretion to select what he feels is a good moment for a snap.

Many prominent men get fidgety when they see the camera trained on them, and for this reason I always used an 'angled' view-finder, which allowed me, as it were, to take a photograph round the corner. The President of Czechoslovakia was very nervous, and the old gentleman was obviously tired and feeling the effects of his long journey. Moreover, he was facing the most important decision of his life. If he signed, he was surrendering the independence of his country.

I saw all too clearly the struggle that was going on within him, and I noticed, too, the observant manner in which Hitler followed the nervous, agitated gestures of the old gentleman's hands. The negotiations seemed to be becoming more and more dramatically tense, and, discreetly, I left the room.

A little later, while I was in the ante-room, Morell came in. He had been sent for, he said, as Hacha had been taken suddenly ill. Together we entered the conference room.

Hacha was in an armchair, breathing heavily, and it was obvious that he had suffered a nervous breakdown. But an injection sufficed, and very quickly the old gentleman recovered his calm, and the negotiations continued. Quite a considerable time elapsed before I was sent for to photograph the final historical act of the signing of the treaty. Red and hectic in the face, Hacha signed with a trembling hand, and then, turning to Morell, he thanked him for his professional administrations.

Later, as we sat at table in our intimate circle, Hitler expressed his great satisfaction at what had occurred. 'I was sorry for the old gentleman,' he said. 'But sentimentality, in the circumstances, would have been out of place and might well have jeopardised success.'

The vain Morell was most anxious to have some recognition shown of his timely professional intervention, and he let it be quite plainly understood that, but for him, the treaty could never have been signed.

'Thank God,' he said, with a sidelong glance at Hitler, 'that I was on the spot and in time with my injection!'

'You go to hell with your damn injection!' retorted Hitler. 'You made the old gentleman so lively, that for the moment I feared that he would refuse to sign!'

For us, sleep that night was out of the question. Within a few hours of the signing of the treaty, we were in the special train and on the way to the Czechoslovak border. At the frontier itself we were met by a fleet of armoured half-tracked Mercedes cars, in which we continued our onward journey, and on the evening of 15th March 1939, in the middle of a severe snowstorm we entered Prague, unrecognised and unobserved.

Hitler's arrival came as a complete surprise, and in view of the secrecy that had surrounded it, no preparations had been made. We drove straight up to the Hradschin, the famous Prague fortress, where we took up our quarters. In great haste a banquet in honour of the event was arranged and was held at midnight.

The Hradschin had not sufficient sleeping accommodation for so numerous a party, and I and several others had to spend the night on camp-beds, which had been hastily collected. A telephone exchange was swiftly installed, and in it, Professor Morell and I bedded down for the night. There was, however, but little rest for us – or for anybody else; the telephone bells rang without ceasing, and there was an endless coming and going throughout the night. At last, however, overcome by fatigue, and helped by the copious toasts we had drunk at the banquet, we fell asleep. All I can remember is that people kept on waking us up, complaining that our snores were interfering with business and making the official telephone conversations all but impossible.

When Hacha arrived in Prague a few days later, he was more than a little astonished to find that all the preparations for the proclamation of the protectorate had already been made.

The next day I had many golden opportunities of taking truly historic photographs, which formed the backbone of my book *With Hitler in Bohemia and Moravia.*

Life had been hectic enough in all conscience in the decade that preceded Hitler's assumption of power and that had culminated in electoral tours all over the country, often for weeks at a time. But in comparison with what happened from 1934 onwards, it was child's play; the incorporation of Austria, the return to the Rhineland, the Olympic Games, the formation of the Berlin-Rome Axis, the occupation of the Sudetenland, the signing of the Russo-German Pact all followed each other in bewildering array.

The atmosphere of feverish activity in which we lived is well summed up in a joke that went all round Germany:

'Well – how go things with the rest of the family, and where are they all?'

'Fine. I'm here, Dad's in the SA and Mum is working in the NSV. Heinz is in the SS, sister Gertrud is with BDV and young Fritz is doing his whack with the HJ; but we all meet each year on Party Day in Nuremberg and have a lovely time!'

And if this is a fair reflection of what things were like with an ordinary family, it requires little imagination to appreciate what life for us in Hitler's immediate entourage was like.

Those of us who formed part of his immediate entourage had to reconcile ourselves to the sacrifice of a very large measure of our private lives; for us there was, and could be, little or no home life, and we seemed to live in plane, train and hotel more than under our own roofs. Hitler, too, had a queer kink, almost of jealousy, and while he was always charming to our wives and welcomed them most graciously whenever they accompanied us, he had to come first in our devotion, and it irked him grievously if family ever seemed to take precedence in our minds.

Neither in the early years, nor, indeed, throughout the brief reign of the National Socialist régime, did there ever exist any Nazi social circle as such among the élite of the Party. It must be remembered that the vast majority of Hitler's high officials were men of modest and often most humble origin, selected originally for their zeal, their efficiency and their devotion to the Führer and his cause. Most of them, of course, had already married into the humble social environment from which they themselves had emanated; and, as is so often the case with self-made men, their wives were unfitted and were totally unable to keep pace, socially or mentally, with the ever widening circle of their husbands' interests and responsibilities. With but few exceptions, they found themselves embarrassed, gauche and out of place in the glitter and glamour of the social and diplomatic worlds into which their husbands had been drawn, and they much preferred to be left at home in peace, in the cosy surroundings to which they had always been accustomed. Their appearances, therefore, were restricted to the minimum possible, and it was only at certain official functions, primarily of a Party nature, at which it was felt that their presence was highly desirable, that they were called upon to fulfil any social obligations.

All this, as may well be imagined, could not but have serious repercussions on the family life. The husbands met so many women younger, more elegant and charming, more witty and intelligent than their wives, and inevitably a very great number of marriages came to grief; by some, indeed, Hitler's immediate entourage was somewhat cynically dubbed the Ante-Room of the Divorce Court.

As the daughter of popular theatrical parents, my wife, fortunately, had been accustomed from her earliest childhood to a life of constant flurry and movement; indeed, I think she rather enjoyed the excitement of it all. She was rather thrilled, too, by my success and growing importance, but only so far as my professional and artistic activities were concerned; of all the political comings and goings she was somewhat contemptuous, and sometimes she made things a little awkward for both of us.

'You'd have had just as great a success anywhere else in the world,' she would suddenly exclaim, 'and abroad at least we'd have led a sane and peaceful existence. The trouble with you is that you married too young and got stuck in this country! What a name you'd have made for yourself in the great big world outside!' And things like that, as can well be imagined, didn't go down at all well in Party circles.

We used to see each other when and where we could; very often she would hop on to a plane or train and meet me for a few fleeting days as I passed from place to place, and on such special functions as the Bayreuth Festival and Party rallies she would join me, but very seldom did we ever start or complete a journey together.

During the Olympic Games, at which my assistants and I took over 6,000 photos, both for the winter sports in Garmisch (a sport in which, incidentally, she was herself no mean performer), and at the Games proper in Berlin, she enjoyed herself immensely. Thanks to her knowledge of languages, she had been asked to help with the entertaining of the vast numbers of foreign guests who had poured into Berlin from all over the world. Throughout the Games there were parties and receptions of some sort every day, and when the Games ended, happy but quite exhausted she said jestingly to me, 'Well, Heini – now I must leave you for a couple of years or so, if I am to accept all the kind invitations to stay with them that have been showered on me by our grateful guests!'

Only once did we have the chance to take a really private trip together. That was in 1935, when, following a serious illness, I spent several weeks convalescing on the Lido. But we also had two less peaceful but very pleasant interludes together.

In the autumn of 1936, Dr Goebbels with his wife paid an official visit to Greece and very kindly invited us to join them.

My relations with the little Doctor had always been very friendly. We sometimes had our minor differences, as over his attempt to discipline me with his famous armband, and when on one occasion I had told Hitler of my experiences as a film producer and script writer, and he insisted on seeing the film, of which I still had a copy.

It was accordingly shown in the Reichs Chancellery, and Hitler, Goebbels and I sat in the front row. When the hairdresser, Pinselweich, as I had called him, first appeared, in three-quarter length on the screen, Hitler turned to Goebbels. 'Very good characterisation,' he said appreciatively. But as the film progressed, I had a real shock. Good heavens! I thought, I'd clean forgotten that! At the same time Goebbels reacted sharply. 'Very bad taste on your part, Hoffmann,' he whispered indignantly and got up and left the hall. It was nearly twenty years since I had produced the film, and I had clean forgotten that the hairdresser had a club-foot!

Sometimes, too, I was the target of his mordant and extremely sarcastic tongue; but although he was quick to take offence, he was not one to bear malice, and he had a keen sense of fun and humour. He was vain, he was ambitious and he was very sensitive on the subject of his deformity; but equally he was undoubtedly one of the foremost brains and one of the personally most courageous men in the whole Nazi hierarchy.

We flew to Athens in Goebbels' special plane and spent a most enjoyable week, though overburdened somewhat with official receptions, in that beautiful and historic land.

The ever-increasing demands of my growing personal business and the constant travelling with Hitler left me but little time to ponder over the events that were succeeding each other with such bewildering rapidity, or to give much thought to how and when it would all end. By this time, too, no one in his entourage would have dared, unasked, to express any personal opinion; and though they had most probably never heard it, his intimate circle followed the principle implied in the British Sergeant-

Major's classic remark: 'You're not paid to think, my lad, but to do what you're told!'

In my capacity as a private friend with no official status, I was frequently asked for my opinion – not, it is true, on the merits or otherwise of this or the other political move – but for an unbiased, unvarnished account of what the people themselves thought about things. Even so, Hitler very much disliked having to listen to things that were displeasing to him (and that it was my doubtful privilege to have practically the monopoly of bringing to his attention), and as often as not he would interrupt with a curt: 'I'm disagreeably surprised, Hoffmann, that you should give any credence to such stupid rumours.'

Among the masses the progress of events had been followed with conflicting emotions. Initially they were fearful at the great risks he was apparently taking; but as one resounding diplomatic success succeeded another, confidence – and even enthusiasm – grew, and 'leave it to Hitler' became the slogan of the German people. And to this attitude I subscribed without further ado; he obviously knew what he was doing, and if at times I doubted the wisdom of some move, why, then, obviously, I was wrong.

My wife's reactions were very different. She had a large number of friends and acquaintances in the artistic and musical worlds, and in society that had nothing to do with Party circles; and as her political outlook was well known to them, her friends were inclined to talk much more freely and openly to her than, for example, to me. On more than one occasion, when I happened to join her with some of her friends, she would make some such remark as: 'Well! here he is! Now you can tell him all this yourselves, so that he'll see it is not always I alone who am the carping element!'

She was an ardent pacifist, with an intelligent and perceptive imagination that enabled her all too clearly to see the dangers that were looming ahead; nor did she make any secret of her fears and her horror of war in Hitler's presence, and I was more than surprised at the docility with which he listened to some of the opinions she expressed. On one occasion, some time in the autumn of 1938, when we were staying with Hitler at the Berghof, conversation turned to the subject of war.

'War!' exclaimed Erna with horror. 'I've only read one war book, thank you – Remarque's *All Quiet on the Western Front* – and I cannot conceive how any decent human being can even think of the possibility of war with complacency!'

Such remarks, admittedly, would have been impossible in Hitler's presence, once war had been declared. But again and again I had good cause to fear that even my influence with Hitler and his genuine affection for me would not suffice to keep my wife outside a concentration camp. Indeed, shortly after the declaration of war she was subjected to quite a long period of house-arrest for 'opposition to State Authority' – and she was lucky to have been dealt with so leniently!

'The Chief is very touchy this morning,' whispered one of Hitler's adjutants to me.

He was pacing up and down the 25 yards of the length of the Obersalzberg hall, not saying a word and showing clearly by the expression on his face that he did not wish to be disturbed in his silent peregrinations.

In these days of intense political tension in August 1939, the eyes of the world were turned on Hitler and the world's press was full of his doings and sayings. I could well understand the excitement that gripped him; but it was not that alone that made him pace up and down in this fashion. I recognised the signs, and I knew him too well – something was in the air! 'I bet that in a very short time we shall have another surprise,' I thought to myself. 'Another of those surprises that makes the world stand on its head and completely discountenances all the diplomats.'

Of what was in store for us I had no idea. I knew, of course, that from the time he assumed power Hitler had made no secret of his conviction that the world was approaching a crisis, which could be solved only by force of arms; a clash, he asserted, was inevitable, but it was axiomatic with him that this would be a struggle between West and East, a struggle of ideologies, in which he fondly hoped that he would have the support of the other Western Powers – and most particularly that of Great Britain – but a struggle that nevertheless he was prepared, if necessary, to wage alone.

Suddenly, the telephone rang. Schaub answered it and reported to Hitler that Ribbentrop was on the line. With a swift movement Hitler seized the receiver from his ADC' ... Marvellous! I congratulate you! Yes, come up at once!' With a beaming smile he put down the receiver and turned to us, a picture of smiling delight. 'Chaps,' he cried, 'Stalin has agreed! and we are to fly to Moscow, to conclude a pact with him! And won't that just make the world sit up again!' And in a mood of complete abandonment, such as I have seen on only one other occasion – and that was later, when France capitulated – he slapped himself delightedly on the knee.

'That,' he exclaimed, 'will really land them (*the Western Powers*) in the soup!'

We were all tremendously excited and pleased. Kannenberg, his majordomo, brought champagne, and joyously we clinked glasses and drank a toast to this great diplomatic coup. Hitler, obviously delighted at our enthusiasm, became more expansive than ever, though he touched no drink.

To me in my political innocence this complete *volte-face* was more than a little disconcerting. From the time of his earliest beginnings 'Communism the Arch-Enemy of Humanity' had been the corner-stone of his whole political edifice and he had convinced and carried his followers with him in a thousand eloquent and compelling speeches. And now?

A little later, when we were alone together, I could not hide my preoccupation from him.

'Cheer up, Hoffmann!' he cried, still in high good humour. 'Now what's biting that mighty brain of yours?'

'Well,' I replied, 'I – it's all a bit sudden, isn't it! For twenty years you've been damning the Bolsheviks in heaps and now – it's – let's kiss and be friends! I don't know, of course, but I can't help wondering what the Party will think of it all; but I'm afraid they won't be too pleased.'

'The Party,' retorted Hitler, 'will be just as astounded as the rest of the world, but my Party members know and trust me; they know I will never depart from my basic principles, and they will realise that the ultimate aim of this latest gambit is to remove the Eastern danger and thus to facilitate, under my leadership, of course, a swifter unification of all Europe.'

In the event, Hitler was not quite correct in his appreciation of Party members' reactions. The next morning in the garden of the Brown House many hundreds of Party badges were lying on the ground where they had been pitched by enraged and disillusioned members. But quite a number of them, I suspect, very soon repented their all too hasty action and very quickly bought themselves a new badge.

Very shortly after this, Ribbentrop arrived from Fuschl, his Schloss in the Salzkammergut, and he and Hitler withdrew for private conversation. When they came out again, I asked Hitler if I was to go with Ribbentrop.

'Naturally,' he answered. 'Apart from the photography, I have a special task for you. Go off at once and see Ribbentrop, and make sure that you've got a place on the plane.'

Ribbentrop greeted my request with a negative gesture. Out of the question, he said, all seats in the machine had already been allotted, and in any case, his own photographer, Laux, was going with him. Much as he regretted it, he could not dispense with a single one of his gentlemen – it simply couldn't be done!

This was more or less what I had expected. My relations with Ribbentrop had always been poor. As with Bormann and Goebbels, I had in him another enemy, intent on undermining the friendly and private character of my association with Hitler. His deprecating smile, as he rejected my request, was not entirely free from a measure of malicious satisfaction.

But poor Ribbentrop had no luck. I went straight to Hitler, and that was that. 'You can leave one of your own people behind,' he directed Ribbentrop. 'Hoffmann's task is one which I am not prepared to entrust to one of your colleagues!' And Ribbentrop retired with a very red face!

After Ribbentrop had left Obersalzberg, Hitler sent for me. 'I have informed our Ambassador in Moscow, Graf von der Schulenberg, that I have appointed you as my special emissary, to convey my greetings and good wishes to Stalin. I am departing from the formal and accepted procedure deliberately, as, by sending these messages through a private individual rather than through an accredited diplomat, I hope to give a personal turn to this contact with Stalin, on which we are just embarking. All this, naturally, won't interfere, however, with your photographic activities. But in addition, I want you to give me an objective and unbiased impression of Stalin and his entourage.'

Hitler broke off and started pacing up and down the great hall of the Berghof, throwing an absent-minded glance through the giant windows at the unbelievably beautiful panorama of the Untersberg and his beloved Salzburg mountains. Then he turned once more.

'I am interested in trivialities, which often go unnoticed, but which often give a much clearer clue to a man's character than all the reports of some silly fathead in the Foreign Office! So – in Moscow, keep your eyes open, Hoffmann!'

In high spirits Hitler bade me a hearty farewell. His joy and satisfaction over this great success were plainly written on his beaming face.

The journey, naturally, was kept strictly secret. Even so, I wanted at least to let my wife know that, for the time being, I could not get back to Munich. Being a woman, she was very curious to know more about this mysterious journey.

'Top secret! Don't ask me!' I retorted.

'Heini – if it's what I think it is, then I'm delighted. I think it's the best idea Hitler has ever had!'

My second wife was no very great admirer of Hitler, and her caustic comments, often very much to the point, caused me more than a little embarrassment. To her last gambit, therefore, I vouchsafed no reply at all; one never knew who might be listening in!

The next day we were in the air – and the world knew nothing about it! We landed at Königsberg, where we spent the night. It so happened that on that very evening the new bar of the hotel, Deutsches Haus, was due to be opened. This was an opportunity not to be missed, and we had a cheery night.

I went straight from the bar to the airport, where I found the engines of our aircraft already running; a few minutes later we took off – this time for Moscow. Lulled by the rhythmic hum of the motors, I wriggled comfortably down into my seat and was soon fast and blissfully asleep. A moment later – or so at least it seemed – some busybody tapped me on the shoulder, and still half-asleep, I heard a voice say: 'We land in three minutes!' I had slept like a babe for five solid hours!

The first thing that caught my eye on landing was something that a few days before I would have regarded as inconceivable – flags with the Hammer and Sickle were flying side by side with the Swastika banners! After the reception at the airport, our Ambassador, Graf von der Schulenberg, invited us to take up our quarters in the German Embassy, where that evening a party had been arranged in honour of our arrival.

The rich and Lucullan abundance of the cold buffet at this party astonished us. We had not expected to find such things in Moscow. But the Ambassador explained – everything had come from abroad – the bread, even, from Sweden, the butter from Denmark and the rest from various countries. That, too, astonished me – but in a different way!

At this party we met all the diplomats accredited to Moscow, among them General Koestring, the German Military Attaché, who had been there for a number of years. Koestring's authoritative opinions were most illuminating and shed much new light on Stalin and his policies. 'There have been endless rumours that Stalin is at death's door – such a sick man that he's only a figurehead and so on. Don't you believe it!' he told us. 'The man is both absolutely fit and possesses a tremendous capacity for work.'

On broader political issues his opinions were equally interesting. Politically, he told us, Stalin was turning his eyes primarily towards the Far East, in which he saw the greatest field for the expansion of Russian influence and power.

'And what, General, do you think are his real feelings towards Hitler and National Socialist Germany?' I ventured to ask.

Koestring had no doubts on the matter.

'Nobody,' he declared emphatically, 'could have been more genuinely friendly and helpful towards both Graf Schulenberg and myself than Stalin. He has told us again and again – and I'm quite sure he meant it – that he had the deepest respect both for the Führer, his policy and the German people, and that in spite of fundamental differences of principle between National Socialism and Communism, he saw no possible reason why the two systems should not live side by side, in peace and to their mutual benefit.'

Of the pact that we had come to conclude he said that it was, of course, no love match, but rather a *mariage de convenance,* an arrangement beneficial to both parties, but one which, for all that, would probably survive for many years to come.

Hitler, incidentally, later showed but little gratitude for the efforts of his negotiator-in-chief, Graf Schulenberg, who ended on the gallows as a result of the July 1944 bomb plot. General Koestring, whom I saw again at Nuremberg in 1946, died a short while ago in the small mountain hamlet in Bavaria in which he had peacefully spent the last few years of his life.

For the next day the Embassy placed a car at our disposal and we went sightseeing. The Kremlin made a great impression on us, as did also the handsome, wide streets and squares, and particularly Red Square, with the great mausoleum of Lenin in the middle. It was, however, not a good time for sightseeing, for a memorial week for Lenin coincided with our visit to Moscow. From all parts of Russia people flocked into Moscow to see his grave and file past the great mausoleum; a vast queue, composed of hundreds of thousands and stretching for miles, filed, day and night, slowly past, paying their respects to the spiritual father of the Union of Soviet Socialist Republics.

Photography, in general, was forbidden, but von der Schulenberg did not think there would be any objection to my taking a few discreet snaps. 'You ought to visit the cemetery where Stalin's first wife is buried,' he said. 'Perhaps you'll have a chance to tell Stalin about it – and that, I know, would please him.'

This grave is one of the most beautiful I have ever seen. The monument, of white marble, is of no great stature, but its charm lies in the pure lines and the living grace of its lovely and beautifully carved female figure.

On the way back, we visited a convent, which had been turned into dwellings. When the car stopped, we were immediately surrounded by a crowd of very raggedly dressed children, and we were surprised that one and all they carried enormous brightly coloured rubber balls, playthings that only the children of the rich enjoy in other countries. Later we were told that these balls were distributed by the State for propaganda purposes and also to assist the development of the State rubber factories.

Before returning to the Embassy we also stopped at a large hotel, from the upper balconies of which we had a wonderful view of the exquisite panorama of the Kremlin. The great emblems of the hammer and sickle on the top of the central cupola – illuminated in brilliant red at night – afforded an unforgettable sight. And in the hotel, for a bottle of champagne and a quarter of a melon, we were invited to pay thirty-five roubles – our complete day's allowance in foreign currency!

We had already been two days in Moscow, and I was still awaiting the permission of the GPU to visit the Kremlin. At last, about nine o'clock on the evening of 28th August, it arrived.

But permission to visit the Kremlin was a very different thing from permission to take a photograph of Stalin. To get that I had to rely on the skill of Graf von der Schulenberg, who, with Ribbentrop, was conducting the negotiations with Stalin and Molotov.

However, armed with our pass, Laux, Ribbentrop's photographer, and I set out in an Embassy car for the Kremlin. In the drive, about 100 yards short of the entrance gates, we were stopped by two armed sentries, who carefully scrutinised our passes and waved us on. At the gates themselves there was a further check, and again we were allowed to go forward. At a walking pace the car drove through a dark park towards the block of buildings in which Molotov had his office; as we drove on, we were accompanied by the regular tolling of a bell – a signal to the sentries patrolling the park that the car passing through was doing so with official permission. When the car halted before the buildings, the tolling also ceased.

Up a spiral staircase, past the numerous GPU sentries we made our way to Molotov's office. We had to wait nearly an hour and a half in the ante-room, for arrangements for the signing of the pact were not yet complete. I had, therefore, plenty of time to have a good look round the room. There was, however, nothing very remarkable about it, and the only thing that caught my eye among the somewhat meagre furniture was a table with about twenty telephones on it.

In front of the door leading into Molotov's office was seated an officer in white tunic and armed with a gigantic pistol, lolling, rather bored, in his armchair, with his legs stretched out before him and his hands in his trouser pockets. A servant, dressed like a hospital nurse, appeared and carried a tray, discreetly covered with a napkin, into Molotov's room. As she opened the door I got a glimpse of the smoke-laden room beyond. It was a big room, furnished in brown, and before the door closed, I caught sight of Stalin himself, standing beside Molotov's desk.

'Look! Stalin!' I said, rather loudly and excitedly to Laux.

The effect on the lackadaisical officer on guard was electric. Apparently he had no idea that Stalin was in Molotov's room (he must have entered by some other door) – and he sprang hastily to his feet, smoothed his uniform and stood stiffly to attention.

Shortly after this episode Graf von der Schulenberg came along, offered me a cigarette and told me that he had informed Stalin about me and my mission.

Ten minutes later we were invited to enter. Molotov came forward to meet me, and after a short and formal introduction he led me to Stalin, who received me with a friendly smile and a hearty handshake.

The actual signing of the pact had been delayed in order to give us the opportunity to take some photographs, an opportunity of which we took full advantage. Using specially rapid plates and discarding flashlights, Laux and I quickly got to work. A Russian photographer – presumably Stalin's personal photographer – was also present. He had a sort of Leica camera, but it was an obvious imitation of the original and a very shoddy affair. And as it was incapable, in the light conditions, of taking a photo without flashlight, he was at a distinct disadvantage.

He was determined, however, to take a group photo. Producing an antedeluvian tripod, which must have come out of the Ark, he proceeded laboriously to fix an enormous, prehistoric camera on it. Next he poured a truly handsome amount of black powder into the tin pan and touched it off by means of a bit of fuse. The resultant explosion rattled the windows and filled the room with dense smoke; and what the photo – if any – was like I have no idea!

After the signing of the historic Pact, Stalin with a friendly gesture invited me to come to his end of the table, where there were glasses that Molotov was already busy filling from the first bottle of champagne. At the same time the official participants in the ceremony drew a little to one side, and I found myself in the centre of the stage.

Stalin clapped his hands, and there was an immediate silence.

Expectantly every eye was fixed on Russia's Mighty Man, who turned and raised his glass to me: 'I make greeting … to … 'enery 'offman, Germany's most big photograph-worker … long … long … long … he may live!'

Afterwards, the Ambassador told me that Stalin had had great fun trying to learn this greeting in 'German' by heart. Anyway, it was a most flattering compliment to me! Once more Stalin clapped his hands. 'Pogale … Pogale!' he cried. For a moment, I didn't understand what he was driving at, but then I realised that the 'Pogale' (glasses) of the rest of the company were being filled. Initially, Molotov had filled only three glasses – for Stalin, for himself – and for me. I noticed that the Red Tsar drank from a tumbler – presumably to prevent any exchange of glasses.

The time had now come for me to say my piece. 'Your Excellency,' I began, 'I have the very great honour of conveying to you the hearty greetings and good wishes of my Führer and good friend, Adolf Hitler! Let me say how much he looks forward one day to meeting the great Leader of the Russian people in person!' This, obviously, made a great impression on Stalin. Through an interpreter he declared that he, too, was most anxious that there should be a lasting friendship with Germany and her great Führer.

Next Ribbentrop proposed the toast of: The Pact, Stalin, and the Russian People; to which Molotov replied with a few suitable words.

While all this was going on, there occurred an amusing little interlude. Just as Stalin raised his glass to me, my colleague, Laux, took a snapshot; I noticed that Stalin made a gesture, showing obviously that he did not wish to be photographed while drinking, and I at once turned to Laux and asked him to be good enough to give me the film. This he did readily enough, taking it out of the camera and handing it to me then and there. I then turned to Stalin. 'Your Excellency,' I said, 'I realised from your gesture that you did not want this snap to be taken. Let me say at once that I had and have no intention of publishing it. But it would be both a great honour and a great joy, to be allowed to keep this picture for myself and my family as a memento of a most historic evening.' With these words I offered the film to him. When the interpreter had translated my remarks, Stalin smiled and pressed the film back into my hands. I need hardly add that I kept my word; and when Goebbels wanted to publish it for propaganda purposes, after the outbreak of war with Russia, I refused to let him have it. Goebbels insisted, but Hitler supported my point of view, and so this photograph, at least during Stalin's lifetime, never saw the light of day.

We all stood around, while Molotov zealously filled the glasses with an excellent Crimean champagne, and very soon there was quite a handsome battalion of empties standing in a row near the wall, and fresh, unopened battalions continued to appear on the scene.

Remembering my special mission, I started to observe Stalin minutely. My conversation with him and Molotov was conducted through an interpreter, and when I tried to talk to Molotov in English, he declared that his knowledge of that language was as sketchy as his knowledge of German; but I had the firm impression that he understood much more of both languages than he pretended.

The conversation turned to Munich, and Molotov told me that, like Lenin, he, too, had studied there as a young man. When I told Stalin that I had visited his first wife's grave and had been profoundly moved by the beauty of the memorial statue, he was both pleased and impressed.

The conversation became more and more animated, and Stalin never ceased raising his glass to me. Then someone tapped me discreetly on the shoulder. It was one of the gentlemen from the Foreign Office. 'We are breaking off in a moment,' he whispered. 'Be careful, Professor – Stalin takes a great delight in drinking his guests under the table!'

'Don't you worry,' I retorted. 'Even Stalin won't do that. It's a game I learnt to play very long ago!'

When we took our leave, Stalin was – there's only one expression for it – well and truly lit up! When I said how truly sorry I was that we had to leave Moscow the next day, Molotov chipped in. 'We'll meet again, you see – either here or in Berlin!'

We landed at the Templehof airport, and Ribbentrop hastened at once to the Chancellery, to report to Hitler, while I hastened to my laboratory, where I intended to develop these historically very important photographs myself. An hour later I was with Hitler, who was expecting me, with a whole set of excellent pictures. After a terse greeting, which gave plain evidence of his impatience, came question number one: 'Well – what's your general impression of Stalin?'

'To be quite honest, I was both greatly pleased and deeply impressed. In spite of his somewhat squat figure, he is a born leader; his voice is pleasing and melodious, and in his eyes there is a look of equally proportioned intelligence, bonhomie and shrewdness. Towards us he was a quite delightful host, standing on no ceremony and yet shedding none of his dignity. His subordinates, I think, have a very deep respect for him.'

Hitler was most interested in my account of Stalin's attitude towards his entourage.

'Does he actually issue his orders?' he asked, 'or does he cloak them in the guise of wishes?'

'As a general rule, he uses Molotov as his mouthpiece,' I replied, 'and then adds a few polite words of his own. The thing that struck me, though, was the way in which, with a look or a brief, almost imperceptible movement of the hand, he seemed to keep control of the whole gathering.'

Hitler smiled. 'You seem to be completely fascinated by the great Stalin, my dear fellow,' he said. Then he frowned and stared fixedly at the lapel of my coat. 'And what, may I ask, have you done with your Communist Party Badge?' he asked.

'It's not there – yet. But – you never know!' I retorted.

Hitler took my pleasantry in good part, although one never knew how he would react to things of that sort. From my long and intimate association with him, I would say that his reactions to any given thing were almost invariably the exact opposite of what one expected.

I told Hitler about the little episode of the officer outside Molotov's door.

'What about his health? They say that he is a very sick man, and for that reason has a whole crowd of doubles. Or do you think that the man you saw was one of these mysterious Stalin manifestations?' asked Hitler jokingly.

'Judging from the way he smoked like a chimney, drank like a fish, and finished up looking full of beans, I should say it was quite likely,' I retorted with a laugh.

'Does he really smoke so much?' Hitler shook his head; smoking was a habit he could not understand.

'Well – to judge from that one historic reception, I should say that he was an out and out chain-smoker.'

'Tell me – how did he shake hands with you?'

'With a firm and hearty grip, which pleased me immensely,' I said, quite truthfully. Hitler had once told me that he could not abide a man who gave one a limp and unresponsive handshake.

'When he directed you to convey his greetings to me, do you think it sounded like a mere polite gesture, or had you the impression that there was a measure of sincerity in it?'

'I'm quite sure that there was more to it than a mere formality, Herr Hitler. I honestly believe that he is perfectly sincere in his friendship for you and for the German people.'

Hitler took up the collection of photographs, examining each one in turn and asking pertinent and searching questions about each one of them. 'What a pity,' he said at last in a doleful voice and shaking his head. 'There's not a single one we can use!'

'What?' I ejaculated, startled. 'Why – what's the matter with them?'

'In every single one Stalin has a cigarette between his fingers,' he replied angrily. 'Just think, Hoffmann – suppose I appeared in all my photos with a cigarette in my hand! Out of the question.'

'But a cigarette-smoking Stalin is exactly typical of the man,' I objected. But Hitler wouldn't have it. The German people, he asserted, would take offence.

'The signing of a Pact is a solemn act,' he said, 'which one does not approach with a cigarette dangling from one's lips. Such a photograph smacks of levity! See if you can paint out the cigarettes, before you release the pictures to the press.'

Knowing his hostility towards smoking, I said no more; the cigarettes were duly expunged from the photographs, and in all the newspapers Stalin stood there, pure and smokeless! I could not, however, resist the temptation of praising the excellent champagne from the Crimea, knowing full well that I should draw a sharp retort from such a rabid teetotaler. To my surprise, he didn't rise to the bait. But he did get in an unexpected backhander! 'In Moscow,' he said, 'alcohol was an essential adjunct to the circumstances, and I'm only delighted to have sent the drink-proof Stalin a boozer worthy of his mettle!'

Chapter 5

With Hitler in Poland

IN THE TENSE days of August 1939, I ventured once, when Hitler and I were alone after one of Henderson's visits, to voice the fear that Britain would certainly go to war.

'Don't you believe it!' retorted Hitler abruptly. 'England is bluffing!' and then, with that rather impish grin that so rarely came on his face, 'And so am I!' he added.

The actual declaration of war by Great Britain caused a sharp slump of Party stock among the masses – how vividly I remember the contrast between the wild enthusiasm of 1914 and the abysmal despondency of 1939 – and something akin to consternation in our immediate entourage.

I was in the Chancellery at the time, and I saw Hitler for a brief moment just after Ribbentrop had left him. He was sitting slumped in his chair, deep in thought, a look of incredulity and baffled chagrin on his face.

With his hand he made a rather pathetic gesture of resignation. 'And for this, my friend,' he murmured, 'we have to thank those fools, the so-called experts of the Foreign Office.'

I knew, of course, exactly what he meant. Again and again I had myself heard Ribbentrop, with an aplomb and self-confidence out of all proportion to his knowledge and his faulty powers of judgment, assure Hitler that Britain was degenerate, that Britain would never fight, that Britain would certainly never go to war to pull someone else's chestnuts out of the fire and so on; and there is no doubt whatsoever that in the game of political chess that ended with this disastrous *dénouement,* it was, above all, the promptings of Ribbentrop at his elbow that had led Hitler to make the miscalculations and false moves that eventually brought him to his death and his country to destruction.

Scarcely had I left him than I received an urgent telephone call from my wife. Never, before or since, have I known her to be in such a state of despair. Normally an animated but controlled creature, she could hardly speak for emotion. She had just been listening to Daladier's solemn words, and the futility of what she said to me was a striking reflection of the state she was in. 'Heini!' she cried, and there was a sob in her voice, 'Oh Heini, go – go, I beg and implore you, at once to Hitler and use every ounce of your influence over him to stop this awful thing before it is too late!'

It would have been farcical – if it had not been so tragic. What, in God's name, did she think that I, the crony and – as I was sometimes and perhaps with justice called – the Court Jester, could do at this stage to stop the vast machinery of Fate that Hitler had put in motion? 'For once I was right and he was wrong,' I thought gloomily to myself, 'and a fat lot of comfort that is!'

On 1st September 1939, the Blitzkrieg against Poland was launched. As reports of the surprisingly swiftly won successes began to flow in, I travelled with Hitler and his staff to the Polish front in the special train that was to become his Headquarters throughout the whole of the three-week campaign. From there he was able to follow the progress of the German armies, and each day, either by aircraft or with a small protective motorised column, we went up to some part of the front line.

These drives were by no means without danger, for large bodies of the disintegrated Polish cavalry had taken refuge in the woods on either side of the roads. Had they but known who was travelling with the diminutive column and had they but realised the weakness of the protective picquets – one rifleman every hundred yards – it would have been the easiest thing in the world for them to have destroyed Hitler and the whole of his entourage. We had a number of lucky escapes and narrow shaves, but our luck held, and we came through unscathed; and for myself, at the risk of being thought somewhat irreverent, I must confess I got a bit bored with hearing again and again how mercifully Providence was protecting us!

For the first time in my life I saw a battlefield. On the Tuchler Heide on both sides of the road for as far as the eye could see, lay a confused mass of broken and abandoned guns, rifles, machine-guns, first-aid boxes, cast-off equipment of every sort and horribly mangled corpses of man and horse, rapidly putre-fying in the hot September sun. An appalling stench hung over the whole countryside, and it was a terrible and ghastly sight that I shall never forget and that robbed Guderian's brilliantly conceived and executed plan of all its glamour for me.

When we returned late each night to Headquarters, we were so filthy and covered with the yellow dust of the Polish roads, that we were unrecognisable. Fortunately, however, the special train was well equipped with baths and a handsome barber's shop, and by midnight we were transformed once more into civilised human beings and seated at tea for the usual nightly conference.

During the campaign I did not obtain nearly as many really good photographs as one would expect from an experienced press photographer; nevertheless, those that I succeeded in getting were incorporated into a volume, *With Hitler in Poland,* and make a valuable contribution to the pictorial history of the war.

Between the conclusion of the Polish campaign and the opening of the offensive in the West, Hitler remained for the most part in Obersalzberg. For me as a press photographer it was a very dull time. With one exception there was nothing interesting to photograph.

On the afternoon of 8th November 1939, I was sitting, as usual, with Hitler in the Café Heck in Munich.

'Are you coming to Berlin with me, after the anniversary celebration in the Bürgerbräukeller?' he asked.

'I don't think I can,' I replied.

'Oh! do try and come – think it over!'

He seemed particularly anxious that I should go to Berlin with him, and in the Bürgerbräukeller, just before he mounted the rostrum to make his speech, he asked me again: 'Well, Hoffmann, thought it over? Are you coming?' And when I excused myself on the grounds of urgent business he seemed to be very disappointed.

That he was uneasy about something was obvious. His speech was much shorter than usual, and when he left, he did not shake hands with his old comrades, as had been his invariable wont every year at this reunion. Some feeling of haste and urgency seemed to be impelling him forward, and 'the old guard' watched with disappointment as he turned abruptly and swiftly left the hall. After his departure the hall swiftly emptied, and within a few minutes I myself had packed up my camera and likewise departed. Only a few of the old comrades and the serving staff were left.

As we drove over the Ludwig bridge on our way to the Ratskeller, I heard a detonation.

'What's that?' I asked my driver. 'It sounded like an explosion!'

The chauffeur shrugged his shoulders.

When we arrived at the Ratskeller I was immediately called to the telephone. It was Gretl Braun, Eva's sister, calling.

'The Bürgerbräukeller has been blown sky-high!' she said excitedly.

'Nonsense! That's a damn silly rumour!' I retorted angrily. 'I was there myself only ten minutes ago. Don't take any notice of such rot!'

I returned to my table, when I suddenly remembered the detonation I had heard. Was it? I wondered. Once more I was called to the phone. This time it was Eva herself. 'Father has just come home covered with chalk and dust. A bomb exploded in the Bürgerbräukeller!'

I dashed back to the Bürgerbräukeller to see the damage. Most of the roof had fallen in, doctors were busy tending the wounded, and there were many, alas, beyond all aid. The bomb had been built into the pillar behind the speaker's rostrum and had been exploded by a time-fuse.

Had Hitler, in a moment of inexplicable intuition, not cut short his speech, he would undoubtedly have fallen a victim to the plot – and the greater part of the assembled company with him.

There were all sorts of rumours and explanations; some said the British were at the bottom of it, while others asserted that it was a put-up job, to arouse public indignation and enthusiasm for the war. A watchmaker named Elser was arrested. He confessed that he had placed the bomb in position, but he refused to say who his accomplices were or who had employed him to do it. A day or two later I was talking about it to Hitler.

'I had a most extraordinary feeling,' he said, 'and I don't myself know how or why – but I felt compelled to leave the cellar just as quickly as I could.'

The political horizon was clear and empty; there were a few mass meetings, collections for the Winter Aid Fund and so on, and these I left to my assistants. I was therefore very relieved when we at last returned to Berlin.

At the Kaiserhof Hotel, which was always my headquarters when in Berlin, I received a telephone call. One of the Führer's adjutants was on the line: 'Will you please come at once to the Chancellery!' Something doing, at last, I thought!

When I got there, the Adjutant himself received me. 'You must maintain the strictest silence about the journey you are about to undertake. Your camera must be seen by no one, and you must take only the absolute minimum of luggage with you, so that your departure will not be observed!' Telling me to return

to the hotel and prepare, he added that, on leaving the hotel to
return to the Chancellery, I was not to use the hotel lift, but was
to slip out by the back door.

Before we got into the waiting cars, I had a chance to exchange
a few words with Hitler. 'Where to, Hitler, Norway?' I asked.

'Yes,' he replied. 'Who told you?'

'No one told me – I'm just guessing,' I said hastily.

Hitler looked at me appraisingly for a moment. 'Right – but
not a word to anyone else, Hoffmann!'

The convoy set off in the direction of the Staaken airport,
but to everybody's surprise did not stop there, but drove straight
on. Only the last car stopped, to bar the road to all on-coming
traffic. On we went, and it seemed as though we were intending
to make the whole journey by car. Suddenly, however, we pulled
up at a closed levelcrossing; and beside it stood the Führer's
special train. We were told to get aboard as quickly as possible,
and in a few moments were on our way northwards. The whole
company foregathered in the restaurant car, and speculation was
rife. We were travelling in the direction of Hamburg, and the
consensus of opinion was in favour of Norway. Hitler merely
smiled and encouraged us in our speculation. He turned to me.
'Well, Hoffmann, have you brought your water-wings with
you?' he asked.

'No, Herr Hitler, I haven't,' I replied. 'In the first place, I can
swim, and in the second, I'm quite sure they won't be wanted,
because you can't swim, and you haven't brought yours!'

At Celle the train stopped. Dietrich, the Press Chief, brought
the latest telephone messages from Berlin, and then the train
went on into the night. Hitler glanced through the messages and
then retired, rather earlier than was his habit.

At about midnight I saw to my astonishment that we were
passing through Celle again. At dawn, unusually early for him,
Hitler appeared for breakfast, and now it became clear that the
whole of the night's run had been a camouflage to hide the real

destination. As it became lighter, Hitler pulled his watch from his pocket and laid it on the table before him. After a while he picked it up again, started counting the seconds, and then said solemnly: 'Gentlemen, it is exactly five forty-five – the first shots are being fired – now!'

It was 10th May 1940. The offensive in the West had started! Another of Hitler's surprise packets!

The date, I was now told, had been postponed several times. Hitler had made the opening of the offensive dependent on meteorological reports, and the forecast had caused him to decide on 10th May. The expert responsible for the accurate forecast was afterwards rewarded by Hitler with a handsome gold chronometer, suitably inscribed.

In bright sunshine we reached Euskirchen, near Cologne, where we changed into the waiting cars. An hour later we arrived at the 'Felsen-Nest,' the first of the Führer-Headquarters, near Münster on the Eifel.

In June 1940, in his Wolfsschlucht Headquarters at Bruly la Pêche, near Brussels, Hitler received the news of the French capitulation. For a moment he threw to the winds his dignity as Supreme Commander of the Armed Forces and slapped himself gleefully on the thigh; and it was then that Keitel, carried away by this burst of emotion, coined the fateful phrase: 'Mein Führer, you are the greatest Military Commander of all time!'

Quite close to the Wolfsschlucht Headquarters stood a pleasant little house, from which the occupants, for security reasons, had been evacuated. The soldiers billeted there showed me the small notice they had found tacked onto the door:

> 'The owner of this cottage is the local German Teacher. He asks all who may occupy it to respect his property. God will reward them!'

'You ought to see, Herr Hitler, with what affection his countrymen are looking after his little garden for him, and how careful they are with everything in the house,' I said, when I told Hitler about it. He was obviously very pleased.

'I do not wish my soldiers to behave in France in the way the French behaved in the Rhineland after the first war!' His face assumed a stern expression as he continued: 'I have ordered that anyone found looting will be shot on the spot. I want to come to a real understanding with France. I shall impose very easy armistice terms, and I will conclude a most magnanimous peace with the French, in spite of the fact that they declared war on me.'

Then we went to Compiègne. I could not refrain from giving Hitler my impressions. 'This place has become a sort of historical pilgrim centre for the French,' I said. 'Normally when on a pilgrimage, one buys holy pictures and texts. But here, everyone buys postcards and coloured pictures of the signing of the armistice in 1918!'

'I don't blame the French for that,' said Hitler, with an inviting gesture towards me. 'But now it's our turn, Hoffmann! Come on – let's get on with it!'

In this way I preserved in photographic form the historic happenings in that self-same railway carriage in the forest of Compiègne; and, like those of my French colleagues in 1918, my 1940 photographs went to the ends of the earth.

While we were on the way from the Wolfsschlucht to the fallen Paris, Hitler said: 'I am so very glad that Paris was spared. It would have been a most serious loss to the culture of Europe if this wonderful city had been damaged.'

One experience that he never forgot was his first visit to the Opera House.

'That is my Opera House,' he cried, joyously. 'From my earliest youth it has been my dream to gaze upon this magnificent example of French architectural genius!' War, power, politics – everything was forgotten, and he went through the building as if he were determined to carry every little corner in his memory for ever.

He also visited the Invalides, where he stood in such long and reverent contemplation, that it almost seemed as though he were holding converse with the great Emperor. When at last he turned and left, he was profoundly moved.

'That,' he said softly, 'was the greatest and finest moment of my life.'

In the autumn of 1940 preparations for 'Operation Sealion' – the invasion of Britain – were complete; the troops detailed were already concentrated at their embarkation bases along the Channel coast, some units had already embarked, the Navy and the Air Force stood ready, and Hitler had but to press the button for the operation to commence. Britain, too, was standing to arms in hourly expectation of the onslaught; and yet – nothing happened.

The abandoning of the operation has given rise to a great deal of speculation. It was common knowledge that, with France defeated, Hitler was determined to crush Britain; but at the last moment he changed his mind, later decided to attack Russia instead and thus gave the prosecution of the war a turn, with the repercussions of which historians will busy themselves for a long time to come.

I myself knew nothing at all about the plans or details for 'Operation Sealion', for in this case, as in all cases, vital or trivial, Hitler had followed his inflexible principle that each individual should in advance be given only those details of any enterprise that was essential to the execution of his own part in it; and for this reason the events of that autumn evening in 1940 – I think it was about 19th or 20th September – did not make any out-standing impression on me – at the time.

I was dining as usual in the Chancellery in Berlin, and when I got there I sensed a feeling of great tension among my fellow guests. I gathered that very sharp differences of opinion had been expressed at that afternoon's War Situation Conference, and the whole company, while awaiting Hitler's appearance, was obviously still on tenterhooks.

'If he persists and gives the orders tonight at ten o'clock,' I heard one staff officer say, 'we are in for a stupid and senseless sacrifice. It will cost thousands of lives, and most of the fleet will be destroyed.'

While I was pondering over this cryptic remark, a naval staff officer and an air force staff officer drew me to one side. 'Herr Hoffmann,' said one of them, as soon as we were out of earshot of the rest, 'in weather like this it is essential that Hitler should not put his plans into operation, and our chiefs have instructed us to ask you urgently for your help in persuading him to abandon his intentions.'

'What intentions?' I interjected.

'That, for the moment, I can't tell you. But it is a gigantic operation, which if launched in this stormy weather, will end in a national catastrophe.'

'And what, gentlemen, do you expect me to do? You know as well as I do that once Hitler has made up his mind nothing and nobody, not even Göring or Raeder, can make him change it; and any attempt to dissuade him only hardens his determination.'

'Just so! And that's exactly why none of us Service people dare to try and argue with him. The staff did its best at this afternoon's conference, but all the change we got was that Hitler would make his final decision at ten o'clock tonight.' The officer's voice assumed a note of extreme urgency.

'For God's sake, Herr Hoffmann, think up some of your famous anecdotes and do your utmost to keep him happy and interested till after ten.'

Seated, as usual, on Hitler's left, I had plenty to think about. Though I was completely in the dark as to what it was all about, the problem, whatever it was, was obviously a vital one. Then another thought struck me. What if Hitler were right and his Service advisers wrong? Such a thing had been known to happen before, and it was asking rather a lot of a photographer to butt in and try and influence the decision. But opinion among the staff was obviously so unanimous that I decided to try and do as they asked.

At the table itself Hitler was always averse to talking 'shop', and as soon as we rose I plunged into the news of the day, cracked a few of the latest jokes and passed from the anecdotes of the moment to those of the 'good old days', which, as I knew, Hitler loved so well. I talked about the 1918 revolution in Bavaria and the subsequent events in 1919. At first Hitler seemed distant and absent-minded, but those were times of stirring interest, and as I myself had been in the thick of it all, the story lost nothing in the telling. Gradually I held his interest and finally had him completely engrossed and firing questions at me. These questions were a godsend, for they enabled me to spin out a yarn that was rapidly wearing thin and to digress at random and at will. My own head was beginning to spin a bit, when Hitler suddenly rose to his feet.

'Gentlemen,' he said. 'I am tired out. There will be no conference tonight.' I glanced at my watch. It was nearly midnight!

There was an enigmatical smile on Hitler's face as he withdrew. The tension broke at once. My two staff officers hastened over to me.

'Hoffmann, when the German people learn what you have accomplished tonight they will be eternally grateful to you.'

It was only very much later, in 1954, that I heard from Doctor Kurz, who had been on the staff at the time, that the point at issue had been nothing less than the launching of the invasion of Britain!

Whether my action was right or wrong I shall never know. But I am confident that Hitler had already come to the reluctant conclusion that the staff were right and that he would have to cancel his original orders; and he had seized the golden opportunity given him by my babblings to do so tacitly by default and had thus avoided the discomfiture of 'losing face'.

After the conclusion of the campaign in France and the signing of the armistice at Compiègne, Hitler paid a brief visit to the troops on the French front and then retired to Obersalzberg. Although he was then quite convinced that final victory was in his grasp, he was too restless to allow himself any long period of real relaxation. His mind was constantly occupied with the idea that this lull in hostilities by no means denoted that the war was ended, and he set to work with great concentration to formulate the plans that would bring swift and final victory and peace.

From the frequency with which Russia became a subject of conversation at our evening gatherings, it is obvious that he was already toying with the idea of a campaign against the Russians; at the same time, as though to justify himself in advance, he frequently complained that Russia was failing punctually to fulfil the clauses of the Russo-German pact dealing with the exchange of goods, and this failure he attributed to the inadequacy of the Soviet communication system.

But when he heard that Russia was taking measures that must inevitably lead to war, he decided that he must return to Berlin and take up residence in the Chancellery; and so our peaceful days at Obersalzberg came to an end, and, except for very brief periods, they were gone for ever. Notwithstanding our departure, work on the vast underground network of tunnels continued with undiminished speed at Obersalzberg. These tunnels joined the Berghof to the nearby SS barracks, while branch tunnels led to the residences of Bormann and Göring. Apart from giving complete protection against any air attack, these tunnels, with the large storerooms that were recessed at frequent intervals along them, contained food supplies and provisions sufficient for years to come and were also a safe asylum for a large and very valuable collection of works of art and important State documents. As soon as we arrived in Berlin, reinforcement of the Chancellery air shelters, based on recent experience of aerial bombardment, was immediately put in hand.

'When it came as come it must,' as Hitler said on the outbreak

Above: I met Lord Simon and Mr Anthony Eden only once, at the Chancellery in Berlin. *Below left:* I caught Ambassador Henderson in my camera as he left Berlin – 1st Sept., 1939. *Below right:* Simon and Eden chat with Hitler. *Below right bottom:* One of the informal pictures I took of the four-power conference, Munich, 29th Sept., 1938.

Success of a mission – Hitler congratulates Ribbentrop after the signing of the Russo-German pact.

The Chancellery: an informal chat with his henchmen.

Hitler decorates General Galland – Chief of the new German Air Force?

High command conference: Paulus, Hitler, Keitel, Halder, von Brauchitsch and Häusinger – now Chief of Military Staff in Germany.

Top left: English prisoners at Dunkirk – my son's photograph. *Top right:* Hitler dances for joy at the capitulation of France. *Centre:* Chiefs of Staff with Hitler at Compiègne, 1940. *Below:* Hitler and Pétain – in Hitler's private train.

Top: No fake – von Paulus in Russian hands. *Centre:* The shattered room after the bomb plot – 20th July, 1944. *Below:* Hitler, Göring and Mussolini – a few minutes after the 1944 attempt on Hitler's life.

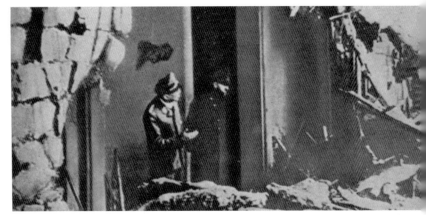

Hitler inspects the bomb-shattered Chancellery, 1945.

The Victory Arch that was to be erected after the war.

One of my last pictures of the Führer: decorating Hitler Youth during the Battle of Berlin

Göring and I.

My wife Erna, with Max Schmeling, a great friend of ours.

Far from the war – the famous Berghof terrace in the Spring.

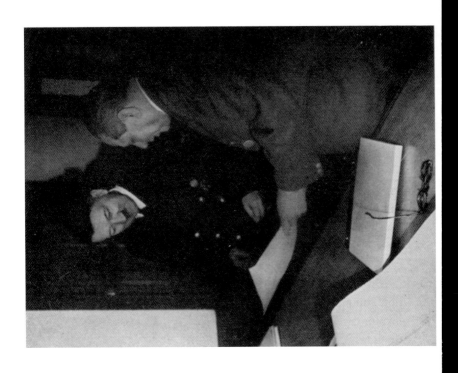

of the Russian conflict, we moved at once to the newly con-
structed Führer Headquarters, the Wolfsschanze, a few miles
from the small provincial town of Rastenburg in East Prussia.
Although it lay at the extreme eastern end of East Prussia, the
place, cleverly camouflaged in the middle of a forest of firs, was
ideal from the point of view of security and throughout the whole
campaign we were not subjected to a single air raid. Comfortably
installed though we were, however, we could not rid ourselves of
a feeling of being 'behind the wire', as in a prison; nor could such
amenities as a Turkish bath, an officers' club, a swimming bath,
cafés and cinemas dissipate our malaise.

It was summer 1941. Like Napoleon before him, Hitler had
now conquered almost the whole of Europe. My mind returned
involuntarily to his first visit to Paris a year before. What
thoughts, I wondered, had passed through his mind at that time,
when France lay prostrate and he, the victorious leader of the
German people, stood reverently before the last resting-place of
the Great Corsican?

And now? A few days before, our troops had started their
invasion of Russia. It had been a declaration of war that evoked
no enthusiasm among the German people; on the contrary, there
was a general feeling of gloomy apprehension; even Napoleon,
people remembered, had only just managed to reach Moscow –
and at what a cost! At Headquarters, in spite of the air of confidence that everyone paraded, the same underlying atmosphere
of pessimism was plainly to be discerned.

Sitting alone with Hitler in the East Prussian Wolfsschanze
Headquarters, I ventured a question. 'How is it,' I asked, 'that
this new war has come about?'

I had the impression that he was expecting such a question.
'Through a concatenation of circumstances,' he replied. 'I was
compelled to take the first step in what is a war of prevention –
and let me emphasise, it must be explained with the utmost clarity
to the German people, that this is indeed a war of prevention. It
was vital that I should get my blow in first, before the Russians

struck! The others (*by which he meant the British*) have not the slightest intention of seeking peace. God knows, I waited long enough; but now I have no option but to risk the hazards of war on two fronts. We need oil for our aircraft, oil for our armour, and the thrust towards the Russian oilfields must at all costs succeed.' He gazed with unseeing eyes into the distance. 'I could not do otherwise,' he concluded.

Chapter 6

Hitler – Religion and Superstition

DURING THE EARLY years of our acquaintanceship, Hitler's attitude towards the two great denominations of the Christian faith were never discussed between us. It was only later, when divergences of opinion came to light, that he defined his attitude to this very intricate problem.

In the course of twenty-five years, Hitler underwent a complete spiritual metamorphosis, which changed the whole method of his approach towards matters of religious faith; in spite of this, however, his attitude towards the Church never acquired that violent aggressiveness, which characterised the attitude of some of his subordinates and Gauleiters.

'I have need of the Church in exactly the same way as had the monarchy and other past forms of government.'

A few years before the outbreak of war, the struggle behind the scenes became much intensified, and Hitler intervened.

'There is too much back-biting on both sides,' he said. 'But while I cannot tolerate the type of fight the Church is waging against us, I must equally condemn the countermeasures taken on our side. I have made it quite clear to all my collaborators that, in the event of war, we shall have need of the Church.'

One of the most fanatical opponents of the Church in the

whole Party was Bormann, and although Hitler generally con-
doned his attitude, there were many repressive measures introduced by Bormann, which Hitler felt compelled to countermand.
In spite of his predilection for avoiding unpleasant things, Hitler
always called upon me to give him the plain unvarnished truth
about public opinion; and of this privilege I made frequent use,
regardless of whether I aroused Bormann's hostility by so doing.

On one occasion, while I was in Vienna during the war,
Baldur von Schirach, a delightful young man, partially of
American descent, with the slim, well-proportioned body of
an athlete, a keen intelligence and a great enthusiasm for the
modern school of art who had married my daughter Henriette
in 1933 and who had become Hitler's Youth Leader, begged me
to invite Hitler's attention to the measures being taken against
the Catholic Church that were bringing the Third Reich into
disrepute in Austria. He had approached me, I explained to
Hitler, because the letters he had written had been suppressed
before they reached the Führer by Bormann. Hitler, however,
ignored my protests and contented himself with saying
somewhat disconsolately: 'I know absolutely nothing of these
incidents in Austria; have you any further unpleasant things of
the same sort to tell me?'

'I regret to say that I have. Do you know, Herr Hitler, that
the crucifixes have been removed from the schools in Bavaria?
Gauleiter Wagner is said to have ordered their removal on
instructions from Bormann.'

'Are you quite certain of that, Hoffmann?' 'I can produce
witnesses! Further, Bormann has instituted a search throughout
all the monasteries for certain classes of books, which he proposes
to add to his vast anti-clerical library. Various monasteries have
simply been closed down, and the old nuns, who had dwelt in
them from their early youth, have been sent to their homes,
where most of them will end their days in the almshouse. I'm
sure, Herr Hitler, you have not forgotten the visit we paid to the
Munich hospital, where the nursing was in the hands of Catholic

nuns? You were, if you remember, greatly impressed with the selflessness they displayed, and you said you would forbid all Party members to interfere or impede these Sisters of Mercy in any way.'

Hitler sent for Bormann at once, and in my presence he said abruptly: 'This sort of thing has to be stopped immediately!'

Bormann, with his attaché case under his arm, sprang to attention. 'Very good, my Führer, I will immediately pass on your orders by teleprinter to all appropriate authorities.' Then, with a disgruntled glance in my direction, he left.

Bormann collected all the files of cases against the clergy he could find and incorporated them into a book. When this book was published, Cardinal Faulhaber appealed to Hitler and was invited to lunch at Obersalzberg. In their ensuing conversation, the Archbishop of Munich petitioned Hitler to order the suppression of this very questionable work. His arguments convinced the Führer, who at once ordered Bormann to destroy all copies.

When relating the details of this interview to a few of us in his own intimate circle, Hitler displayed a moderation towards Church affairs – not, it must be admitted, without a tinge of political expediency behind it – which was entirely absent in the later war years. Apart from the fact that he fully recognised the high intelligence of Cardinal Faulhaber and the great influence he wielded, he reminded us that Bavaria was a devoutly Catholic country, and that a statesman who tried to ride rough-shod over the deep convictions of a people was no statesman.

'A real leader of men,' he declared, 'gains control of his people not by force, but by convincing them that he is right. Only against those who, notwithstanding public opinion, still oppose him to the detriment of the common cause, should he use force; and then he should, indeed, he must, be utterly ruthless.'

There were many dignitaries of the Church who enjoyed Hitler's particular esteem. Abbot Schachleitner visited him frequently, to discuss Church matters with him. When visiting the Rhenish monastery Maria Laach, Hitler had a long and animated discussion with the Abbot of that famous pilgrim centre.

In 1925, I decided that the time had come for my nine-year-old son to go to boarding school, and I consulted Hitler on the subject.

'I strongly recommend you to send him to a convent school,' he said. 'For young people the convent school is the best educational institution we have. The Simbach convent, on the Inn opposite Braunau, had a great reputation when I was a young man.'

This advice rather astonished me, for Hitler, of course, knew that I was a Protestant. But I took his advice, and he drove my son down to the convent in his new Mercedes and personally handed him over to the Mother Superior. 'See that you make a decent man of him,' he admonished her, on departing. And on the drive home he turned to me. 'You should make a present of a really good picture to the convent,' he said.

When next I visited my son, I took with me a fine oil painting of the Holy Family, for the chapel, and it was accepted with great joy and gratitude.

Unfortunately, the Church did but little to try and bridge the ever-growing rift between itself and National Socialism.

The attitude that Cardinal Innitzer recommended all Catholics to adopt towards National Socialism in Vienna in 1938 was observed, for the most part, in theory only. Again and again from the pulpits came political exhortations, which had no result but to give Bormann a legitimate excuse to intervene; and in consequence many a preacher found his way into the concentration camps. They were interned in this fashion *only* after they had been tried and condemned by a properly constituted court.

'I would release any priest,' declared Hitler, 'provided he were willing to sign an undertaking not in future to interfere in politics, but to restrict himself to his spiritual duties. But this they refuse to do – a proof, to my mind, that they attach greater importance to political affairs than to things spiritual. If these gentlemen are determined to play the martyr – so be it!'

Even so, there was never any really tragic conflict between Church and State. At the New Year's reception the representative of the Vatican, Monsignor Orsenige, was invariably present to give Hitler, as Head of the German State, the good wishes and blessing of the Pope.

At dinner one evening Hitler told us that he had ordered the arrest of Pastor Niemöller – the same Niemöller who, in 1935, had spoken of 'the mighty work for the unification of our people, which has begun among us.' Bormann nodded appreciatively. 'The monitoring service submitted a report to me, which contained a verbatim transcript of a telephone conversation between Niemöller and some other *frater in Christo*. Therein Niemöller not only spoke most spitefully about me personally, but also expressed views of a highly treasonable character. I sent for him, and when he started unctuously to pay his respects, I told him quite bluntly that his devotion to me was nothing but sheer hypocrisy. I then handed him the report from the monitoring service, refused to listen to any further explanations, and had him handed over to the Gestapo.'

Some years later, I asked Hitler why Niemöller was still in prison.

'He'll stay where he is, until he signs the undertaking,' declared Hitler categorically. At the same time, he had given Himmler orders that Niemöller was to be kindly treated in captivity.

Hitler was very fond of visiting churches; and although his interest was concentrated on the architecture, the sculptures and the paintings, he always adhered strictly to religious observances.

Our common interest in art led us to visit a great number of churches and religious institutions during the years of our association. Among others, we visited the Naval church in Wilhelmshaven.

As we were leaving I took a photograph of Hitler. Hitler came slowly down the steps, and when the golden cross of the great gates was exactly over his head, I snapped him. From my point of view, it was an interesting and original snap. But the clerical opponents of the Party held violently opposed views. When the picture appeared in my book, *Hitler as No One Knows Him,* I was accused of trying to represent him as a devout churchman. Even Hess demanded that the photograph should be withdrawn, but I submitted the whole thing to Hitler himself for his personal decision. 'That I visited the church is a fact. What my thoughts were, you could not photograph, and it wasn't you who put up the cross which happens to be just above my head in the snap. Leave it just as it is, Hoffmann – if the people think I'm a devout man, well, no harm will come of that!'

Hitler firmly believed that he had been chosen by Fate to lead the German people to hitherto undreamed of heights; and his rise to power, the great success he achieved immediately after his assumption of power, only strengthened this belief, not only in Hitler himself, but also in his adherents.

When in his speeches he referred to Providence, he did not do so simply to achieve rhetorical effect; he really believed what he said, and this conviction could not but be strengthened by the truly miraculous manner in which he was again and again preserved.

It started with the march on the Feldherrenhalle in 1923. Hitler was marching at the head of the column; all around him his comrades were shot down – and he escaped with a dislocated shoulder. The attempt on his life in the Bürgerbräukeller in November 1939, was so organised that it could not possibly fail. What mysterious power was it that persuaded Hitler, against his usual custom, to leave early? Even in the attempt on 20th July 1944, he was the only one who was not seriously injured. What could have persuaded Colonel Stauffenberg to remove the second charge from his attaché case at the very last moment? Had he left it where it was, the result desired by the conspirators would inevitably have been achieved.

Nor was it only in these cases that his life hung on a thread. In the period of struggle, during his election journeys he was constantly exposed to the gravest of dangers. Many a great stone was hurled at his head – but not one hit him; by train, car and plane I travelled hundreds of thousands of miles with him and saw with my own eyes how often he escaped death by a hair's breadth.

In principle, Hitler rejected astrology. He admitted that the juxtaposition of the stars might well have some influence on the fate of mankind, but he felt that the interpretation of the cause and effect had not been scientifically mastered; he appeared to be an exponent of the exact sciences, but this did not prevent him from being, in many respects, a superstitious man. Often, when he was hesitant over some decision, he would take a coin and toss for it; and though he would laugh at his own stupidity in appealing thus to Fate, he was always obviously delighted when the toss fell the way he hoped it would.

He believed firmly in the chronological repetition and faithful reproduction of certain historical events. For him November was the Month of Revolution; May was a propitious month for any undertaking, even when eventual success followed but later.

In 1922 he read a prophecy in an astrological calendar that exactly fitted the events of the putsch of November, 1923, and for years afterwards he used to talk about it. Even though he would never admit it, this prophecy undoubtedly made a lasting and profound impression on him.

During the course of our twenty-five years of association I had numberless opportunities of seeing how prone he was to premonitions. Quite suddenly and for no reason that he could explain, he would become uneasy. On the occasion of the Bürgerbräukeller attempt, too, he had this mysterious, impelling feeling that there was something in the air, that something was wrong, and he altered all his plans, without really having the least idea why he did so.

Shortly before the end of the war a discussion arose in his intimate circle as to which of the three leading men on the Allied side would die first and whether the death would have any decisive influence on the course of the war. 'Roosevelt, I think, will be the first to die,' declared Hitler. 'But his death will not alter the course of the war.' A fortnight later, Roosevelt was dead.

Hitler read many books on astrology and the occult sciences, but he never tolerated the presence of a 'resident astrologer'. After 1945, I was told, with a wealth of corroborative detail, that, like Wallenstein, he had kept his own particular brand of 'Seni'. I can only congratulate my informant on the brilliance of his imagination!

I shall never forget the disconcerted expression on Hitler's face when he was laying the foundation stone of the Haus der Deutschen Kunst in Munich in 1933. At the symbolic stroke, the silver hammer in his hand broke in two. Very few people noticed it, and Hitler immediately ordered that no public mention was to be made of the untoward incident. 'The people are superstitious,' he declared, 'and might well see in this ridiculous little misfortune an omen of evil.' But looking at him, I realised how taken aback he was; it was not of the people, but of himself that he was thinking!

Such little incidents invariably left an unpleasant impression on him. We never mentioned them again, for fear of depressing him.

Once – after Hitler had come to power – someone in our intimate circle started to talk about the centuries, the prophecies of the famous astrologer, Nostradamus. Hitler was very interested, and told one of his officials to get the books for him from the State Library, but on no account to say for whom he was getting them. As it was, a deposit of three thousand marks had to be put down before the Library would give him the books.

In the prophecies mention is made of a mighty mountain, over which a great eagle is sweeping, and Hitler compared the mountain to Germany and the eagle to himself. He went through the prophecies sentence by sentence, and said that although he could not claim that they all had direct bearing on himself, he did feel that they constituted an inexplicable phenomenon; and in this connection, he quoted Hamlet: 'There are more things in Heaven and earth …'

It happened one day, long before 1933, when we were sitting together in the Café Heck, both immersed in our newspapers.

Suddenly Hitler looked up. 'I've just been reading that there's been another serious motor accident at the seventeenth milestone. That's the fourth in the last week or so – rather mysterious, isn't it?'

An interesting discussion followed, and as no other explanation for these accidents was forthcoming, we came to the conclusion that they must have been caused either by some subterranean water stream or by some sort of earth disturbance – an earth-ray or something of the sort. Impulsively Hitler said: 'Let's all go to this mysterious seventeenth milestone and see for ourselves!'

Off we all went along the mathematically straight road, but nothing happened to us and for any explanation we sought in vain; there were neither subterranean currents, nor earth disturbances nor anything else.

'Completely inexplicable,' said someone.

'When a man is faced with a puzzle which he cannot solve, he dismisses it as insoluble,' retorted Hitler. 'A religiously-minded person would say "Providence" or "Fate."'

It was during the Spanish Civil War, in 1936. Hitler had attended the ceremonial burial in Wilhelmshaven of the sailors killed by Red bombers on board the cruiser *Deutschland*, off the Spanish coast. For the return journey to Berlin he had directed that his special train should travel by night, and it was a rather silent company, fresh from the solemn ceremony we had just attended, which gathered in the saloon-car.

Hitler's glance happened to fall on the speedometer with which his carriage was equipped, and finding that the train was travelling at the exceptionally high speed of 80 miles an hour, he immediately directed an orderly officer to tell the driver to go more slowly. The officer returned almost at once. The train superintendent, he said, had explained that the special had been scheduled at short notice and was compelled to maintain a definite average speed, in order to avoid a major dislocation of the main-line traffic.

Hitler at first made no comment. Then suddenly he said: 'In future, my special train shall travel at 35 miles an hour. For many years I used to travel at high speed both by train and car. But I have limited the speed of my car to 35 miles an hour, and now I shall impose the same limit on my special train. There it is – I have a feeling that to continue travelling at these high speeds must inevitably some time or other lead to a disaster, which would be the end of us all.'

After a short pause, he continued, almost apologetically, 'I don't know why,' he said; 'but today I feel very uneasy. The ceremonial interment has depressed me, and perhaps that's the reason; or, maybe, I'm getting old and more nervous.'

His glance wandered speculatively over the silent company. 'Normally,' he continued, 'I never give a thought to the dangers of everyday life. Not even when I'm speaking – if I had a fixed idea that at any moment some madman in the crowd might attempt to take my life, I should be quite incapable of stringing two consecutive sentences together.'

His medical man, Dr Brandt, thought that this queer malaise was probably due to nervous tension. Scarcely had he begun to speak, however, than the train began a series of most violent jerks, which pitched us pell-mell out of our seats. There was a moment of consternation; what had happened – a derailment? Sabotage? The brakes screamed, and the train came to an abrupt stop. We jumped out into the pitch black night.

With the aid of a torch, I went slowly along the length of the train. The first thing I saw was the wheel of a motor vehicle. A little further on a body mangled and entangled in the wheels of the train ... then another ... and another. I stumbled over the main shaft of the vehicle, lying beside the line, and came then to a level-crossing, its steel barrier buckled and smashed, and dead and dying people lying all around it. The Führer's personal bodyguard came hurrying to the scene.

There had been a frightful accident, from which we had had a miraculous and hair-breadth's escape. A travelling theatrical company of twenty-two members was returning home in a motor coach. The driver, who was well acquainted with that stretch of the road, knew that at eight o'clock at night no train was due to pass, and he assumed that the level-crossing barrier would be open; but of the special train, of course, he knew nothing. Too late he realised that the barrier was closed; to brake was impossible and he crashed straight into the jaws of the oncoming express.

Instinctively I had taken my camera and flashlight apparatus with me, and I took some photographs, which were afterwards of great value in the enquiry into the cause of the accident.

All the unfortunate actors had been killed, and Hitler was deeply shaken by the catastrophe, which he alone had foreseen; and from then on, his special train was limited to a speed of 35 miles an hour.

One night we were driving from Berlin to Munich through a frightful storm – a regular cloudburst – which reduced the chauffeur Schreck's visibility to practically nothing. We had just passed through Lohof, some 15 miles from Munich, when a man suddenly appeared in the headlights in the middle of the road, waving us to a stop. Schreck braked violently and just managed to pull up in time. Hitler opened the door of the car.

'Can you tell me the way to Freising?' asked the man in a somewhat wild manner. It was an astonishing question in any case for the Freising road is on the other side of Munich. 'My friend is on the other side of the road,' the man continued, 'stopping cars coming from that direction.'

Hitler became suspicious and immediately slammed the door and told Schreck to drive on as fast as possible. Hardly was the car well and truly under way, than three pistol shots rang out behind us.

The next day the newspapers reported that several cars had been shot up at the same spot, and that in one case a bullet had passed through the back of the car and out through the windscreen, without, however, hitting anybody. Schreck thereupon examined our car most carefully; and in the upholstery he found three entrance and exit bullet holes. Had anyone of them been but a few inches lower, the episode would have had a very different ending!

During their investigations the police found a man in the vicinity of Lohof, almost naked and very badly injured. He turned out to be an inmate who had escaped from a nearby lunatic asylum and who, presumably, had been run down by some car and had been dragged a considerable distance by it.

Hitler's adjutant, Schaub, and I went to the hospital to see whether this man was the same man who had fired on our car. But the man was so swathed in bandages and so badly hurt, that any identification was impossible.

When we returned from the hospital Hitler said: 'You know, I just don't know what made me slam that door like that; it was that same, funny, inexplicable feeling!'

Once again, as so often before, a sixth sense had warned him of imminent danger.

Chapter 7

Women and Hitler

'MY BRIDE IS GERMANY,' Hitler was wont to say; and although it was jestingly said, there was also an undercurrent of seriousness in the remark. Much as he enjoyed the company of beautiful women, he was determined to remain a bachelor, as he always emphasised, whenever the question of marriage cropped up.

After he had assumed power, he often asked Frau Goebbels to invite a few young actresses to tea, and he took a delight in attending these tea parties, at which he showed himself to be a charming and gallant guest. To each of the girls invited he used to present a bouquet of flowers and a bonbonnière.

On one of these occasions I said to him: 'Herr Hitler, you have but to make your choice. No woman, I'm sure, would turn you down.'

'You know my point of view, Hoffmann. It's perfectly true that I love flowers; but that's no reason why I should become a gardener!'

He had no preference for any particular type of beauty; personality and a sympathetic character were the things that attracted him. A simple Gretchen or a sophisticated woman of the world, the fashionably slender or the voluptuously curved – each delighted him after her own particular fashion. If he had any preference at all, then I should say that it was a leaning towards the elegant, slim figure. Nor did he object to lipstick and painted fingernails, which were so scornfully castigated in Party circles.

In the old days, when bobbed hair came up at a Party discussion, the more conservative members pleaded that 'women with hair cut short should not be admitted to Party gatherings'; but Hitler decided in favour of the bob.

He rejected the original uniform designed for the Bund Deutscher Mädchen (the German counterpart of the Girl Guides), declaring that in the matter of feminine uniforms we should do well to follow the example of associations abroad. At the first march-past he saw, he turned to my son-in-law, Baldur von Schirach, who was then Reichs Youth Leader.

'In old sacks like that, the poor girls won't attract a single masculine glance. The Party isn't here to bring up a race of old maids!'

On Hitler's orders, a well-known Berlin modiste was ordered to design new uniforms for the feminine sections of the Hitler Youth movement, and these much more attractive garments were taken into immediate use.

While he was struggling to achieve power, he had a lively appreciation of women as a political influence, and he was convinced that feminine enthusiasm, tenacity and fanaticism would be the deciding factor. At his meetings, a special role was assigned to the women. Long before the beginning of the meeting, armed with their knitting and sewing, the 'incorruptibles' would take their seats in the front rows, thereby preventing opponents, who always showed up at these meetings, from getting too near to Hitler himself.

Their enthusiastic interruptions and the frantic applause with which they greeted Hitler's speeches were usually decisive in ensuring the success of those early meetings. These women were the best propagandists the Party had; they persuaded their husbands to join Hitler, they sacrificed their spare time to their political enthusiasms and they devoted themselves utterly and selflessly to the cause of the Party's interests.

Although he was very often embarrassed by them, Hitler had no option but to accept the veneration and enthusiasm that these single-minded supporters showered on him – often, it must be admitted, in a most importunate manner! And while it is true that in the building up of the Party the women played a decisive role, it is also a fact that their excess of zeal raised many a storm in the political teacup.

In the directing of Party affairs, however, the activities of the women were severely restricted, and no woman played a leading role in the Third Reich.

'I allow no man to stick his finger in my political pie,' said Hitler to me on one occasion. 'And most certainly no woman!'

Many indeed are the New Year's Eves that I have celebrated with Hitler, but none were so happy and carefree as those of the early days. Hitler even in those days drank nothing, and while this had a certain restraining influence on the company, it did not spoil the party, but it did keep the fun within reasonable bounds.

After the Berghof had been enlarged and a number of guest rooms had been added to it, Hitler used to invite the members of his immediate entourage and their wives to stay and see the New Year in. These were really cheery parties, though the uproarious fun usually only started after Hitler had retired, which he generally did very shortly after midnight. He took a keen pleasure in the traditional New Year's Eve games, and his interpretation of the grotesque leaden figures was both clever and amusing.

Very much in keeping with the occasion was the ceremony of the Berchtesgaden Mountain Rangers, who, punctually at twelve o'clock, greeted the New Year with salvoes from their huge fowling-pieces. The thunderous reverberations re-echoed through the surrounding hills, and as the last echo died away, the chiming of the bells of Berchtesgaden church was wafted upwards through the winter night to the terraces of the Berghof. The beauty and solemnity of that moment always moved us profoundly. The ceremony of 'shooting in the New Year' was centuries old, and Hitler supported it by making each year a liberal donation of powder to the Mountain Rangers, a deputation of whom always came, after the ceremony, to give him their thanks and good wishes for the coming year.

My mind goes inevitably back to New Year's Eve 1924–25, which Hitler spent in my Munich home. It was a small party of some twenty young men and women from among the intimate friends of our artistic circle. The rooms were gay with flowers, Chinese lanterns and brightly coloured paper decorations; in the bay window of the dining room stood the Christmas tree still in all its pristine glory, crowned with a little figure of the Infant Jesus and its 'snow' shimmering and glistening in the flickering light of its many, multi-coloured candles. The meal was of the cold buffet, help-yourself type, and the table was loaded with all the confections in which Germans delight and in the preparation of which my wife was such an adept – *die belegten Brötchen,* slices of bread and butter, garnished lavishly with a variety of delectable sausage and other *delikatessen,* salads of all sorts in profusion, and a large and tempting array of colourful jellies, custards, cakes and sweets of every kind; at convenient intervals stood large bowls of hock- and claret-cup, lovingly prepared by my own expert hand, while for those gentlemen who felt the need for something more bracing or something less sweet, schnapps and beer invitingly beckoned to them from little tables at the side.

In short, an ordinary New Year's party, a cheerful carefree affair of intimate friends on enjoyment bent, with music and games, a little flirting, much laughter and good spirits and lots of kissing under the mistletoe and good wishes, when the final hour struck.

The party had hardly begun, before I was asked whether Adolf Hitler was expected.

'No,' I said, 'I did ask him, but I don't think he can get away this year.'

'Oh! Heinrich! what a disappointment,' cried one young maiden. 'I do so want to see him. Couldn't you phone – just once more – and try and get him to come?'

The company was very insistent, and so I decided to try my luck once more. To my great surprise, Hitler accepted, 'but only for half an hour'.

Everybody now awaited his arrival with great excitement. With the exception of myself no one knew him personally, and when finally he did arrive, there was great enthusiasm – particularly among the ladies.

Once more I was able to observe what a great influence he exercised over women. In his cutaway coat he looked very smart. He had not yet started to wear the lock of hair hanging over his forehead, and his air of very modest reserve only served to enhance his charm. The women were charmed by his little moustache, though to me personally it was an eyesore.

One of the ladies was completely fascinated by Hitler. She engaged him in a long conversation and very cleverly managed to manoeuvre him under the mistletoe. (I so liked this English custom that I had started it in my own house.) Having got him where she wanted him, the lady, a young woman working in my studio and as pretty as a picture, then flung her arms round the unsuspecting Hitler's neck and gave him a hearty kiss. I shall never forget the look of astonishment and horror on Hitler's face! The wicked siren, too, felt that she had committed a *faux pas,* and an uncomfortable silence reigned. Bewildered and helpless as a child, Hitler stood there, biting his lip in an effort to master his anger. The atmosphere, which after his arrival had shown a tendency to become more formal, now became almost glacial.

'You mustn't take this ancient custom too seriously,' I said, in an attempt to cover up his moment of confusion. 'I'm only glad that it didn't happen to one of the more elderly among my guests. But then, you've always had luck with the ladies, Herr Hitler!' But there, apparently, I had deceived myself.

There was nothing Hitler loathed more than to be given so-called good advice, and this was probably one of the reasons why he restricted his social activities to consorting with only a very few families. 'Political aunts,' as he called the women who felt called upon to give him good advice, were anathema to him.

Of his relatives he spoke but seldom. During the whole twenty-five years of our association, he never once mentioned his brother, Alois Hitler, who had a restaurant in the Wittenberg-platz in Berlin; and never once was Alois Hitler seen in the Chancellery. His younger sister Paula, who lived in Vienna, kept up a desultory correspondence with him, but I remember how, after she had paid him a fairly long visit in Obersalzberg, he broke off all communication for more than three years.

But his views were well known to me from the numberless conversations we had had through the years, when, sitting just the two of us in companionable solitude, he sought relaxation and chatted about art or literature, philosophy and anything that came into his head. He held strong and precise opinions on such subjects as nepotism and heredity.

'The fact that one member of a family shows greatness,' he declared, 'is no reason for presuming that all his brothers and sisters must also have talent.'

Nepotism he regarded as being not only dishonestly abhorrent but also fundamentally dangerous and stupid; and Napoleon was his favourite example in support of his dictum.

'By putting totally unsuitable brothers and relatives of extreme mediocrity in positions of power and on the thrones of the lands he had conquered, he not only made himself both ridiculous and unpopular, but by so doing he contributed to his own downfall. For in his hour of need, it was just these very mediocrities who turned against him in a selfish and desperate endeavour to retain the wealth and power, with which his bounty had originally endowed them.'

And so he continued along the path that destiny had mapped for him, deliberately unmindful of the rest of his family. Alois, as far as I know, is still in Berlin; and his sister, a sweet, simple and gentle creature, still lives in the modest and contented obscurity of her Bavarian home.

On the question of heredity his convictions were equally concise. 'History,' he said, 'abounds with proofs of the fact that seldom if ever is the son of a great man himself also great. And in the nature of things this must be so. Eugenically, a son nearly always inherits the characteristics of the mother, and as most great men choose for their wives a woman who will be a complete antidote to the affairs of State he is conducting, it must follow that his son will rarely inherit those attributes which are essential to his assumption of the mantle of his father's greatness.'

His conviction that his successor must be a man of a mental stature equal to his own, that he himself could never beget a son with the necessary qualities, and that the problem of potential succession would be complicated, to the detriment of Germany's future, by the very presence of a son, was undoubtedly the major reason why he decided never to marry.

His step-sister, Frau Raubal, who was older than Hitler, was later his housekeeper for a long time in Obersalzberg and was completely devoted to him. She had two daughters and a son, who was a schoolteacher in Linz. During the war he was shut up in Stalingrad, and when Hitler was approached with the suggestion that he should allow his nephew to be flown out, he brusquely refused, saying that he could make no special exceptions. Frau Raubal's elder daughter, Angelica, was known to all of us as Geli.

At Hitler's personal table in the Café Heck, the centre of Munich's café – frequenting community, men predominated. Very occasionally a woman would be admitted to our intimate circle, but she never was allowed to become the centre of it, and had to remain seen but not heard. Hitler, admittedly, was never wanting in his charming compliments and gallantry, but for the rest, the lady had to conform to the customs of the circle. She could, occasionally, take a small part in the conversation, but never was she allowed to hold forth or to contradict Hitler.

One day in 1927, however, there came to the table a lovely young woman, who, with her artless and carefree manner, captivated everybody. It was Geli Raubal, Hitler's niece; and from that moment, whenever Geli joined us, she became the centre of the party, and even Hitler was quite content to take a back seat.

Geli Raubal was an enchantress. In her artless way and without the slightest suspicion of coquetry, she succeeded, by her mere presence, in putting everybody in the best of good spirits; each and every one of us was devoted to her – especially her uncle, Adolf Hitler. She even managed to get him to go shopping with her – a great feat! I well remember Hitler telling me how he hated it when Geli tried on hats or shoes, or inspected bale after bale of material, engaged the shop girl in earnest conversation for half an hour or more, and then, finding nothing that suited her, walked out of the shop; and although he knew that when he went shopping with Geli, this was bound to happen, he always followed her like a faithful lamb.

Under her influence, his social life became much more active; they frequently went to the theatre and the cinema together, but best of all, Hitler delighted in taking her for a drive and a picnic in some secluded beauty spot in the neighbouring woods.

By this time, in 1927, Hitler had already acquired great popularity; whenever he appeared in a bar or a restaurant, he was immediately surrounded by Party members and autograph hunters and he therefore preferred to spend his leisure hours with his little circle of intimate friends in the quiet and comforting solitude of the forest. Even there, however, he maintained his reserve. His attitude towards Geli was always decorous and correct; and it was the way in which he looked at her, the tender voice in which he addressed her, which alone betrayed the depth of his affection for her.

When he moved into the house at 16 Prinzregentenstrasse he installed her in a beautiful room, most delightfully furnished in a style appropriate for a young maiden by the foremost of Munich's furnishing establishments. There was a certain air of homeliness about this bachelor establishment. Hitler lost no opportunity of praising Geli's art as a cook; that she excelled therein is not to be wondered at, for her mother, who later ran the household for a considerable time, was a cook of quite exceptional merit.

Geli was deeply revered, indeed worshipped, by her uncle, and any idea of an affair between them most certainly never entered his head. To him she was the personification of perfect young womanhood – beautiful, fresh and unspoiled, gay and intelligent, and as clean and as straight as God had made her. He watched and gloated over her like some savant with a rare and lovely bloom, and to cherish and protect her was his one and only concern. For many years he had her voice trained by a well-known singing master; but in his attitude towards her private life he was less generous and seemed obsessed with the desire to keep her always under his own personal supervision.

But Geli, a high-spirited young girl of twenty, wanted to be free, to move about and to meet people, not to sit quietly at the same café table day after day with the same rather solemn faces. At Shrovetide her dearest wish was to go to a ball, but Hitler would not hear of it. But Geli persisted and gave him no peace till he finally consented – but only on condition that Max Amman, the proprietor of the *Völkischer Beobachter* and a very old and trusted friend of Hitler's, and I went with her. We were to take her, he directed, to the Deutsches Theater – the scene of the famous Bal Pares, and Amman and I had to promise faithfully that Geli would leave the ball with us punctually at eleven o'clock!

I was given the task of obtaining designs from the famous dress designer, Ingo Schröder, for an appropriate dress for Geli for the occasion. When I submitted them to Hitler he rejected the lot. The designs, he said were excellent and very decorative, but far too conspicuous; Geli was to wear ordinary evening dress.

When Geli, flanked by us two guardians of her virtue, left the ball at eleven o'clock, she was in anything but a festive mood; and I must admit we sympathised with her. In a ball of this kind, the fun and excitement doesn't begin till after midnight.

The theatre photographer had taken a photograph of us – not, of course, at ease in our loge with foaming glasses of champagne in our hands, but a stiff, formal group, with Geli in the middle and the two old watchdogs on either side of her; and this photo Geli duly presented to her uncle the following day.

I told Hitler straight out what I thought. 'Herr Hitler,' I said, 'the restraint under which Geli is living is not only a great strain on her, but it is also making her thoroughly unhappy. That much was quite obvious at the ball. Far from giving her any pleasure by permitting her to go to it, all you've done has been sharply to accentuate the intolerable restraint you impose on her.'

'You know, Hoffmann,' replied Hitler, 'Geli's future is so dear to my heart, that I feel myself in duty bound to watch over her. Right! I love Geli, and I could marry her; but you know my views and you know that I am determined to remain a bachelor. Therefore I reserve to myself the right to watch over the circle of her male acquaintances until such a time as the right man comes along. What Geli now regards as restraint is in reality wise precaution. I am quite determined to see that she does not fall into the hands of some unworthy adventurer or swindler.' Hitler, of course, had no idea that Geli was deeply in love with someone else, someone whom she had known in the old days in Vienna.

Who he was, what had passed between them, whether he returned her love and if so, why they did not marry, nobody knows for certain. Geli was a very reserved girl, not wont to open her heart or mind to anyone. Her greatest friend was my wife, Erna, who loved her deeply and admired her, not only with an artist's eye for the beautiful, but also for the many sterling virtues of her mind and character. Intimate though they were, only once did an unhappy Geli, burdened perhaps beyond endurance and seeking the solace of an older woman's comfort, lift the edge of the veil that shrouded her innermost thoughts. Even then, as if regretting the impulse, she stopped almost before she had begun. 'Well – that's that! And there's nothing you or I can do about it. So let's talk about something else,' she said abruptly; all my wife had gathered was that Geli was in love with an artist in Vienna and was desperately unhappy about it; nor could her gentle sympathy and offer of any help in her power elicit another word.

The good spirits that she invariably paraded were nothing more than a blind. It was nattering to her, admittedly, that the otherwise so serious and unapproachable uncle, who veiled all his feelings from the sight of everyone else, should be so devoted to her and should fling his reserve to the winds in her presence. She would have been no woman if Hitler's gallantry and generosity had made no impression on her. But this rigid supervision of her every step, this prohibition against making the acquaintance of any men or of indulging in any normal social intercourse without Hitler's knowledge were intolerable to a character that was as free as nature itself.

I was, perhaps, the only one who fully realised how she felt. My efforts to persuade Hitler to change his ways failed completely. So great was his fear of losing Geli, that he was convinced that only by his present methods could he guard against the danger.

Geli knew, of course, that Hitler was in love with her; but she had no inkling of the immensity of this love, so deep and, like all great loves, so utterly selfish. But her eyes were opened in a terrifying manner by a quite innocent episode.

One day my friend, Emil Maurice, one of the oldest Party members, who had been Hitler's chauffeur for many years, came to me pale, agitated and in a great state. Still quivering under the influence of his experience, he told how he had dropped in to see Geli, a perfectly innocent visit, during which they had laughed and joked and chatted as one always did when one was with Geli. Suddenly, Hitler had come in. 'Never in my life have I seen him in such a state,' said Maurice. Livid with rage and indignation Hitler had raved at him; and there had ensued a scene so terrible, that Maurice seriously thought that Hitler meant to shoot him on the spot.

Innocent? On Geli's side, most certainly so; on Maurice's – perhaps, for the good Emil had a roving eye and but little discrimination or discretion. Had he been misguided enough to try and make some advances to Geli, Hitler's keen sense of observation – almost a sixth sense, where Geli was concerned – would certainly have been alarmed and forewarned; and to have found his suspicions apparently justified would have driven him to boundless fury.

It was a very long time indeed before Hitler regained his self-control sufficiently to tolerate Maurice's presence without flying into a rage.

On 17th September 1931, Hitler invited me to go on a fairly long tour with him up north. When I got to his house, Geli was there, helping him to pack. As we left and were going down the stairs, Geli leaned over the bannisters and called, 'Au revoir, Uncle Adolf! Au revoir, Herr Hoffmann!' Hitler stopped and looked up. For a moment he paused, then he turned and mounted the staircase again, while I went on to wait for him at the front door. Very shortly, Hitler joined me.

In silence we got into the car and drove off in the direction of Nuremberg. As we drove through the Siegestor, he turned suddenly. 'I don't know why,' he said, 'but I have a most uneasy feeling.'

I did my best to cheer him up. It was the weather, this 'Föhn' – the south wind – that always had a depressing effect on one. But Hitler remained unresponsive, and in silence we drove all the way to Nuremberg, where we stopped, at the Deutscher Hof, the Party hotel.

We had left Nuremberg behind us and were driving towards Bayreuth, when Hitler saw in the driving mirror a car coming up on us. For security reasons, our habit at the time was never to allow any other car to overtake us. Hitler was about to tell Schreck to speed up, when he noticed that the approaching car was a taxi, and that a page-boy from the hotel was sitting next to the chauffeur and signalling frantically to us to stop.

Schreck drew up. The boy, panting with excitement ran to Hitler and said that Hess wished to speak to him most urgently from Munich and would hold the line. We turned and raced back to the hotel.

Before even the car stopped, Hitler leapt out and rushed into the hotel, with myself following as quickly as I could. Throwing his hat and crop onto a chair, he hastened into the telephone booth. He did not even bother to shut the door, and so every word was clearly audible.

'Hitler here – has something happened?' His voice was hoarse with agitation. 'Oh God! how awful!' he cried, after a short pause, and there was a note of despair in his voice. Then in a firmer tone, which rose almost to a scream: 'Hess! answer me – yes or no – is she still alive? … Hess! on your word of honour as an officer – tell me the truth – is she alive or dead? … Hess! … Hess!' his voice rose to a scream. He seemed to be getting no answer. Either he was cut off, or Hess had hung up to avoid having to answer! Hitler rushed out of the telephone booth, his hair awry over his forehead and a wild and glazed look in his eyes. He turned to Schreck.

'Something has happened to Geli,' he said. 'We go back to Munich – get every ounce you can out of the car! I must see Geli alive again!'

From the fragments I had heard, something, obviously, had happened to Geli, but I knew no details, nor did I dare ask.

Hitler's frenzy was contagious. With its accelerator jammed to the floorboards the great car screamed its way back to Munich. In the driving mirror I could see the reflection of Hitler's face. He sat with compressed lips, staring with unseeing eyes through the windscreen. Not a word was spoken; each of us was plunged in his own gloomy thoughts.

At last we arrived at his house and heard the dread news. Geli had already been dead for twenty-four hours. She had taken a small 6.35 pistol from Hitler's armoury and shot herself in the vicinity of her heart. Had help been immediately forthcoming, the doctors said, she might perhaps have been saved. But she had shut herself in her own room, no one had heard the shot, and she had bled to death.

From the doctor's examination, it appeared that she must have shot herself very shortly after our departure. The body had already been returned from the coroner's court, and when we arrived, it was already lying in state at the cemetery. Her mother, poor woman, met us with mutely streaming eyes; and with her were Hess, the Reichs Treasurer Schwarz and Frau Winter, Hitler's housekeeper.

Frau Winter told me what had happened in the house after our departure. As I have already related, Hitler returned to bid her a second farewell. Fondly stroking her cheek, he had whispered some endearing words in her ear; but Geli had remained disconsolate and angry.

'Really,' she had said to Frau Winter, 'I have nothing at all in common with my uncle.'

Hitler actually had only returned that very day to Munich from some journey, and although he had known that he would be there only for a few hours, he had sent for Geli and her mother, who, at the time were in Obersalzberg; and the preparations for the journey that stood before us had robbed him of any opportunity of devoting much attention to her.

Geli was depressed, Frau Winter said, and was not happy living in Hitler's house. With that I agreed, but what followed only tended to confuse the issue. To the best of my knowledge Geli was secretly in love with someone else, but Frau Winter insisted that it was Hitler she loved, and many little episodes and remarks had quite convinced her that this was so.

Did Hitler know the reasons for Geli's suicide, or had he just a premonition of evil? 'I have a most uneasy feeling' – were these words of his simply the expression of some instinctive malaise, or had his last farewell with Geli given him some good cause for anxiety? These are questions that will remain unanswered for ever, and the real reasons for this lovely girl's suicide will never be known.

Geli was the very reverse of the hysterical, suicidal type. She had a carefree nature and she faced life with a fresh and healthy outlook, which make it only all the more incredible that she should have felt impelled to take her own life.

In her room was found an unfinished letter to a Viennese singing master, saying that she wanted to come to Vienna and take lessons from him; whether this letter was in any way prompted by the discovery of a letter from Eva Braun, which she had by chance found in one of her uncle's pockets, must remain an open question. But Geli was no more; she had died by her own hand, and the why and the wherefore and the rest of the story is, and must for ever remain, a matter of pure conjecture.

According to Frau Winter, Geli had told her, shortly after our departure, that she was going to the cinema with a friend and had asked Frau Winter not to prepare any supper. That being so, Frau Winter was not in any way anxious when she did not see Geli again that night.

It was only the next morning, when Geli did not appear as usual for breakfast, that she went up and knocked at her door. Getting no reply, she had tried to peep through the keyhole; but the key was in it, and the door had been locked from the inside. Thoroughly alarmed, she called her husband, who broke open the door. A horrible picture presented itself; Geli lay dead in a pool of blood on the floor, and the pistol was lying in a corner of the sofa. Frau Winter immediately informed Geli's mother and sent word to Rudolf Hess and to Schwarz.

On her mother's instructions, her body was taken to Vienna and there laid to rest.

Hitler's veneration for Geli's memory assumed all but the form of a religion. With his own hand he locked the door of her room, to which no one but Frau Winter, he ordered, was to have access; and for many years, on his instructions, Frau Winter daily placed in the room a bunch of fresh chrysanthemums, Geli's favourite flowers.

He commissioned a number of famous artists to paint portraits of her from a variety of photographs, and these, together with bronzes of a most lifelike bust, sculpted by Ferdinand Liebermann, occupied an almost shrine-like place of honour in all his various residences and in the Reichs-Chancellery.

For two days, I saw nothing of Hitler. Knowing his nature so well and realising that in these terrible circumstances he would prefer to be alone, I did not go near him. Then suddenly at midnight my telephone bell rang. Sleepily I rose to answer it.

'Hoffmann, are you still up? Can you come round for a few minutes?' It was Hitler's voice, but a strangely unfamiliar one, desperately tired and apathetic. A quarter of an hour later I was with him.

He opened the door to me himself. Looking grey and desolate, he gave me a silent handshake.

'Hoffmann,' he said, 'Will you do me a great favour? I cannot remain in this house, where my Geli died; Müller has offered me the use of his house in St Quirin on the Tegernsee lake; will you come with me? I want to stay there for the few days until she has been buried, and then I shall go to her grave. Müller has promised me that he will send all his servants off on holiday. Only you will be there with me. Will you do me this great favour?' His voice had a note of pleading urgency, and of course I assented at once. The next day we set out.

In St Quirin the housekeeper handed the keys of the house over to me and, with an astonished and pitying look at Hitler, who seemed to be a completely broken man, he left us. Schreck, too, who had driven us down, was sent away; before he went he managed to whisper to me that he had taken Hitler's revolver, as he feared that, in his desperation, he might be tempted to do away with himself. And thus we two were left completely alone – Hitler in a room on the first floor, and myself in the room immediately beneath him.

Hitler and I were entirely alone in the house. Even as I was leaving him after having shown him to his room, he clasped his hands behind his back and started pacing to and fro. I asked him what he would like to eat, but he merely shook his head without a word. I took up a glass of milk, however, and a few biscuits, and then I left him.

In my own room I stood at the window, listening to the dull rhythmic sound of the pacing feet over my head. Hour after hour, ceaselessly and without pause it continued. Night came, and still I could hear him, pacing, up and down, up and down. Lulled by the monotonous beat, I dozed for a while in my armchair. Suddenly something jerked me back to complete wakefulness. The pacing had ceased, and a deathly quiet reigned. I sprang to my feet. Could he have ...? Softly and with great caution I slipped up to the floor above. The wooden stairs creaked a little as I mounted. I reached the door, and then, thank God, the pacing started again. With a lighter heart I crept back to my own room.

And so it continued, hour after endless hour throughout the long night. My mind went back to our previous visits to this idyllic little house, nestled beside the Tegernsee. How very different everything had then been!

Geli's death had shaken my friend to the depths of his soul. Had he a feeling of guilt? Was he torturing himself with remorseful self-reproach? What would he do? All these questions went hammering through my head, but to none of them could I find an answer.

Dawn began to lighten the night sky, and never have I been more thankful for the coming of the day. I went up again and knocked gently at his door. No answer. I went in, but Hitler, oblivious of my presence, took no notice; with hands clasped behind his back, his eyes gazing unseeing into the distance, he continued his eternal pacing. His face was grey with anguish and drawn with fatigue; a hairy stubble disfigured his face, dark shadows were blackly smeared beneath his sunken eyes, and his mouth was set in a bitter yet desolate line. The milk and biscuits were untouched.

Would he not try, please, and eat something, I asked? But again there was no reply, only a slight shake of the head. Something he must eat, I thought, or he will collapse. I rang up my house in Munich and asked how to cook spaghetti – a favourite dish of his. Following exactly the precise instructions I had received, I tried my hand at the art of cooking. The result, in my own opinion, was good. But once again I had no luck. Though it was his favourite dish, though I praised my cooking of it to the skies and implored him to try and eat just a little, it seemed as though all I said passed him by unheard.

The day dragged slowly to its end, and another night came, more horrible even than the one before it. Almost at the end of my tether, I could hardly keep awake; but from above me the footsteps went on and on, drumming and boring through my skull. A terrible agitation seemed to keep him on his feet, and nothing made him tired.

Another day came. I was myself all but comatose; my movements and actions became mechanical and instinctive. But the footsteps never ceased.

Late in the evening, we heard that Geli's funeral was over and that nothing now stood in the way of Hitler's pilgrimage to Vienna. We left the same night. Silently Hitler took his place beside his driver, Schreck. The almost intolerable strain, which had held me, snapped, and for an hour or so I slept exhaustedly in the car. We reached Vienna in the early hours of the morning, but throughout the long drive, Hitler spoke no single word.

We drove straight through the city to the Central Cemetery. Here Hitler went alone to the grave, where he found Schwarz and Schaub, his personal ADC, awaiting him. In half an hour he was back and gave the order to drive on to Obersalzberg.

Scarcely had he got into the car, than he began to talk. His eyes gazed fixedly through the windscreen, and he seemed to be thinking aloud. 'So,' he said. 'Now let the struggle begin – the struggle which must and shall be crowned with success.' We all felt a tremendous and blessed relief.

Two days later, he was speaking in Hamburg, and thereafter he rushed furiously from city to city, from meeting to meeting. His speeches were fascinating and compelling as never before, and an almost superhuman power of persuasion seemed to emanate from him the moment he mounted the platform. To me it seemed as though he were seeking in the turmoil of political meetings an anodyne for the frightful pain in his heart.

If there were anyone whom he ardently desired to marry, it was his niece, Geli. His love for this beautiful and intelligent girl was as great as was the political urge that possessed him; and while she would not have hindered the vast work of internal regeneration that he most certainly accomplished, it is quite possible that in the ties of home and family, in the contentment of domestic bliss by which he laid such store, coupled with Geli's restraining influence, he would have lost his zest for those international adventures that brought him to his ruin.

Round no woman in modern times has sensation hovered more eagerly than round Hitler's mistress and later wife, Eva Braun. Only a few people were aware of her existence, and those few kept silent.

My wife and I know perhaps more than anyone else of the inside story of Hitler and Eva Braun, and let me say at once that those who turn to this chapter in eager anticipation of a sensational and glamorous love story will be sadly disappointed. Hitler himself was a personally modest and intensely shy person, and as far as we ourselves knew or noticed, there never was any love story.

The middle of three daughters of Fritz Braun, a master craftsman, she was educated in the Catholic Young Women's Institute in Simbach on the Inn, the town on the opposite bank to Hitler's birthplace, Braunau; after completing a commercial course, she came in 1930 as a saleswoman to the shop that I ran in conjunction with my studio, and in spite of her nineteen years, she had a somewhat childish and naive air.

Of medium height, she was greatly preoccupied with her slim and elegant figure. Her round face and blue eyes, framed by darkish blonde hair, made a picture that can only be described as 'pretty' – an impersonal, chocolate-box type of prettiness. As she was so fond of telling all my employees, she made most of her clothes herself, and they were both skillfully made and tastefully designed; to lipstick and painted fingernails she had at the time not yet aspired.

She showed but little leaning towards music, and preferred the jingle of a dance hall; it was only later that she displayed a measure of interest in the theatre, but more still in the cinema.

With a few short interruptions, Eva Braun worked for me until 1945. From 1943 onwards, when all women were enlisted for war work, she came back to me, at Hitler's request, and worked in my Art Press.

Her younger and much more fastidious sister, Gretl, was also one of my employees. In 1944 she married Himmler's aide-de-camp, Hermann Fegelein, who, on the collapse of Germany, was shot as a traitor by order of Martin Bormann.

Hitler knew all my employees, and it was among them that he first made the acquaintance of Eva Braun, with whom he sometimes chatted in the normal, quite inconsequential manner; occasionally, he would come out of his shell a little and pay her the sort of little compliment he was so fond of paying women. Neither I myself nor any of my employees noticed that he paid her any particular attention. But not so Eva; she told all her friends that Hitler was wildly in love with her, and that she would bring him up to scratch and marry him.

Hitler on the other hand had no inkling of what was going on in Eva's mind, and he certainly had not the slightest intention of entering into a binding relationship, either then or later, with her. To him, she was just an attractive little thing, in whom, in spite of her inconsequential and feather-brained outlook – or perhaps just because of it – he found the type of relaxation and repose he sought.

Frequently when he intended coming to see us for an hour or so, he would say casually: 'Ask that little Eva Braun of yours to come along, too – she amuses me.' On other occasions he would rise and say: 'I think I'll pop in and see little Eva for half an hour; give her a ring, like a good chap, and ask her if I may'; and very often, indulging in his favourite relaxation, we would all go on a picnic together to one of the beauty spots, in which the surroundings of Munich abound. But never, in voice, look or gesture, did he ever behave in a way that suggested any deeper interest in her.

He gave her gifts in abundance; but they were flowers, chocolates, trinkets of modest value and the trivialities of the ordinary gallantry in which he delighted.

One day in the summer of 1932 she did not come to work. I did not worry about it, but towards midday, my brother-in-law, the surgeon Dr Plate, came in looking very serious.

'This is a bad business,' he said. 'During last night Eva rang me up. Speaking softly and with great difficulty, and obviously in great pain, she told me that she had shot herself through the heart with a 6.35 pistol. She had felt so lonely, she said, and so neglected by Hitler that she wanted to end it all.'

My brother-in-law returned at once to the hospital. A little later Hitler came in, and I told him what had happened.

'Is the doctor a man who will hold his tongue?' was his first question, and I told him he could rely on Plate's discretion. Hitler insisted on speaking to my brother-in-law, and from what he said, I gathered that he had received a letter of farewell from Eva. That same day he and Plate met in my house.

'Doctor – please tell me the truth. Do you think that Fraulein Braun shot herself simply with the object of becoming an interesting patient and of drawing my attention to herself?'

My brother-in-law shook his head. 'The shot was aimed directly at the heart,' he said; and from his further observations it was obvious that he considered it a genuine case of attempted suicide.

When my brother-in-law had gone, Hitler started pacing up and down the room. Suddenly he stopped and faced me.

'You hear, Hoffmann,' he said in an agitated voice. 'The girl did it for love of me. But I have given her no cause which could possibly justify such a deed.' He turned and continued his pacing.

'Obviously,' he continued, more to himself than to me, 'I must now look after the girl.'

'I see no obligation,' I objected. 'No one could blame you for what Eva has done.'

'And who, do you think, would believe that? And another thing – what guarantee is there that something of the kind might not occur again?'

To this I could find no answer.

'If I take on the responsibility of looking after her,' he declared, 'that doesn't mean that I intend to marry her. You well know my views. The great thing about Eva is, that she is no political blue-stocking. I loathe politically-minded women. The *chère amie* of a politician must be quietly discreet.'

And in this manner Eva Braun got her way and became Hitler's *chère amie*.

Even so, at that time there was established no liaison between them, in the accepted sense of the word. Eva moved into his house, became the constant companion of his leisure hours and, to the best of my knowledge, that was all there was to it. Indeed, I can think of no more apt simile than once more to liken Hitler to some ardent collector, who preferred to gloat over his latest treasure in the privacy of his own seclusion.

Eva was rigidly excluded from all official functions, whether of an internal or international nature. Even in the intimate circle, if any visiting generals or officials were present, she did not appear or come to table with us. She accompanied Hitler on none of his journeys, and she did not visit him in any of his headquarters, but remained in his house in the Prinzregentenstrasse in Munich, where Hitler saw her as occasion offered, or went to the Berghof in Berchtesgaden when Hitler was there in residence. And it was only at the Berghof, where she had her own private suite of apartments, and in the exclusive company of Hitler, his aides-de-camp and immediate personal entourage that she emerged, as it were as one of the family.

That Eva became his mistress some time or other before the end is certain, but when – neither I nor, I think, anyone else can say. Not at any time was there any perceptible change in his attitude towards her that might have pointed to the assumption of more intimate relations between them; and the secrecy that enshrouded the whole affair is most strikingly emphasised by the profound astonishment of all of us in his most intimate circle, when, at the bitter end, the marriage was announced.

Whether Eva at that time was really in love with him is hard to say. She was an ordinary, pretty little shop girl, with all the frivolity and vanity of her kind, and she was undoubtedly flattered and thrilled beyond words at the attention and compliments that this rising power in the land was paying her. In the make-believe of her own romantic imagination, she saw herself, I think, in a role, to which she was in reality so lamentably unsuited, as *a femme fatale* of the future, a sort of modern Madame Pompadour, a *dea ex machina,* influencing, behind the scenes the fate and destinies of nations at the side of the Man Who Loved Her. Nothing could be farther from the truth. As other men turn to soft-beslippered feet on the mantelpiece, a book and a pipe when the day's work is done, so Hitler turned to the company of attractive young women – and deliberately I emphasise the plural, 'women'.

Later, under the influence of the tremendous events through which she lived, and as the war years marched towards their grim conclusion, Eva's mental stature grew, and her character broadened and deepened; and by her final gesture and decision to remain at the side of her protector to the end, she attained heights that more than atoned for the vanities and frivolities of the past.

For a long time Hitler's friendship with Frau Winifred Wagner was of world-wide interest. He had made her acquaintance as long ago as 1922, and his very sincere feelings were primarily the reflection of his deep veneration for Richard Wagner and his works. He was not interested in Frau Winifred alone, but in the whole of the Wagner family and the Bayreuth Temple of Art, which he supported most generously. Nor was this happy relationship in any way disturbed when the eldest daughter, Friedelind, went to England and there criticized her mother's admiration for the Führer.

For years he regularly attended the Bayreuth festival and by his presence there he set the fashion for the whole constellation of Party chiefs and the diplomatic world.

At the 1932 Festival, much to the annoyance of Eva Braun, there now appeared upon the scene a woman in whom Hitler showed very particular interest – Unity Valkyrie Mitford, the daughter of Lord Redesdale.

Financially independent, Unity Mitford led the life of a female globe-trotter and was full of enthusiasm for Hitler and his ideas. In Munich she was in the same set with the Bruckmann and Hanfstängl families and became particularly friendly with Putzi Hanfstängl's wife, who was an American by birth. Hitler raved over her as the personification of perfect Germanic womanhood – a fact that drew from Eva Braun many acid comments, which were zealously collated and faithfully repeated to him.

In Unity Mitford, personal encounter with Hitler quickly transformed what had hitherto been a fervent, but impersonal and theoretic admiration of an idea and the brain from which it had emanated, into an intense and passionate devotion to the man himself and all that he stood for. In her car, decorated with the Union Jack and the Swastika, she drove all over Europe, everywhere taking up the cudgels in favour of the object of her adoration and his ideas.

Hitler admired her tremendously as an example of his *beau idéal* of womanhood; but he was even more aware of the value, for propaganda purposes, of Unity and her blind devotion to him. During the many times she returned to Germany, she was frequently to be found in Hitler's circle at the 'Osteria,' the Schwabing wine booth, sometimes accompanied by her sister, who later married Mosley, the leader of the British Fascists.

In his conversations with Unity and her sister Hitler always made a point of talking about his unrequited love for Britain; and all the hints and remarks of this nature that he let drop, often in a light and conversational manner, were made with the sole object of ensuring that through this channel, they would certainly be repeated in the right quarter. All this gave rise to considerable conjecture in political circles.

I met Unity Mitford on many occasions and under a great variety of circumstances – in Bayreuth, in Nuremberg and elsewhere. She was an intense woman – intense almost to the verge of hysteria. Coupled to her great personal devotion to Hitler was her even greater and more passionate devotion to her heart's desire; with every fibre of her being she yearned to see Britain and Germany closely united. She often said to me, she dreamed of an impregnable and invincible alliance between the Ruler of the Seas and the Lord of the Earth; the land of her birth in unison with the country of her hero could, she was convinced, achieve a world dominion, so strong that none could withstand it, yet so just and benevolent, that all would welcome it. 'To few women,' she said she felt, 'had been granted so great an opportunity to work for so great a cause; and to the furtherance of this great ideal she was prepared to devote, and if need be, unhesitatingly to sacrifice her life.'

Hitler's admiration of her, she realised, was purely aesthetic, and his interest strongly tinged with political self-interest and expediency; but the sacrifice of her purely personal desires as a woman was but small a price to pay, when placed beside the tremendous issues at stake.

She may, too, have cherished the secret hope, unadmitted perhaps even to herself, that once the Grand Alliance on which she set her heart had been achieved and the prospect of a peaceful, Utopian domination was in sight, the more intimate alliance, in which she would find her own personal happiness, might easily follow.

The gathering storm-clouds that steadily dimmed the bright sunshine of her fair visions filled her with frantic despair; and the declaration of war was the final, cataclysmic explosion, which shattered for ever and beyond repair everything that she had hoped and lived for. It was more than she could bear, and life no longer had any meaning or attraction for her.

To the kindly and well-meant suggestion of the Gauleiter of Munich Adolf Wagner – a wealthy Alsatian mine-owner, and previously Minister in the Bavarian Government – that she should leave Germany and return to her own country she turned a deaf and uncomprehending ear; and shortly afterwards she was found, lying dangerously wounded in the English Garden.* She had shot herself through the head!

Hitler at once sent for the best doctors available and was most assiduous in his attentions; every day he sent her flowers, and on her bedside table stood a photograph of him, personally autographed.

When she had recovered sufficiently to be able to travel, Hitler sent her to Switzerland, accompanied by Professor Morell, his personal physician. From there she returned to England, where she died in 1948.

Unity's attempted suicide made a profound impression on Hitler. Shortly after this tragic event he said to me, in a most unhappy tone: 'You know, Hoffmann, I'm beginning to be frightened of women! Whenever I happen to show a little personal interest – by a look or by paying some little compliment – it is always misinterpreted. I bring women no luck! And that's

---

* One of Munich's famous parks.

a fact which repeats itself in a most unusual and fateful way throughout my life!'

Involuntarily my thoughts went back to the death at an early age of his mother, to Geli's suicide, to Eva's attempt to take her own life, and then to Unity ....

There is another woman, too, of whom the world knows nothing, who tried to end her life because of her unrequited love for Hitler. In 1921, when Hitler was still quite unknown, this woman tried to hang herself in a hotel room; but fortunately she was found in time.

Many years later, Hitler brought her, now a happily married woman, to my studio to have her photograph taken.

The fascination he held for women was quite astonishing. During his struggle for power, the more elderly women used to rave about him like young flappers; and the letters he received later! Virtuous, married women wrote and begged him to become the father of their children; others wrote with an excess of exuberant extravagance that showed them to be obviously abnormal. And in Hitler's private office was a voluminous set of files with the generic subject title:

'CRACKERS!'

Chapter 8

Hitler and the Arts

HITLER'S PASSION for the arts was no pose. He had a discerning and highly appreciative eye for quality and was himself a water-colour artist of very considerable merit. Some of his pictures, in both composition and treatment, were exquisite, and had he devoted his life to painting, as he would so dearly have liked to do, he would, I think, have gained for himself an honourable place among the watercolour artists of our times.

In the first, early days of our friendship, he was greatly interested in my modest collection of paintings, among which those by Grützner held a particular attraction for him. 'As a young man in Vienna, I once saw a Grützner in the window of an art dealer's – a picture rather like that one,' said Hitler, pointing to the painting of an aged monk. 'Rather timidly I went in and asked the price. It was quite beyond my reach. Oh dear, I thought to myself, I wonder if I shall ever succeed well enough in life to afford to buy myself a Grützner!'

Twenty-five years later, Hitler possessed a collection of about thirty Grützner masterpieces.

Here is another story he told me of his Vienna days.

'Thanks to a recommendation I was asked to call and see a lady who lived in a delightful house in the very fashionable vicinity of the Hofburg. An elderly and charming Viennese lady received me in a most friendly manner. Very shortly, she informed me, she would have been celebrating her golden wedding, had her husband been still alive, and to mark the anniversary she very much wanted to have an aquarelle of the interior of the Capucin church in which she had been married.

'I at once started work on the commission. It was a task which afforded me endless delight, and with loving care I reproduced every minute detail of the interior of the very beautiful baroque church. At last the picture was finished, and as I entered the house to deliver it, I resolved to ask two hundred kronen for it. Slowly I mounted the staircase, step by step. Two hundred kronen, a bit too much, I thought, for as a general rule I was at the time getting about fifteen kronen for my pictures. The higher I mounted, the lower my courage sank. I handed over the picture to the old lady, and she was enchanted with it; and then came the question which I had been dreading: What, she asked, was the price? My courage failed me completely. "That, madam, I would prefer to leave to you," I muttered. More I could not bring myself to say.

'With a benign smile she disappeared into a neighbouring room, to re-appear a few moments later with a sealed envelope. By the time I reached the staircase I was already inquisitively fingering my precious envelope. Why, oh why, hadn't I demanded my two hundred kronen? My curiosity was too strong for me, and ere I reached the door I hastily tore open the envelope and, with eyes boggling with incredulity I saw – five one-hundred kronen notes!'

'Well, you were a good deal cheaper as a painter than you are as a photographic model,' I said, laughingly.

'For me in those days five hundred kronen was a lot of money; but for the Party thirty thousand dollars are no more than the proverbial drop in the ocean. You must learn to differentiate between the individual me and the Party, Herr Hoffmann!'

After the fire in June 1931, in the Glass Palace, the famous

Munich Art Gallery, in which so many of the principal works of the German Romantic painters were destroyed, Munich for many years possessed no appropriate and representative building for the holding of art exhibitions; and it was not until 1937 that the Haus der Deutschen Kunst (The House of German Art), designed by Professor Troost, was built in the Prinzregentenstrasse, and the Munich artists again had a place worthy of their works.

Hitler's instructions that I should be entrusted with the organisation of the Annual Art Exhibition were not given through any representation on my part, but as the result of a quite spontaneous decision of his own.

The first exhibition in the Haus der Deutschen Kunst was to be opened on 18th July, 1937 and a jury of twelve professors had been appointed to make selections from the 8,000 works submitted. A few days before the exhibition was due to open, Hitler asked me to accompany him on a tour of the various galleries. It was no very pleasant spectacle that presented itself to our eyes; the pictures had not yet been hung, and that air of 'organised chaos' prevailed, which seems to be an inevitable feature of any exhibition.

Hitler went through the various rooms, and I could see that he was not particularly edified by what he saw; apart from that, it had come to his knowledge that the twelve professors of the jury intended to hang their own pictures in the best places. Disappointed and angry, he suddenly declared: 'There will be no exhibition this year! These works which have been sent in show clearly that we still have in Germany no artists whose work is worthy of a place in this magnificent building. I hereby dissolve the Jury of Selectors!'

Consternation! 'That will be a terrible blow to the Munich artists, Herr Hitler,' I ventured. 'Think of all the hopes that will be dashed.' I pressed him further. 'Herr Hitler,' I continued, 'surely you can't be serious. There are about eight thousand pictures submitted, and out of that lot, surely we can find fifteen or seventeen hundred worthy to constitute an exhibition.'

For a while he hesitated and considered; then he agreed.

'If you think you can find sufficient pictures, worthy of the type of exhibition we have in mind, to fill these galleries, telephone to me in Obersalzberg, and I'll come and inspect your choice. But don't allow yourself to be influenced by anybody!'

In this way I found myself quite unexpectedly responsible for the exhibition. It was no easy task that my plea on behalf of the Munich artists had placed on my shoulders. But I knew Hitler's views, and I had a fairly good idea of what would find favour in his eyes.

'I cannot abide slovenly painting,' he used to declare frequently, 'paintings in which you can't tell whether they're upside down or inside out, and on which the unfortunate frame maker has to put hooks on all four sides, because he can't tell either!'

And so, in order not to jeopardise the success of the exhibition, I determined to adhere strictly to what I knew to be his taste, and from the 8,000 works submitted I chose some seventeen hundred, to which I felt he could take no possible exception.

Every year we could have filled a complete room with 'Portrait of the Führer' – there were normally anything up to a hundred and fifty of them, of all sizes and in all poses, most of them copied from photographs that I had myself taken. As a result Hitler directed that only one portrait of himself should be exhibited each year, and that he himself would select it. In 1938 he chose a portrait by the Tyrolese painter, Lanzinger, *Hitler in Knight's Armour*. This portrait had been bought by the town of Munich and then been recommended to Hitler for exhibition; and though 'Armoured Adolf' had many critics, it equally found many admirers.

I had always wanted to create an opportunity for the modern school of painting to show its work in the exhibition, and so, with the connivance of the Director of the Haus der Deutschen Kunst, I prepared a surprise for Hitler and devoted one gallery to the moderns.

When we entered it together, I confess my heart was beating a bit rapidly. Hitler looked at a picture by a well-known Munich artist. Then he turned to me. 'Who hung this one?' he asked, and his tone was not exactly friendly.

'I did, Herr Hitler!'

'And that one?'

'Yes, Herr Hitler – I chose them all!'

'Take the whole damned lot away,' he rasped and stomped angrily out of the room; and that was the end of my attempt to curry Hitler's appreciation for modern art!

In 1938, among the paintings submitted was one by P. M. Padua, entitled *Leda and the Swan,* and it would, I thought, be all the more interesting to exhibit the treatment, by a modern artist, of a subject that, of course, has been a favourite with artists throughout the centuries. Its technique was magnificent, but the boldness of the artist's approach was perhaps a little too direct, and I put it to one side, intending to ask Hitler what he thought.

He, too, was greatly impressed with the work, but he feared that it might cause offence to a certain number of the visitors to the exhibition, and he hesitated to give a ruling; then he had an idea. 'A picture like that can be properly judged only by a woman. I will ask Frau Professor Troost to decide!'

Having studied the picture for quite a while, Frau Troost declared that she could see no reason why it should be rejected.

'There you are, Hoffmann! You see – you're more prudish than the ladies! and to me, that's quite a new side of your character,' jested Hitler. Frau Troost's verdict had removed all his misgivings, and he directed me to hang the picture – which I did, in a prominent position.

In the middle of that very same night I was awakened by the ringing of my telephone. It was Frau Troost. 'I haven't had a wink of sleep, Professor! The question of that picture gives me no peace! I've thought the whole thing over again, and I've come to the firm conclusion that Padua's picture cannot be publicly exhibited. Do, please, have a word with the Führer and get him to change his decision!'

'Knowing Hitler, I don't think he'd ever change a decision he has once made, Frau Professor,' I replied.

When I told Hitler the next day about this nocturnal call, he was half angry and half amused.

'How like a woman, Hoffmann! You can't rely on any of them! Frau Troost should have thought of all her objections before. Now that I've taken the decision, I shall stick to it!'

As I expected, Padua's picture aroused great controversy – some in its favour and some against it, and it remained a centre of interest; and many of the leading members of the Party, including the Women's Section of the Party, demanded its removal. But there were just as many patrons of the arts who were so enthusiastic, that they wished to acquire the picture. But Martin Bormann beat them all to it!

When the Haus der Deutschen Kunst closed its doors in 1945, I heaved a sigh of relief at being rid of an honorary appointment that I had certainly not wanted.

In the summer of 1937 another great cleaning-up process of the museums and art galleries was initiated at the instigation of Dr Goebbels; and with 'Degenerate Art' as his slogan, he removed all the works that, in his opinion, were 'unpalatable' to the German people.

The climax of the campaign was an exhibition, arranged by Goebbels, of 'Degenerate Art'. This met with by no means unanimous approval, and many even of the very conservative members of the Party felt that he had gone much too far. I did not hesitate to give my own views very frankly to Hitler, and I told him that I thought Goebbels had gone quite the wrong way about things.

When Hitler visited the exhibition, I accompanied him, and much to Goebbels' displeasure, Hitler drew his attention to several pictures that, in my opinion, certainly did not deserve the stigma of inclusion; and it was a source of great satisfaction to me that I succeeded in persuading Hitler to instruct Goebbels to withdraw at once a very considerable number of pictures. Among them, I remember, were the *Walchensee* by Lovis Corinth, a Richard Dix, which was a masterpiece of technical execution, in no way degenerate, but with a slight tendency towards pacifism, and some drawings by Lehmbruck and others.

'If Goebbels insists on having his exhibition of Degenerate Art, he would be much better advised to concentrate his attack on artistic trash, and particularly on some of the trash which we ourselves are producing,' I told Hitler. 'Of the pictures submitted for acceptance in the Haus der Deutschen Kunst at least a third come in this category. Many artists seem to think that as long as the National Flag, the Swastika, heaps of Party uniforms and standards, masses of uniformed SA, SS and Hitler Youth on the march are included in a picture, that in itself gives it a right to demand acceptance!'

I waged perpetual warfare with the protectors of this type of 'artist'. Whenever I rejected a picture, the painter would complain to his Gauleiter, who in turn would approach Hitler and petition for the inclusion of the picture. As a rule, however, Hitler gave me a free hand and never interfered.

The Exhibition was such a success, judged by the numbers who visited it, that Dr Goebbels decided to send it on tour round Germany.

As a result of this exhibition I received innumerable letters from artists who were by no means degenerate, but whose works had been included, and who thought, erroneously, that I had been the instigator and organiser of the exhibition.

For Hitler, Vienna was the City of Disappointment. He had no love for it, and in his mind it was associated with the days of his poverty, misery, and the desperate struggle for his daily bread. But the Vienna of those days, the Imperial City, with its majestic buildings, its glorious picture galleries and cultural institutions, was, for all that, the source from which the enthusiastic young artist, Hitler, drew all his learning and inspiration.

The greatest disappointment of his life was his failure to pass the entrance examination into the Vienna Academy of Art, and it must be admitted that, with the exception of his very early efforts, his watercolours, which he used to sell to keep body and soul together, were well above average. Only on the occasion I have already related did he receive a 'princely' honorarium, and for the most part he sold his wares for twenty or thirty kronen apiece.

Later, of course, his pictures fetched fantastic prices. In 1944, for example, one of his watercolours was bought for thirty thousand marks – a tribute, I think, to Hitler, the statesman rather than to Hitler, the artist. I myself published a folio of his paintings in facsimile, and in 1936 the well-known American magazine, *Esquire,* had an article on Hitler as an artist, with reproductions of his works in colour.

Even after the collapse of Germany, the Americans continued to show the greatest interest in Hitler as an artist. Two of his watercolours, *The Ratzenstadl in Vienna* and *The Old Courtyard,* which belonged to me, were shipped to America on 29th June 1950 and, as far as I know, they are still in a museum in Washington.

When Hitler migrated to Munich, he was delighted to gain the *entrée* into artistic circles. He dreamed of the day when he would possess his own picture gallery, and when the publication of his book, *Mein Kampf,* began to bring him in a lot of money, he started to transform his dream into reality.

He collected, however, in a very haphazard way, and would acquire whatever happened to please him. In his Munich residence he preferred to have pictures by Munich artists, among which were the well-known *Bismarck in Cuirassier Uniform* by Lenbach, *The Sin* by Franz von Stuck, *A Parkland Scene* by Anselm Feuerbach, many Grützners, of which he was particularly fond, a painting by Heinrich Zügel and a large number of Spitzweg's works.

It was from a Munich art dealer that Hitler acquired the

picture *Thought is Free of Tax*, which is one of the best known of Spitzweg's paintings and depicts a scene at a frontier station. As he always did when purchasing a valuable picture, he sought a guarantee of authenticity before completing the deal. The picture was submitted to the scrutiny of three experts – Alt of the Helbing Gallery in Munich, who had catalogued all Spitzweg's works, Uhde-Barnays, the art historian and publisher of many books on Spitzweg, and Spitzweg's own great-nephew.

Hitler intended the picture to be his birthday present to Minister Hjalmar Schacht, the President of the Reichsbank, and a suitable brass plate with his greetings and a facsimile of his signature was attached to the frame. Hitler's ADC, Wiedermann, presented the picture and told Hitler how delighted Schacht had been to receive it. One day an art expert, who happened to be paying Schacht a call, expressed doubts as to its authenticity.

Hitler was furious, and directed me to investigate and try and find out whether the picture was a forgery or not. Further, he wanted to know whether the expert opinions given to him were given in good faith, and whether, if they were, the experts concerned were still willing to stand by their guarantee of authenticity.

The results of my investigations were somewhat conflicting. The famous Dorner Institute of Art Technology declared that the picture was a forgery, while other art experts were equally emphatic that it was genuine. I myself had a collection of sixteen Spitzwegs, and I was a little hesitant. When I placed these conflicting opinions before Hitler, he said: 'Well – whether it's genuine or otherwise is not really important; the fact remains that it is such a masterpiece, that Spitzweg himself could not have improved on it.'

So, as far as Hitler was concerned, the picture remained a genuine Spitzweg.

Not long afterwards the great Spitzweg forgery case was heard in Stuttgart, and the picture was sent there and produced in evidence. But once again the experts could not agree as to its authenticity.

In the course of the case, the identity of the painter who was said to have painted the alleged forgeries was disclosed, and counsel suggested that I should ask this man whether he had, perhaps, painted our picture.

Toni Steffgen, a completely unknown artist, lived in Traunstein and devoted himself to making copies of Spitzweg's pictures. But Steffgen was no forger; he signed each picture with his full name and with the note: 'A copy, after Spitzweg.'

One day two men entered the chemist's shop in Traunstein to make some small purchase and to their surprise saw a 'Spitzweg' hanging on the wall.

'That's a valuable picture you've got there,' said one of them. But the chemist shook his head. 'No, gentlemen – it's only a copy of a Spitzweg. The painter of it lives here in Traunstein, and I bought it from him for a few marks. He's in very poor circumstances, and if you gentlemen would buy one or two of his pictures from him, he would, I know, be delighted.'

The two men needed no second bidding, and in a few minutes were introducing themselves to Steffgen. Agreement was swiftly reached. In future, Steffgen was to work exclusively for his two new friends.

This stroke of fortune gave Steffgen new courage. He improved on his technique to such an extent and finally mastered that fluidity that is the hallmark of Spitzweg's work so perfectly, that even art experts could no longer distinguish between his work and that of Spitzweg himself.

The two swindlers, too, did not do badly out of the deal; they sold each picture for round about ten thousand marks – and paid Steffgen twenty or thirty apiece!

This Steffgen, then, was the man whom, with our picture under my arm, counsel and I set off to visit.

When we entered the 'studio' – a small room that served as workshop, living room and kitchen, all in one – the painter himself was sitting at the solitary window. His sick wife, with hollow cheeks and wracked by a violent coughing, was lying on a sofa, which was upholstered in washable oilcloth. Even two good antique pieces of furniture could not disguise the extreme poverty of the establishment.

In a friendly fashion I explained to him the object of our journey. 'Herr Steffgen,' I said, 'we have brought a picture with us and we want to know whether you are the painter of it. As counsel has already told you in court, if any picture has been painted by you, you can say so openly and without fear of any consequences. Please examine this picture very carefully; take your time before answering, but when you do answer let there be no doubt about it.'

For a long time Steffgen gazed at the picture. At length, however, he made up his mind. 'Yes,' he said, 'certainly, that picture was painted by me.' And that, as far as counsel was concerned, was the end of the case of the picture *Thought is Free of Tax.*

For the satisfaction of relieving, temporarily at least, the straitened financial circumstances of the family, counsel and I each ordered a picture for three hundred marks, and gave him a hundred marks apiece in advance. But we never received them.

When the case ended – the swindlers received a heavy sentence of penal servitude – the Public Prosecutor sent me the picture, because the person of the Chancellor of the Reich could not be connected with a court case, and for many years it hung, unnoticed, in a corner of my office.

In May 1945, when all my property and my art collection was confiscated by the Americans, this copy of *Thought is Free of Tax* found its way, with the rest, to the Collecting Point, the depot for all confiscated works of art. But from the cellars of the Collecting Point many hundreds of pictures were stolen – among them, the questionable Spitzweg, which then went on to Switzerland, purchased for a goodly sum of solid Swiss francs by a rich industrialist.

Now this picture was regarded by the Americans as a sensation;

they sought it everywhere and eventually traced it to its new Swiss owner. On the grounds that it was stolen property they demanded its return, but without success.

'I am a Swiss national; I bought this picture for a considerable sum of money,' sturdily declared the Swiss, 'and I would not dream of surrendering it – to you or anybody else!'

The Americans played their last trump card. 'The picture,' they told him, 'is a fake!' and to this they received the laconic reply: 'I don't care whether it's a fake or not; its interest for me lies in the fact that it once belonged to Hitler!'

On one occasion when Goebbels was paying him a visit, the Doctor noticed among the paintings one by Loewith, which, Hitler told him, had been a present from me.

Goebbels examined the picture with great care. 'A fine picture, mein Führer,' he said, with a malicious glance in my direction. 'And I don't wonder, for Loewith, of course, was one of the most talented among the Jewish painters!'

'Quite!' retorted Hitler with a laugh. 'That's why I've hung him!'

Hitler's favourite birthday or other anniversary present to his immediate collaborators and to the leading personalities of Party, State and armed forces was a valuable painting; and from his very wide collection, he used to choose a picture the motif of which fitted in some way with the character, the habits or the profession of the recipient.

Dorpmüller, the then Minister of Communications, received on his seventieth birthday a landscape by Spitzweg with a railway as its motif, and Ohnesorge, the Postmaster General, was given *The Old Post Coach* by Paul Hey. Grand Admiral Raeder received *A Naval Battle* by Willem van der Velde; to Göring, the passionate hunter and Master of the Hunt, he presented *The Falconer* by the Viennese artist, Hans Makart. Doctor Ley, the alcohol-proof creator of the Arbeitsfront, was rewarded with *The Carousing Monk* by Grützner; and for Goebbels' fifth wedding anniversary he chose – Spitzweg's *The Eternal Honeymoon*.

Hitler made a sharp distinction between those pictures that he acquired privately, mostly from Munich or Berlin art dealers or at auctions, and those that were confiscated in the course of the campaign 'For the Safeguarding of Jewish Artistic Property' by Rosenberg and his staff. The latter he refused to accept for his private collection.

Alfred Rosenberg, who had his headquarters in Paris, thought he would give Hitler great pleasure by presenting him with two most valuable pictures; one was the famous Vermeer van Delft, *Der Astronom,* from the Rothschild gallery, and the other the no less famous *Madame Pompadour* by Boucher, from the Louvre.

Whenever Hitler came to Munich from Berlin or from his Führer-Headquarters, his first act was always to visit the 'Führerbau', to inspect the pictures he had recently purchased or that were being offered to him by the art dealers. On one such visit, the majordomo of the house gave him the two pictures that Rosenberg had presented to him. Hitler, who was fully aware of their priceless value, was anything but pleased. With a contemptuous gesture he turned to the discountenanced major-domo. 'Tell Rosenberg,' he said stiffly 'that I am not in the habit of accepting presents such as these. The proper place for these paintings is an art gallery, and a decision as to their fate will be made when the war ends!'

Hitler was determined that Art should occupy a pre-eminent place in the life of the Third Reich. Living artists were to be given every opportunity of developing their talent – those of them, that is, whose works were based on sound and accepted academic principles; but against the Degenerates he was equally determined to wage a merciless war. Goebbels, however, to whom Hitler had entrusted the direction of the National Academy of Culture, strove to make art the hand-maiden of his political activities.

He instructed Adolf Ziegler, the President of the Academy, to remove from the German galleries all pictures that were not acceptable to the National Socialist régime; and it was his intention to burn the lot!

When I got word of this mad idea, I hastened to the Reichs-Chancellery.

'It's simply not done, Herr Hitler!' I remonstrated. 'Even from the point of view of your own cultural policy, to destroy such works would be an act of irresponsible vandalism! Why – you will certainly find purchasers for them abroad, and collect quite a lot of foreign exchange into the bargain! You might even be able to arrange for an exchange of pictures with some of the foreign galleries, for among those condemned are the works of such artists as Franz Marc, Lovis Corinth, Liebermann, Gaugin, Renoir and Van Gogh!'

I persisted in my arguments, and I succeeded in persuading him that such wholesale destruction was mere stupidity. He directed Goebbels to appoint a commission to examine the question. Most of the members were art dealers, and from Hitler I received orders to attend the commission's meetings.

'It would give me great pleasure,' he said, 'if you were to succeed in exchanging a Picasso or a Pechstein for a Dürer or a Rembrandt!'

Hitler's enthusiasm for Art communicated itself to the other leading personalities of the Third Reich, with Göring in the van. Ribbentrop and Goebbels, however, were not to be outdone, and they, too, sent representatives to all the big art auctions. So zealously did they bid against each other, that most of the pictures were sold for far more than they were worth; and this rivalry also led to some highly diverting episodes.

On one occasion, Hitler refused to buy a picture, *Bismarck*, by Lenbach, because he thought that the price, thirty thousand marks, was too high. Shortly afterwards, the picture was put up for auction at Lange's in Berlin. 'Get it!' ordered Göring. And when the third hammer-stroke fell, he was seventy-five thousand marks out of pocket over the deal!

I happened to be there when Göring presented the picture to

Hitler as a birthday present. The latter was astonished to receive as a gift a picture that he himself had refused to buy; but when he heard the price paid, he flew into a real rage.

The net result was that he instituted 'The Führer's First Refusal'.

By order, no picture of historical and artistic merit could be sold without the previous consent of the Führer. If Hitler were interested in any picture, he would direct Posse, the Director General of the Dresden Gallery, and when he died, his successor, to fix the price.

Göring, however, did not feel himself bound by the order of the Führer, and one picture all but caused a real break between the two men.

An Amsterdam art dealer offered a Vermeer, *Christ and the Sinful Woman,* to Hitler, and the latter immediately denoted that he was very interested. When Göring heard of this and found out the price that Hitler was offering, he outbid him handsomely; the price paid was one and a half million guilders, and the picture passed into the possession, not of Hitler, but of Göring.

Hitler was very angry, but he consoled himself with the thought that Göring would present the picture to him for the gallery he was planning in Linz. In this, however, he was doomed to disappointment, for Göring did no such thing! 'The great thing is,' he said, 'that the picture should remain in Germany; and that is assured by my "Führer prerogative" decree.'

One picture over which he exercised this prerogative was Vermeer van Delft's famous *The Artist in his Studio,* from the Czernin collection in Vienna. He maintained that a work of this nature should not be kept in a private collection, where it would be seen only by a limited and privileged few, but should become the common art property of the nation.

The picture was accordingly earmarked for the Linz Gallery, and the funds for its purchase came from the Reich Postal Service, from the money acquired from the sales of a special issue of 'Hitler stamps,' which brought in many millions of marks.

I myself was once present when Ohnesorge, the Postmaster General, handed Hitler a cheque for fifty million marks derived from this source.

In all, some ten thousand pictures were to be purchased for the Linz Gallery. Among them were Moritz von Schwing's most important work, *Aschenbrodel* (Bubbling Ashes), and that most striking picture, *Plague in Florence,* by Makart, which Mussolini had presented to Hitler; and with some of the many millions that he earned from the sale of his book, *Mein Kampf,* Hitler acquired, among others, Leonardo da Vinci's *Leda and the Swan,* A *Self-Portrait* by Rembrandt, *The Honey Thief* by Cranach the Elder, Watteau's famous *Dancing Children,* and a work by Adolf Menzel, called *Construction in Silesia. The Discus Thrower,* the famous statue by Myron, was acquired from an Italian princely house through the intermediary of Mussolini and was also destined for the Linz Gallery. In 1945, however, it was returned to Italy.

I once asked Hitler why he was according Linz such preferential treatment.

'The recollections of the time I spent there as a young man have perhaps something to do with it,' he replied; 'but my primary reason is that I do not think the great capital cities of the world should have a monopoly in art treasures.'

Hitler was very fond of showing me his architectural designs, and I must say that I was astounded at what I saw. Nor was I alone in my admiration; many famous architects found these designs most impressive. Very interesting were the designs that he had made at the age of twenty for triumphal arches. 'These, my friend,' he said to me, 'will one day be erected in Germany!'

The layout and the internal architecture of the Senate Hall of the 'Brown House' were first roughed out on the back of a menu in the Café Heck; and later, with very minor alterations, they were incorporated in the building. In the course of years, he dashed off many hundreds of designs.

While the Brown House was being built, Hitler proved to be no easy foreman; he watched every little thing with an eye like a hawk, and anything that displeased him was mercilessly torn down again.

Thinking of him in this light, I could not refrain from asking him: 'Herr Hitler, why didn't you become an architect? You would have been pre-eminent!'

'Because,' he retorted, 'I decided instead to become the Architect of the Third Reich!'

Chapter 9

With Hitler at Home

STAYING AT THE BERGHOF in Obersalzberg was like living in a gilded cage. In contrast to the Chancellery, where everything had a very formal and official air, life in Obersalzberg was of a much cosier and more intimate character.

The walls of the dining hall, with its great table to seat eighteen, were panelled in pine; the general architectural design was modern and had a pleasing effect, the harmonious ensemble of which was completed by the adroitly placed mirrors and lighting. The ornamentation was by no means lavish, but equally the room gave no impression of bareness.

But the most wonderful thing of all was the superlative view from the windows of the wild massif of the Untersberg, in which, according to the legend, the Emperor Friedrich Barbarossa had taken up his abode.

Strange guests were only very seldom invited to dine in this room, in which Hitler was wont to take his meals with Eva Braun, his aides-de-camp, doctors and immediate colleagues; and the small, intimate circle would sometimes be completed by the presence of friends of Eva's and their children.

The servants came with us from Berlin. The cook and the chambermaids all came from the Berchtesgaden district, and the cuisine was Bavarian in style. Hitler adhered to his vegetarian diet, which a first-class cook from Vienna used to prepare for him, until Bormann discovered that her Aryan ancestry was not all that it should have been, and she was, unfortunately, dismissed. Both in the old house, 'Wachenfeld', and after the remodelling, Frau Raubal, Hitler's elder sister and the mother of Geli, exercised for many years a general supervision as house-keeper. But after the death of her daughter, she and Eva Braun, who almost invariably accompanied Hitler to Obersalzberg, quarrelled so much that Frau Raubal left.

Frau Raubal's attitude towards Eva Braun had always been one of frigid disapproval – the disapproval of a respectable matron, who sees clearly through all the wiles of some little flibbertigibbet of a gold-digger and wonders only at the frailty and gullibility of men, even the most intelligent among them.

After the death of her daughter, Geli, her feelings intensified into a deep dislike akin almost to hatred. She was convinced, and nothing we said could shake her conviction, that her Geli had been deeply in love with Hitler and that the presence and influence of Eva Braun had been both a source of great unhappiness to her daughter and one of the primary causes of her untimely end. She was a prey to conflicting emotions of profoundest resentment against the woman who, she considered, had done her daughter so grievous a wrong, and boundless devotion to this step-brother of hers, whom from the beginning she regarded as the future saviour and leader of her country.

Like all her kind, Frau Raubal was a most excellent house-keeper; and the one contribution she could make to Hitler's cause was, she felt, to see that his household was run in every way with the perfect and effortless rhythm of a superlative machine; and in the accomplishment of this self-imposed duty she was prepared to stifle her own feelings and the strong antipathy, which the presence of Eva Braun evoked in her, and remain at her post.

The atmosphere at Obersalzberg, however, became too much even for her determined devotion to duty. Here, in the quasi-solitude of the mountains, Eva was very much more the chatelaine than was ever possible in the more public surroundings of Munich. Before Bormann succeeded in turning Obersalzberg into a sort of second Berlin Chancellery, Eva was the hostess of the house and, except on such occasions as the visit of the Duke and Duchess of Windsor, she behaved as such. Had she been content to remain aloof, the relations between the two women might well have continued to be one of implacable but tacit hostility. But when she started to give herself airs and not only to interfere, but to interfere capriciously, haughtily and inefficiently, in the management of the household, it was too much. The stern, tight-lipped disapproval of the one and the often somewhat stupidly condescending hauteur of the other were frequently shattered by bitter and venomous mutual recrimination, till Frau Raubal could stand it no longer. For reasons that she refused to discuss, she asked Hitler for permission to relinquish her post.

Hitler, of course, was well aware of the intense friction between the two women; but like most men, he loathed family rows, and particularly rows between the womenfolk, and would go to almost any lengths to avoid being drawn into them. In this case, he took the line of least resistance and let Frau Raubal go without demur. She returned to her home in Munich, where she lived peacefully, until she died in 1948.

In later years the whole of the Berghof was closed to the public, and could only be approached by special permission. Inside the enclosure, about a mile and a half from the house, a little tea pavilion was erected; it was a duck-walled, circular building, whose single room was heated by a large open fireplace. Here, in front of the fire, Hitler would often fall asleep after his almost daily walk to the pavilion; then the gentle murmur of conversation would cease, we would wait till he woke up again and then we would all go back to the Berghof together.

Except for Hitler's wolfhound and Eva's terrier, for whom it was the highlight of the day, this self-same walk, day after day, was not very exciting. After dinner there was usually a film, and the talk round the fireside would continue till long after midnight. There was no end to the variety of subjects that were touched upon, but generally art, theatre and architecture held pride of place. Hitler himself was always ready to hold forth on astrology, astronomy and indeed on any subject from the Ice Age to the discovery of uranium – and in such detail, that sometimes it was very difficult to suppress a yawn.

His memory was phenomenal. He remembered not only every date of any historical importance, but also the units and their tonnage of every fleet in the world. The 'German Fleet Calendar' he knew by heart, and he not infrequently embarrassed his Naval Officers with questions that they either could not answer or answered wrongly. There was hardly a motor car, whose name, model, number of cylinders, weight and God knows what else besides he could not quote accurately, and when he was challenged he would gladly have a bet – and he generally won!

Discussions on the humanities interested him but little. Technical subjects, on the other hand, enthralled him; I don't know how many times I have listened to him holding forth on the theory and practice of bridge construction. He was particularly impressed by the American bridges, and he amassed all the photographs and books on the subject that he could lay his hands on. It was his intention, later, to build a bridge in Hamburg that would surpass the American bridges in size and everything else, and to which he proposed to give the proud name of 'The Gateway of the World'.

The construction and details of a giant public hall, capable of seating three hundred thousand people, was another subject on which he would discourse for hours; and although I did my very best to appear interested and used to nod my head approvingly at regular intervals, I must confess that the only thing I remember now about this mammoth building is that it was to be erected in Berlin.

On one occasion, fairly early on, when we were talking about nuclear fission, I said to Hitler: 'I've read that for many years the Americans have been experimenting in this field; are we ourselves doing anything of the kind?'

'Of course we are!' he replied. 'But these experiments are the greatest danger to which humanity has ever been exposed; just think of it – if some darn' Profax (his favourite term for the scientific Professor) makes a bloomer, he'll probably blow the whole globe to bits! That's the theory, anyway; in practice, thank goodness, we've not yet reached that stage!'

And in those days we used to laugh and thought this was a great joke!

In the evenings, summer or winter, Hitler loved to have a fire in the hearth. He always sat as close to it as he could get, and he took a delight in stirring it up with a poker and throwing fresh logs into the roaring flames. At these gatherings, tea and coffee were always served, for even those among the company who liked a drink were anxious to demonstrate how abstemious they were, really; but for me, of whose tastes Hitler was well aware, there was always 'a drop of what I fancied', and the reflection of the dancing tongues of fire would flicker pleasingly on my wine glass.

In these cosy surroundings, Hitler liked to beguile himself with a little music. He possessed an enormous collection of gramophone records, and in a huge cupboard on the mantelpiece were hundreds of songs and choruses, which had been specially made for him, in every dialect of the German language; most of them, however, had never even been played.

His favourites were extracts from the Wagner operas; then, almost as a concession, would come the Beethoven symphonies and the music of Richard Strauss, while really light music would be represented by *Die Fledermaus* and *The Merry Widow*. At these 'musical causeries by the fireside', Bormann, whom he dubbed 'The Master of the Archives', gave proof of his musical appreciation by taking on the job of putting on the records.

The majestic music of *Tristan* and *Die Meistersinger* invariably took Hitler back to his old days in Vienna. 'I would scrape and save every farthing,' he would tell us, gazing with a far-away look into the leaping flames, 'to get myself a seat in "the Gods" at the Imperial Opera. And the gala performances! What a superb spectacle of pomp and magnificence it was, to watch the members of the Imperial family arriving, and to see the Grand Dukes in their glittering gold uniforms and all the great ladies, adorned with their scintillating diadems, stepping out of their carriages!'

The joy that the eternal repetition of his favourite music gave Hitler was a delight that I could not share with him; a little change now and then would, I thought feelingly, be a decided improvement! My daughter, Henriette von Schirach, seemed to share my opinion, for one day, while she was visiting Obersalzberg, she produced the records of Tchaikovsky's *Symphonie Pathétique*. But Hitler told her quite brusquely to take them away. Tchaikovsky, obviously, could not aspire to a niche among the august Wagner-Strauss-Lehar trinity!

On another occasion Hitler was quite horrified when my wife played Stravinsky and Prokofiev to him; and on the one classical symphony that the latter wrote, his only comment was: 'Even a blind hen sometimes strikes a grain of corn!'

Another thing that delighted him was the medical discussions in which the doctors used to engage, and he would listen, with truly astounding patience and an unceasing stream of questions, to themes that in reality did not concern him in the least; as far as I was concerned, I was quite convinced that I had contracted at least one, if not all, of the diseases whose symptoms had been portrayed with such clarity and in such detail! After one such debate, Hitler became an enthusiastic supporter of the 'Zabel-System,' a diet advised by Dr Zabel of Berchtesgaden.

Occasionally topics would crop up that were not particularly pleasing to him, and I noticed that women showed much more courage in inviting Hitler's attention, within our own small circle, to some shortcoming or other, and that in this way not a few rather delicate questions were ironed out. Sometimes, however, Hitler took strong exception, and this once happened with my daughter.

Henriette had just returned from a visit to Holland and was giving her impressions of Amsterdam. In describing how, from her hotel window, she had watched some Jewish women being taken off to Germany, she used the word 'brutal'. Hitler interrupted her harshly, and an icy silence fell on the little circle.

A little later Bormann took me aside and advised me to tell Schirach to take his wife away, as Hitler had been so angered, that even an intervention on my part would have no effect. Accordingly, the von Schirachs left Obersalzberg, without attempting to say good bye!

As with music, so with films Hitler delighted to have endlessly repeated those that had pleased him; and when I was staying with him, I had no option but to conform. I saw the *Nibelungen* film, with Paul Richter as Siegfried, at least twenty times and the *Fire Tongs Bowl* nearly as often.

Initially, Goebbels used to arrange for a preview of new films at Obersalzberg, before they were generally released. On such occasions, of course, the production would be regarded with a particularly critical eye. Eva Braun would express displeasure at some scene or person in the film, Bormann or one of the others would take exception to something else and so on; and the upshot of it all would be that Hitler would order cuts and alterations, quite oblivious of the trouble and expense involved.

Goebbels was furious and quickly stopped sending any more new films. When I told him that I was 'fed up to the teeth with seeing the same old films again and again,' he retorted: 'And I, my friend, am not in the least interested to hear critiques of my films from some stupid little flapper' – Eva Braun – 'or from a glorified butler!' – Bormann.

Hitler seldom stayed for very long in Obersalzberg; but one of the few occasions when he decided to do so, life became very hectic, and there was a constant coming and going of diplomats, statesmen, high Party functionaries, ministers and generals, there were receptions and banquets of all kinds, but from these the ladies were excluded.

Bormann had gradually succeeded in transforming the idyllic Obersalzberg into a species of political closed-shop, where, with Hitler cut off from the outside world, he created for himself an excellent opportunity for trying to gain his chief's agreement to his own plans and intentions. In time, the whole district was sealed off by a high wire fence, many miles long; a huge barracks was built for the SS, and on the top of the Kehlstein, at an altitude of over six thousand feet, and made of gigantic blocks of granite, was erected a house, which the Americans later named 'Eagle's Nest'. Ostensibly it was to be used as an excursion chalet, and its construction and design were remarkable. An approach gallery over 200 yards long led to a lift, the shaft of which rose 200 feet through the hewn rock. From its battlement windows there was a stupendous view over the whole of the Berchtesgaden district right up to the frontier of Austria itself. Its construction, for which the funds, materials and manpower were placed at Bormann's disposal by German industry and the German Arbeitsfront (Labour Organisation), took many years to complete and cost vast sums of money. But Hitler did not like it, and in all he went there but five times.

Göring, who had his own residence in Obersalzberg, was a very rare visitor at the Berghof, where he only came when he had to do so. One after the other, the Chancellery and the other Government departments all set up their own quarters in Obersalzberg, which in the course of time became a sort of Berlin branch office.

Like Göring, Bormann, too, had his own house, but unlike the Reichsmarshal, he spent all his time with Hitler at the Berghof and even took all his meals there.

Before Bormann's influence had gained the upper hand, access to Obersalzberg was open to all, and a veritable flood of pilgrims would pour in from all over the Berchtesgaden district the moment it was known that Hitler was in residence. In time, this stream grew to such proportions that official action had to be taken to control it. Sometimes more than five thousand people, many of them from Austria, would march past Hitler with hands raised at the salute.

A 'march-past' of this kind often lasted two hours or more, and as the place where Hitler normally stood to receive the enthusiastic acclamations was in the full glare of the sun, a tree was planted to afford him a little shade and protection.

In 1945, everything which had the slightest connection with the previous owner of the Berghof was blown to pieces, and a little later it was all razed to the ground once again. All that now remains is this tree, and I can only hope that what I have just described will not cause it, too, to disappear.

If Hitler was in a good mood, he would summon children out of the crowd and entertain them to tea and cakes on the terraces; sometimes, inevitably, among his little guests were some who were not of pure Aryan descent, and among the many photographs that I took of these kindergarten receptions was one, in which this blemish was clearly visible and that, when published in all innocence in my volume *Hitler among the Children*, caused a great flutter.

On one occasion a very lovely and eager little child attracted Hitler's attention, and he had a long talk with her and invited her mother to bring the little girl often to see him. Little Berneli, as the child was named, became Hitler's admitted sweetheart, and many were the snaps I took of them on the terrace together. Her father, we found, was an ex-officer, who had won the Iron Cross, Class I.

Then one of the many over-zealous busybodies of the Party, who knew the family and had nothing better to do, must needs scurry to Bormann and tell him that the child was not of pure Aryan descent. Bormann immediately forbade the mother and child ever to appear in Hitler's presence again, but – and this was typical of the man – he did not tell Hitler what he had done.

Later, when Hitler enquired what had become of his little friend, Bormann was merely evasive.

A real row started, however, when Bormann saw the photo of Hitler and the little girl together in my book. In great excitement he demanded that the photograph should be forthwith removed, and when I told him that this was technically not possible, he demanded that the whole book should be scrapped. This was too much of a good thing! Without further ado, I went straight to Hitler, told him the whole story and asked him to decide the issue.

Hitler always hated it when he was faced with anything that he found irksome or embarrassing, and this time his scorn was directed against those who had denounced the child. If they had held their stupid tongues, no harm would have been done; as it was, although he did not interfere with my book, he felt he had to be logical and refuse to see the child any more.

'There are some people,' he told me, 'who have a positive genius for spoiling all my little pleasures!'

The first thing Hitler did when he left his bedroom at the Berghof in the morning was to go straight to the magnificent terrace on the ground floor. There, at a particular time, he usually saw a wonderful and inspiring sight – two gigantic eagles sweeping in high circles through the sky; through field-glasses he would eagerly watch the majestic flight of these rare but handsome birds. Then, one day, to his consternation, he saw but one eagle; what, he wondered anxiously, had happened to the other?

For days the subject was anxiously discussed among us, for we all saw how worried Hitler was at the disappearance of the second eagle.

A little later he decided to go again to Obersalzberg for his birthday, and a few days before the event our column set out from Munich. About 30 miles outside Munich we saw a fast-moving car approaching from the opposite direction, and in spite of the speed at which it passed us, Hitler noticed that some great bird with outspread wings was lying on the back seat. Immediately he halted the column. 'I do believe,' he said, 'that that was my eagle!' and he forthwith ordered the Commando escort under Standartenführer Rattenhuber to drive back and overtake the car.

'If I am right, I promise you, gentlemen, that I shall mete out an exemplary punishment to those scoundrels! And not to them alone, but also to the recipient!' he said, and the black look on his face boded no good for the unfortunates who had roused his wrath.

About an hour later we saw the Commando car returning at full speed. We halted, and Rattenhuber came running up.

'You were quite right, mein Führer,' he reported. 'It is the eagle from the mountains.'

'And the recipient?' asked Hitler in menacing tones.

Hesitatingly Rattenhuber continued.

'The eagle was delivered to your Munich residence in the Prinzregentenstrasse. It is mounted on a marble plinth, which bears the inscription:

TO OUR BELOVED FÜHRER FROM HIS MOUNTAINS
April 20th.
From the Local Party Group
NSDAP Berchtesgaden.'

Driving to Obersalzberg, Hitler often preferred to avoid the Autobahn and to take instead the old road that wound round the Chiemsee lake. On this road was situated the Hotel Lambach, of which he was particularly fond and where he often used to stop for a meal or a cup of coffee. This, of course, quickly became known, and the Lambach became a favourite place for excursionists, who gazed at the 'Hitler Room' and the Guest Book with great interest.

If Hitler intended to make any considerable stay in Obersalzberg, he would often transfer his more important conferences to the Lambach.

On one occasion we had stopped there for a short rest and were proceeding gently towards Berchtesgaden, when Hitler suddenly noticed a man lying in the middle of the road. Schreck, the driver, pulled up and the men of our escort jumped out to attend to the man. When he recovered consciousness, he said in a weak voice that he had had nothing to eat for two days. Sandwiches were immediately produced from our hamper, and Hitler further took out his pocket book and gave the man fifty marks.

When we resumed our journey, Hitler gave us a dissertation on the importance of the National Socialist People's Benevolent Society. 'This little incident alone proves how very important the Society is,' he said; 'and how necessary it is that the scope of its activities should be enlarged.'

Later in the day Reichsminister Lammers also arrived in Obersalzberg, and at dinner that night he told us of a curious experience.

'On the way here,' he said, 'I found a man lying senseless in the middle of the road. I stopped to see what we could do to help him, and the poor chap said he'd had nothing to eat for two days. Fortunately I had plenty of food with me.'

'Did you give him any money?' Hitler asked.

'Oh, yes, mein Führer! I gave him twenty marks.'

Hitler laughed. 'Well – that makes seventy marks he got out of the two of us. He deserves it! And it'll be amusing to see who the third mug will be!'

Hitler knew full well how deadly a weapon ridicule could be. At his own table he had often enough seen Goebbels, in his sarcastic manner, make fools of men whom he disliked, for Goebbels was astute enough to realise that anyone, who lacked the gift of ready and sharp repartee and who allowed himself to be made to appear ridiculous, was subsequently not likely to be invited frequently again to the Führer's table.

Hitler himself had a horror of appearing ridiculous. He was always most cautious as regards any new suit or hat that he proposed to wear. First of all he would insist on making sure that the top hat or cap or whatever it was really suited him, and for this purpose, I always had to photograph him in private in his new garments; only if he were completely satisfied with the resultant photograph would he then take them into public use.

After 1933 he gave up wearing his favourite Bavarian leather shorts, and he even went as far as to beg me to make no new prints of photographs of him wearing them and to withdraw from sale any existing ones.

He was very shy in the face of nudity – not in the field of art, in which he encouraged it, but as regards his own person. He was obsessed with the idea that if anyone saw him or took a photograph of him in bathing trunks, he would lose face in the eyes of the people, and he would frequently quote instances of how the publication of some private snapshot had jeopardised the popularity of a statesman.

'I remember a photograph on the front page of the *Berliner Illustrierte*,' he said, 'showing President Ebert and the War Minister, Noske, in bathing trunks; and even though it was in the days of a democratic republic, the loss of prestige was very great. Mussolini frequently exposes himself to ridicule in the same way, and it always angers me when I see photos in the press of him and his family in bathing costumes on the Lido. A really great statesman wouldn't do it.' After a pause he continued. 'What would happen to our reverence for Napoleon, if pictures of him in these ridiculous things had been handed down to us? And it's for this reason that I never bathe in public.'

'But, surely, you could have a private bathing place, mein Führer, where no one could see you,' said one of his secretaries.

'In that case I should have to have my servant with me, and I do not wish to have applied to me the old saying that "No man is a hero to his own valet!" He turned jokingly to me. 'In any case,' he said, 'Hoffmann here would know no peace till he'd taken a snap of me! As it is I am always afraid lest some skilful forger should set my head on a body in bathing trunks!'

Later Morell told me that the Führer was a very difficult

patient and that it was quite impossible to persuade him to allow an X-ray to be taken of him. Whenever Morell had to give him an injection or wished to make an examination, Hitler would first send his servant out of the room and would then expose only the minimum of his person essential to the matter in hand.

I was given another example of his great fear of ridicule, when I took a photograph of him with Eva's little Scotch terrier, Burli. 'You mustn't publish that snap, Hoffmann,' he said. 'A statesman does not permit himself to be photographed with a little dog, however amusingly winning it may be. A German sheepdog is the only dog worthy of a real man; though, of course, Bismarck's bulldog was in keeping with the massive stature of the man!'

As soon as he assumed power, Hitler caused the old Chancellery of the Reich to be completely remodelled. Beside one of the big reception rooms he had built a music room and a dining hall, which were designed by the architect Troost, and whose interior decoration and furnishing were done by United Munich Workshops.

The dining hall was almost a perfect square. On the back wall of this lofty apartment, whose three glass doors opened out on to the historic Chancellery gardens, was hung the great, 20-foot wide painting, *The Entry of the Sun-goddess,* by F. August Kaulbach; in niches stood two life-size bronze statues, *Blood and Earth,* by the Munich sculptor, Professor Wackerle; and a big table, capable, when fully extended, of seating sixty, a number of smaller tables for the personnel attendant on the principal guests, and a buffet completed the furniture. Originally, this was intended to be a purely private dining hall; but later it became a veritable round-table chamber, where visiting heads of states and foreign diplomats could dine officially but intimately with Hitler.

The service was in the hands of SS-men, specially trained for the purpose. They wore short white jackets and black trousers and their service was deft and discreet. The normal meal, other than on State occasions, was usually quite homely and consisted of soup, a meat course with vegetables and a light sweet. If any of the guests present preferred, like Hitler, to have a vegetarian meal, his wishes were at once fulfilled; but the only one I ever saw who exercised this privilege was Martin Bormann. The guests consisted usually of important officials, famous artists and any Gauleiters who happened to be in Berlin on business, and the company was always various and lively.

During the war, only uniforms were to be seen. I myself was the only one in civilian clothes, and even I used to put on a uniform coat, without badges of rank, on official occasions, in order to fit in with the general picture; and Hitler, when he was entertaining some very distinguished guest, usually put me on his left, in order to avoid giving offence to one or other of the numerous Field Marshals or Generals who were invariably present.

In the early days Hitler liked everyone to play his part in the conversation; but later he used to monopolise it himself. Goebbels had a highly specialised parlour trick of his own; by means of barbed and malicious remarks he delighted in trying to make guests, whom he did not particularly like, look ridiculous, and whatever one felt about him, that he possessed both wit and a sarcastic tongue is undeniable.

Whenever Goebbels began his little fencing game with me – which was fairly frequently – the whole table, including Hitler, sat back and prepared to be amused. Here is an example, typical of the numberless little sparring matches in which we indulged. It was during the war, and the British had just carried out a night raid on Berlin. Hitler, who had arrived that day from his Führer-Headquarters, asked: 'Has the bombing had any effect on the night life of Berlin?'

There was a general silence. Goebbels fixed me with a long and ironic look, which irritated me.

"Why are you staring so maliciously at me, Herr Doctor?' I asked angrily.

'That should be pretty obvious, my dear fellow, surely! You are the only expert on the night life of Berlin who can answer the question!'

All eyes were turned on me; Hitler chortled with amusement, and Goebbels started to preen himself.

'What, pray, do you know about experts, Herr Doctor? Every child in Berlin knows that there are no experts in *your* Ministry!' Hitler covered his face with his hands and roared with laughter, and the rest of the company followed suit. Goebbels started to reply, but I interrupted him. 'Chuck it, Herr Doctor,' I said coarsely, 'You won't get any change out of me!' and Hitler, who feared that our exchange might get out of hand, rose and retired with Goebbels for an official conference. The remainder of the party all congratulated me; they took an impish delight in the fact that I had reduced 'the great Hot Air Merchant' to silence.

Goebbels, however, had no intention of taking this reverse lying down, and he leapt in to take his revenge one day, when I was not present at table, and Hitler asked the cause of my absence. 'Hoffmann is a law unto himself,' said Goebbels in a resigned voice. 'It doesn't suit him to work in collaboration with my ministry, he studiously avoids anything in the nature of propaganda work, and he has no sense of political responsibility whatever. All he thinks about is making money!'

But he got a sharp retort from Hitler. 'You leave Hoffmann in peace,' he said. 'He started life as a business man and he's remained exactly as he always was. Others have risen to become Ministers – Herr Minister!'

In view of the esteem in which he was held, it is not surprising that on Hitler's birthday and other anniversaries a whole long row of tables in the Chancellery should be filled with the presents that poured in upon him. There was everything one could possibly think of, from a bit of carving by some Hitler Youth to a home-knitted pullover, from an expertly made model of the Berghof to the latest products of well-known firms, and from bicycles to the last word in elegant motor cars; musicians, writers and poets dedicated their compositions and works to him, and artists presented him with their paintings, some of them very amateurish but some of very high virtuosity. Good things to eat and drink also abounded, and in the cellars of the teetotal Hitler the choicest wines of the Rhine, the Moselle and the Palatinate, which would have brought joy to the heart of a wine-lover, languished, alas, unheeded.

Many a housewife sent him home-baked cakes, never dreaming that these culinary confections would in no case be even tasted by Hitler. This type of present did not even appear on the gift tables, but quietly disappeared, for Hitler always believed that this would be a very easy way of poisoning him; his suspicions in this direction were strengthened when Schreck, his chauffeur, was taken dangerously ill on the way to Stettin, after having partaken of a dish intended for Hitler himself.

On one occasion a Turkish delegation arrived in Berlin and was received by Hitler. After the delegation had returned to Turkey, there arrived a gigantic packing case, filled with the most wonderful sweetmeats – crystallised fruits, chocolates, marzipan, bonbons, and honey, all packed in the most delightfully coloured wrappings. Hitler was delighted with the gift and admired it immensely; but he would not accept it. He ordered that the case should be closed up again and, complete with its marvellous contents, should be buried in the Chancellery garden. When I expostulated that that would be a pity, he retorted, 'I am not prepared to wish on to my friends the things I refuse to touch!'

A little later I saw some workmen, who were busy in the vicinity of this 'grave', enjoying half-moons of marzipan and gold and silver wrapped bonbons with the greatest gusto. I asked one of them where they had found these fine sweets. The man was a Berlin cockney, 'Blimey, Guv'nor,' he said. 'Ain't yer 'eard of the Great Destruction? Well – we quietly dug it all up again! Luvverly grub, we finds it – so does the missus an' kids!'

Another time, on the way to Feldafing on the Sternberger See, we came upon an antiquated car that had broken down. The chauffeur seemed to be at his wits' end, and Hitler pulled up to see whether we could be of any assistance. Schreck very quickly found out what was wrong, and we were soon on our way again. But the owner of the car had made a note of our number plate, and the next day a parcel arrived, containing three tins of super-fine caviare, accompanied by a most gracious letter of thanks from the Rumanian Minister.

Now Hitler had a weakness for caviare. Nevertheless, he returned the parcel by return of post, with an equally gracious letter to say that it was the duty of every motorist to help a fellow motorist in distress and that the little service he had rendered in no way deserved so great a reward.

But to me he said: 'One never knows, Hoffmann!'

In contrast to the custom in Obersalzberg, women were very seldom invited, in the later years, to meals in the Reichs-Chancellery. Göring, too, was a rare guest; Hitler's culinary confections, he declared, were not to his taste. But the lick-spittling Bormann dutifully consumed raw carrots and leaves in his master's company – and then he would retire to the privacy of his own room and devour with relish his pork chop or a fine Wiener Schnitzel.

'Our Bavarian Cannibal' was what Hitler used to call me. He was very anxious to convert me to vegetarianism, but in this he had as little success as I myself had in my attempts to convince him of the delights of alcohol – in spite of the fact that his cellar was filled with the choicest of wine, gifts for the most part from every province of Germany.

'Wine is a wonderful specific against insomnia, Herr Hitler,' I told him. 'Why don't you try a glass before you go to bed?'

'I don't like it. I always think I'm drinking vinegar,' he replied shaking his head and grimacing at the idea. 'I tried drinking wine when I was younger,' he continued. 'But without some sugar, I couldn't swallow the stuff!'

Sugared wine! God, how awful! With every appearance of

outrage I had at him. 'Sugar in wine! You can't put sugar into a noble beverage, Herr Hitler! If a wine merchant did that, he'd go to prison! And in any case you have many choice sweet wines in your cellars, which you'd drink *and* enjoy, without bothering about any sugar!'

'I dare say you're right; and you're certainly far more at home in my cellars than I am, Hoffmann!' And so saying, he sent for a bottle of my own choosing. Emptying his glass in a couple of gulps, he smacked his lips. 'Excellent!' he exclaimed. 'By jove, I like that wine!'

I was greatly pleased at my apparent success, and when a little later Hitler said he was sleepy and was going to bed, my elation knew no bounds. The next day I asked him how my 'medicine' had worked.

'I slept like a top,' he answered. 'All the same, I'm not going to drink any more wine. You know, Hoffmann, wine makes one see everything *couleur de rose;* but dispassionate consideration can only be undertaken on a stone-cold, sober stomach! At first the patient drinks wine as a medicine; then gradually the daily dose becomes a cherished habit. That may be all right for you, my dear fellow; but for me – no!'

So I had failed after all: and all I could think of to say was: 'Well, of course, to abandon this cherished habit at my time of life might well have a very serious and unfortunate effect on my health!' And I left it at that.

On one occasion, however, I rather overshot the mark. In a small circle of our friends Hitler pointed to me as 'a Bohemian held fast in the fetters of all bad habits' – by which he meant a devotee of good food, good wine and good tobacco.

'Well – all I can say is, that these bad habits suit me down to the ground!' I retorted. 'I feel as fit as a fiddle, while you and Hess, who spend your whole lives chewing raw leaves, swallowing pills, having endless injections always feel poorly, and you couldn't carry on without a daily visit from the doctor!'

This was very thoughtless on my part, for to be referred to as a sick man was a thing Hitler could not abide; and for several days afterwards, my usual invitation to join the Führer's table was lacking!

Shooting, which he hated, was a regular conversational hobbyhorse with Hitler; and if Göring, The Reich Master of hunting, were present, he would hold forth at length and with much irony.

'I have nothing against the chase as a profession,' he would say; 'and I have nothing, equally, against those who, through the environment of their upbringing, have indulged from their earliest youth in these animal-slaughtering activities. But nowadays it has become the fashion; every high Party official feels that it's "the thing" to be a member of some shooting syndicate or other and to slaughter indiscriminately the dumb beasts of the earth!'

'Mein Führer, you do us wrong!' Göring would object. 'The German sportsman is the protector and preserver of our forests!' Hitler would laugh. 'Indeed, yes! he protects and preserves the unfortunate beasts until they are old enough to be shot! The professional gamekeeper tells his master exactly when and where an animal will emerge, and the latter, sitting in comfort behind a telescope, spies his victim and slaughters him. Then with a hearty huntsman's cheer he returns proudly to his home.'

'But our new game laws forbid indiscriminate slaughter,' objects Göring. 'And the real sportsman finds his greatest joy in watching wild animals.'

'Then why don't you follow the example of the Duke of Windsor? When I asked him if he was interested in shooting, he said yes, he was – but only with a camera!'

'But, mein Führer, shooting has a political importance, as well. The foreign diplomats are always delighted to accept an invitation to shoot; and problems often seem less thorny when one is out stalking than when one is seated round a conference table.'

'I see. So you think that there exists a sort of freemasonry of the forest? Well – I know nothing of shooting; but if the killing of animals really contributes to better political relations, I shall be only too happy to place our slaughterhouses completely at the disposal of our foreign guests!'

Hitler's words were still sarcastically delivered, but his scorn, obviously, was mounting. 'That's why I praise the poacher. He knows more about nature, by God, than all your Sunday sportsmen put together. He's foolhardy and he's courageous, and it's only lack of money that prevents him from hiring a shoot for himself.'

'You are pleased to jest, mein Führer!'

Then the fat was in the fire!

'Jesting be damned! If you call yourself a sportsman, why don't you face a wild animal in equal combat? If you, Herr Master of the Hunt, were to stand and kill your boar with a spear, then I should be impressed. If that fat old publisher, Müller, ran after a hare and caught it with his own hands, I should praise him for a good and sporting effort. I have every respect for the man who stands and faces a charging tiger in the jungle, but none at all for the would-be Nimrod who takes advantage of the mating season to sit up a tree and shoot down some unsuspecting animal intent on paying court to his mate!'

By now he was in a veritable temper.

'I hereby and with immediate effect forbid any leading member of the Party, in so far as these activities do not constitute part of his profession, either to accept or to issue any invitation whatever to any shoot! I shall instruct the Minister of Justice to modify the penalties for poaching! And I shall direct Himmler to release his poacher prisoners and to form them into a corps of sharp-shooting gamekeepers for the protection of wild animals!'

Actually, having thus blown off steam, he promptly forgot all about it.

Chapter 10

Hitler's Headquarters – And Mine

WITH THE EXCEPTION of the Felsennest in the Eifel, all Hitler's Headquarters bore names that had some connection with the wolf – Wolfsschanze, Werwolf, Wolfsschlucht; this was because at the beginning of his political career Hitler had used the pseudonym, 'Wolf.'

At these Headquarters the invitation to the 'evening' cup of tea usually came about three o'clock in the morning, after the last of the situation reports had been discussed. Usually very few people were present, and the party normally consisted of Hitler's aides and secretaries, a doctor and any liaison officer from Ribbentrop or Himmler who happened to be at Headquarters. Unbeknown to Hitler, these latter had been given the task by their chiefs of reporting every minute detail of what happened in the Führer's intimate circle.

My own quarters were simple but well-found and comfortable, consisting of a sitting-room, bedroom and bathroom, and, to help me to while away my many free hours, I was also given a wireless. In the same barrack with me lived Professor Dr Morell, Admiral Voss, General Bodenschatz, who was Göring's Adjutant, and Obergruppenführer* Wolf, Himmler's Adjutant and

---

* Obergruppenführer = Major General, SS (Translator)

The Lindberghs as Göring's guests.

British Fascists in Nuremberg, 1934, with Unity Mitford's sister in the background.

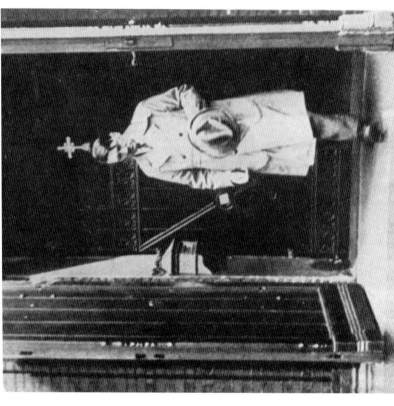

The accidental appearance of a cross over Hitler's head caused a storm of protests.

At ease among his friends Hitler, a teetotaller, confined himself

'Hitler's Sweetheart' – it delighted him to see her at the Berghof until some busybody found she was not of pure Aryan descent.

With young Fräulein Goebbels – a day of rest.

First an autograph . . . and then the honour of being snapped.

Miss Unity Mitford.

The famous sculpture of Geli by Professor Thorak.

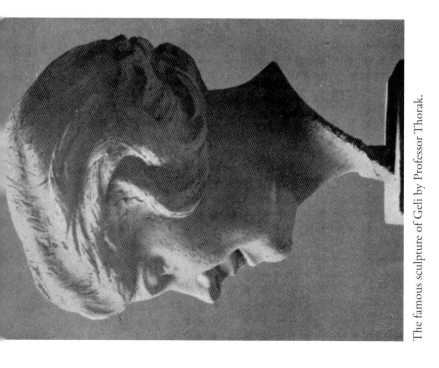

Geli Raubal, Hiler's niece, ward, and one great love.

Geli's suicide left a wound in Hitler's heart. She was a girl of beauty and character, who might have changed the Führer's life.

From shop-girl to Reich Chancellor's wife. Eva Braun, a simple, pretty, inconsequential girl, met Hitler in my studios, and when she attempted suicide, Hitler felt a moral obligation towards her that led to marriage and death together.

Eva Braun borrows my camera to snap Hitler and a little guest at Obersalzberg.

Hitler in glasses and Bormann choose a tiara wedding present for Gretl Braun.

A tea party – Funk, with Frau and Dr Goebbels, Frau V. Dirksen and the author.

Eintopf in the Chancellery – the patriotic 'utility Irish Stew,' which all good Germans ate at least twice a week.

Not for publication – Hitler using a reading-glass.

Censored personally by Hitler – no photograph in spectacles was to be published.

Relaxing with the local paper at Berchtesgaden.

15.1.35: good news from the Saar.

Taking the dog for a run.

The Berghof, at Obersalzberg, near Berchtesgaden; interiors, and fireplace.

Wintersports at Obersalzberg.

Hitler loved family gatherings.

The usual evening call from Berlin to Eva in Munich.

The entrance to Hitler's study at the Reich Chancellery.

was the only person present at Hitler's first National broadcast –1st Feb., 1933.

I clink glasses with Stalin in 1939. Molotov is in the background.

I was present when Hitler welcomed Lloyd George to the Berghof.

the man who later made the first overtures for an armistice in Italy. My job at Headquarters consisted exclusively of taking photographs of officers and men who had come to be presented with various decorations – hardly a full day's work!

Hitler's personal quarters were deep underground, with a cement roof 25 feet thick, dark, windowless and devoid of fresh air; night and day they were lighted by electricity, and a pump did its best to keep the atmosphere healthy.

I just used to sit and wait until Hitler sent for me, either to take a meal or to have a talk. These talks took place for the most part in the middle of the night, and often, by the time I left the Führer's dug-out, the sun was already high in the heavens, and I would fling myself on my bed sleepy, tired out and in a thoroughly bad temper.

Life in this inner ring was both boring and exhausting. As long as Hitler continued to take his meals with us, there was always something of interest to listen to, but once he had decided to eat alone, boredom reached its zenith.

We lived in complete isolation, except for occasional arrivals commanded to attend by Hitler to be decorated by him personally with the Knight's Cross of the Iron Cross, with Diamonds and Swords. While most of these heroes painted the situation at the front in the rosiest of colours, some of them spoke pretty bluntly, much to Hitler's annoyance. When they had gone, he would say that each man could only see the situation on his own tiny bit of the front and was, of course, in no position to venture an opinion on the whole.

A frequent visitor was Field Marshal Rommel, of whom Hitler at first held the highest opinion. I remember taking photographs when Rommel came to submit a report on his unsuccessful offensive against Egypt in the summer of 1942. Rommel, incidentally, was the only man to whom Hitler gave permission to talk to the international press reporters in Berlin. After his crushing defeat at El Alamein by General Montgomery, Rommel realised that his position in North Africa had become untenable, and he flew at once to Führer-Headquarters – this time to be received very coldly.

On various occasions, most of our Field Marshals and senior Generals – von Brauchitsch, von Rundstedt, von Leeb, Mannerheim*, Guderian, who was relieved of his command, and Hoepner, who was dismissed from the Army by Hitler in person – paid us visits, but beyond marking the occasion with photographs, I did not come into contact with any of them.

When, in the winter of 1941 the German armies became bogged down in the snow and terrible cold at the gates of Tula and Moscow, there was a scandal about the inadequacy of the troops' winter clothing. Hitler immediately set to work and himself designed the types of clothing that were to be manufactured, but by the time they were in mass production, it was already too late, and many thousands had died of exposure.

Hitler was completely confident of the ability of the German armies to defeat Russia speedily and decisively. Quite early on, I remember, I ventured to say that I hoped we would avoid making the same mistakes as Napoleon.

Hitler laughed.

'You sound like one of the western propaganda merchants, my dear fellow,' he replied. 'If Napoleon couldn't do it, Hitler can't! – That's the parrot cry with which they are trying to comfort themselves. Don't you worry! Nothing like that can happen to us – I've studied my history far too well!'

One day in 1943 I was having a meal alone with Hitler in 'Werwolf' in the Ukraine, just at the time when the first very disquieting reports about Stalingrad were beginning to come in.

'My officers are a pack of mutineers and cowards. I will no longer admit them into my intimate circle, and I will never have a meal with them again!' The savage contempt and anger in Hitler's voice staggered me; never before had I heard him speak in this manner.

---

*Field Marshal Mannerheim was the supreme commander of Finnish forces, allied to Germany.

'First of all they do their cowardly best to dissuade me from this or that operation, and then, when I carry it through to a successful conclusion, they take the credit and come running and asking for orders and decorations. If I had listened to these – gentlemen, the war would have been lost long ago!'

To my great astonishment, he repeated these trenchant remarks in front of the company at lunch.

A little later, when all chance of relief had gone and the fall of Stalingrad was imminent, we were at the Wolfsschanze Headquarters in East Prussia. The atmosphere was one of abysmal gloom, and I did my best to keep out of Hitler's way. One day I was sitting in a corner in the mess, when General Jodl and Colonel Schmundt, the Führer's Chief Aide-de-Camp, came in. They did not see me, and quite unintentionally I became an eavesdropper of their conversation.

Schmundt told Jodl that he had been entrusted with a special mission by Bormann; on the Führer's instructions he was to fly to Stalingrad and present Field Marshal Paulus with a pistol, with which the latter was to take the logical action, consequent upon the collapse of the Stalingrad front. Greatly moved, Schmundt declared that, with all due respect to the Führer, he would not accept this mission.

'It offends my honour as a soldier,' he exclaimed. 'I know Paulus as an exemplary officer who, during his thirty-five years of service, has always been outstanding. I am quite convinced that whatever his decision, it will be a decision taken in the best interests of his men. An army commander must be given a certain liberty of action. If Paulus were to shoot himself, he would no longer be able to do anything for his men.'

In the event, Schmundt did not fly to Stalingrad. Whether he refused to do so, or whether Hitler cancelled the order, I do not know.

When the first foreign newspapers with photographs of the surrender negotiations arrived at Headquarters, Hitler, obviously, could still not bring himself to believe that Paulus had allowed himself to fall into the hands of the Russians. He sent for me and handed me a photograph.

'I want your expert opinion, Hoffmann,' he said, pointing to the photo. 'Is that an original photograph, or is it a composite picture, into which the figure of Paulus has been inserted for propaganda purposes?'

I could see with what tenseness he awaited my verdict; but I had no option but to assure him that the photograph was an original and had not been tampered with in any way.

I had one experience that might well have ended very badly for me. I was hanging about in the Wolfsschanze Headquarters with nothing particular to do, and I turned on my radio, and found that I was listening to London. Although I knew that this was strictly forbidden, I was very curious to hear what the other side were saying, so I listened for a bit.

'Mr Churchill has arrived in Cairo,' said the announcer, 'where he attended a parade of British troops.'

A little later, Linge, Hitler's valet, telephoned and asked me to come and see the Führer. It was already late at night, and my quarters were in the midst of some tall trees, about 100 yards from Hitler's dug-out. Hitler greeted me with the usual question: 'Well – any news?'

With the British announcement still in my mind, I said quite conversationally: 'That fellow Churchill must have boundless vitality! Fancy his going to Cairo!'

'Who told you that?' asked Hitler with great interest.

My blood ran cold! For obvious reasons I dared not tell him I'd been listening to an enemy wireless.

'Oh – er – a er – a couple of SS-men whom I met on the way here told me,' was the best lie I could rake up on the spur of the moment.

'Must have been men from the telephone exchange,' he said. 'Ring up the exchange and ask them when the news came in.'

Dutifully I rang up. 'They say they know nothing of the report,' I said.

'Tell them to get me Ribbentrop on the phone at once!' It was already three o'clock in the morning, but eventually Ribbentrop came through.

'I have just been informed that Churchill is in Cairo, inspecting British troops – by my photographer! You, of course, and the whole of your Foreign Office know nothing about it!' In a rage Hitler slammed down the receiver, while I stood there with very mixed feelings, imagining the hate that Ribbentrop, too, was probably working up. (In 1945 I found a book on the Foreign Office in which this night is mentioned and a description is given of how the whole Foreign Office spent the rest of the night in a frantic search for the origin of this ominous announcement!)

Hitler refused to be pacified; an hour passed, and still no report. Abruptly he turned and sent for Himmler, whose quarters were 30 miles away. The moment the latter arrived a general parade was ordered, at which all SS sentry-groups and the personnel of the telephone exchange would also be present. Accompanied by Himmler I had to walk down the ranks, looking closely at each individual man. Naturally, I was quite unable to identify my 'informants', and I rather lamely attributed my failure to the darkness of the night. The situation, really, was becoming most painful!

I noticed that Himmler was regarding me with a suspicious stare. Suddenly he turned and said that if the two men in question would step forward, they would not be punished in any way. Not a man stirred, and in silence we returned to the Führer's dug-out. A little later a report arrived from Berlin: 'Your information is correct!' And for the rest of the night Hitler was far less friendly towards me than usual, and it was with a sigh of relief that I made my way back, in the grey of the first dawn, to my own quarters. Later in the morning, Bormann strolled over. 'I only wanted to remind you, my dear fellow, that like the ministers and all the rest of us, you mustn't listen to enemy wireless! The Führer expects strict compliance with this order – even from you!'

Hitler always wished to be kept well-informed about events, but he always hated it when anything unpleasant had to be reported to him.

He disliked having to show clemency, for this he regarded as a weakening of existing laws. In his personal office he had a department under Reichsleiter Bouhler that dealt with appeals on compassionate grounds. Very few petitions were submitted to Hitler himself; and most of them were rejected by Bouhler's office.

As I had assumed no official office after the assumption of power, but had remained a private individual, I was able to approach Hitler in a very different manner. The others came to Hitler to submit their reports; I on the other hand used to go to have a chat with him. Very often the remarks that I threw out conversationally had an ulterior motive, for I should never have been allowed to make a direct approach; but whenever I succeeded unobtrusively in putting some theme into his head in a manner that made him raise the subject himself, I usually got my own way. Not a few regulations were rescinded by Hitler as the result of his agreement with the oblique references that I had ventured to make to them.

Both Bormann and Goebbels regarded me as a rather meddlesome 'informer', for much of what I accomplished rebounded on their heads; nor did it help matters much, when Hitler once said to me, in Bormann's presence: 'Hoffmann, you're the bridge which links me to the people!'

The word very quickly went round that I 'had a way' with Hitler, and I was inundated with petitions and requests of every possible kind.

One of those who appealed to me for help was Hans Moser, who had been banished from stage and screen by Goebbels on account of the non-Aryan ancestry of his wife! In Vienna Moser begged me to intervene and have a word with Hitler, and this I promised to do. The opportunity occurred after the showing of one of Moser's films in the Chancellery, with which Hitler was obviously delighted.

'Moser is very popular with the public,' I said. 'The people won't like it at all if he's forbidden to play simply on account of his wife. Why, you yourself always enjoy his films!' I had struck while the iron was hot; Hitler was still in good spirits after the film, and he agreed cordially with me; and the ban on Moser was forthwith removed.

Scarcely a day passed without my receiving a petition of some sort or another. One that I received moved me profoundly. A distracted mother wrote to me and told me that her son, a most talented young artist, had got involved in some case of high treason and had been condemned to death.

High treason? Death penalty? I didn't see much hope. Still, I told her to send me at once some photographs of her son's artistic works; and a few days later with a folio under my arm I set out for Wolfsschanze in East Prussia.

Hitler was always informed when I arrived, and I would then be invited to lunch, which we generally took alone. This time he greeted me in a very friendly fashion. 'How are you, Hoffmann? What's the news?' I handed him a letter that I had brought with me from Eva Braun and, obviously pleased, he stuck it unread in his pocket. At table he was very expansive. 'You tuck in to the animals' bodies,' he said. 'Don't worry about me!' This reference to my 'anti-vegetarianism' was always the sign of a good mood.

'How's art?'

Thank goodness! He'd given me the opening I wanted. 'I've brought some of the works of a young artist with me. May I show them to you?' Without waiting for his reply, I opened the folio and placed the drawings before him.

What he saw immediately aroused his interest. Anxiously, I watched his expression. There was no doubt about it, the pictures pleased him. He pointed to one sketch. 'Look at that, Hoffmann!' he said, appreciatively, 'this young man has a talent that all but amounts to genius! And they say we have no youngsters coming on! Nonsense! But you've got to find them – and then encourage them!' He looked up. 'How old is this young man?' he asked.

'About twenty.'

'Does he want some sort of salary? Or can we help him in any other way?'

Now for it! 'He could most certainly be helped, Herr Hitler!'

'How do you mean? Is he ill – wounded?'

'No, Sir. But he has been condemned to death for insulting you!'

Hitler's expression hardened. 'Don't talk rot, Hoffmann! Damn it! one doesn't get condemned to death for that!' I refrained from any irritating contradiction. 'Would you read his mother's letter?' I said, handing it to him. Hitler glanced hastily through it and then stuck it, with Eva's letter, into his pocket without a word. He began to pace the room in an agitated fashion; the case, obviously, had moved him. Not another word was said on the subject; but I had a feeling that Hitler would do something to help the young man.

Nor did my instinct betray me. The young artist was called up and drafted into the Army. Later, alas, he was reported 'Missing – believed killed.' Against that tragedy I was powerless; but at least I had saved him from death at the hands of an executioner.

Chapter 11

The End for Both of Us

THE LONGER THE WAR lasted and the more fearful the air raids on the Fatherland became, the more intolerable grew the atmosphere in Führer-Headquarters, where the deepest pessimism reigned supreme. In spite of everything, however, life in Sperrkreis I – the inner circle round the Führer himself – and in particular its nightly gatherings, continued to bear the hallmark of an artificially maintained optimism. But these gatherings had become a torture for us, and no longer did we feel that we were living in a gilded cage, but rather in an iron prison. Hitler had given Bormann absolute and unquestioned authority and himself submitted tamely to many of his decisions.

On one occasion in 1944, when I returned to Headquarters from Vienna, I was having dinner with Hitler and I gave him a message from Baldur von Schirach. 'Schirach,' I said, 'protests against Bormann's accusation that it is now too late to think of organising the anti-aircraft defences of Vienna; he told me that a few weeks after the beginning of the war he had completed his plans for this purpose, but had been instructed by Bormann to take no steps, as premature action would only unsettle the population of the city unnecessarily.'

Hitler seemed to regard this message as an implied criticism of Bormann, for he rounded on me sharply. 'Get this quite clear in your own mind, Hoffmann, and tell it to your son-in-law, too,' he cried. 'To win this war I have need of Bormann! It's perfectly true that he is both ruthless and brutal. He's a bull, and not for nothing has he given his son the nickname of "the bull"; but the fact remains, one after the other, everybody has failed in their implicit obedience to my commands – but Bormann, never!'

His voice rose to a scream; he looked searchingly into my face, as if his words held some special application to me personally. 'Everyone, I don't care who he may be, must understand clearly this one fact: whoever is against Bormann is also against the State! I'll shoot the lot of them, even if they number tens of thousands, just as I will shoot those who babble of peace! Far better that a few thousand miserable and witless nincompoops should be liquidated, than that a people of seventy millions should be dragged down to destruction!'

Never had I heard Hitler talk in such tones, and never in my life had I seen such wild and hate-filled eyes!

In the spring of 1944, in the space of a few short weeks, Hitler changed in a most remarkable manner; and the case of Adolf Ziegler, the President of the National Art Council, comes readily to my mind.

Some little time before, Ziegler discussed with two industrialists, Pietsch and Rechberg, the possibility of concluding a separate peace through the intermediary of the British Prime Minister's son, Randolph Churchill. Hitler got to hear of the discussion and forthwith threw all three of them into a concentration camp.

When, at the request of his wife, I tried to put in a word in favour of Ziegler, Hitler turned to me and said: 'Ziegler can thank his lucky stars that he stands under my protection! The Gestapo would have shot him long ago!' A few weeks later, indeed, he released Ziegler, who had been saved by his Party Insignia in Gold.

But if all this had happened a few months later, it would have had a very different and much more unhappy ending for him!

I was frightened! For the first time in my life I felt nervous at Headquarters! One thought was paramount in my mind: since Stalingrad, Hitler has become a different person; this is not the Hitler of the old days, this is the Hitler face to face with inevitable collapse, eclipse and annihilation!

With such thoughts running through my head, it will be understandable that I should restrict my visits to Headquarters to the minimum possible. But my long absences continually caused Hitler to exclaim mournfully: 'When Hoffmann is not here, something seems to be lacking!' or 'Without Hoffmann, I no longer exist!'

When the impulse moved him, I would be torn from Munich, from my family, my business or from whatever I was doing. 'The Führer says: will you please come at once!' Again and again this same message would be delivered to me, and the same night or early the next morning I would have to hurtle, by train or plane, a thousand miles or so to Führer-Headquarters.

'What's wrong?' I would ask.

'Nothing's wrong, my dear fellow,' Hitler would reply. 'It's only that I'm delighted to see you again!'

Bormann's reaction to these sudden reappearances of mine was the exact opposite, for I shattered the wall of isolation with which he was deliberately surrounding Hitler. I would bring with me a few petitions or a few cases that merited his attention, would tell him what people were saying and thinking and so keep him more or less in touch with the prevailing frame of mind.

For this reason, I was a thorn in Bormann's flesh, but even he did not dare to show his personal antipathy in front of the Führer, and so he hit upon a diabolical plan.

In the autumn of 1944 he came to see me in my rooms at Führer-Headquarters. 'You've been looking very seedy lately,' he said, avoiding, as was his habit when speaking officially, the use of the familiar 'du', 'and Hitler is worried about your state of health. You must let yourself be examined by Morell.'

'I feel as fit as a fiddle,' I protested; 'but if it will please Hitler, of course I'll go and see Morell.'

Morell could find no trace of any latent disease in me, but he could give no definite answer until he had received the result of a bacteriological analysis, which was being made for him in the Health Institute of the SS.

For some time I heard no more and had forgotten all about it. About a fortnight later, I was in Munich and was just about to go out, when a message came through from Bormann's office: Please ring up Morell immediately. Putting through an official call, I was talking to Morell within a few minutes. 'On Bormann's instructions,' he said, 'I have to tell you that, at Hitler's request, you are not to come near him for the time being or to come to Headquarters at all. Your presence would constitute a grave danger for him and for us all!'

I was thunderstruck. 'What the devil are you talking about?' I asked.

'The SS Bacteriological Institute has found traces of typhus bacillus in the blood test sent to them; I'm afraid you have got Paratyphus B – the most dangerous form of the disease! As a doctor it was my duty to bring this fact to the notice of the medical authorities. I did suggest to Bormann that in your case, surely, this would not be necessary, but he refused absolutely to listen to me.'

Morell paused, while I remained in dumbfounded silence.

'I'm awfully sorry, but in the face of Bormann's instructions, I had no option. Tomorrow morning the Munich Public Health people will call for you, according to Hitler's instructions, and take you to a special building, a sort of villa, where you will be well looked after, but will be kept in isolation and under observation.'

In the first shock, it never entered my head to hark back to the background to all these events or to their instigator – Bormann!

I went to the bookcase and pulled out the appropriate volume of an encyclopaedia; there it stood – Paratyphus B, the most dangerous form of the disease!

But I felt fighting fit! I read on: 'There are also "germ-carriers" – individuals who unwittingly harbour the bacillus without themselves suffering from the disease. These individuals constitute a source of public danger and must in no circumstances be allowed to participate in any activities which bring them into close proximity with food.'

Hitler, I knew, had a horror of germs. Then suddenly the scales fell from my eyes and I realised Bormann's plan in all its diabolical entirety! Everything was clear to me, and it was also quite clear that Morell was in no way to blame. He had saved my life in 1936. Just after Hitler and I had returned from a long journey, his driver Schreck and I were both taken seriously ill. A week later, Schreck was dead, and Hitler had lost an old and trusted follower. I myself refused to be moved into a hospital, but hovered between life and death in my own home.

In his anxiety, Hitler sent the famous surgeon, Professor Magnus, to see me, but in my feverish hallucinations I refused to see any strange doctor. My wife then suggested that we should get our friend, Dr Morell, to come down from Berlin to have a look at me, and the latter, when he heard how dangerously ill I was, hastened down to Munich the same night.

When he realised that I should require his constant attention for a long time to come, he stayed, with but the briefest of interruptions, and at no little sacrifice and inconvenience to himself, for many weeks and lavished his unremitting care on me.

Hitler used to come in every day to ask how I was progressing and during my convalescence used to spend a lot of time at my bedside; and it was under these circumstances that he made the acquaintance of Dr Morell and formed a very high opinion of him. He suffered from recurrent pains in the stomach, the heritage of gas poisoning during the first war, and he decided to place himself in the hands of Dr Morell, whose opponents had dubbed him 'The Injection-Doctor'. Hitler, however, swore by him. 'Up till now, no doctor has succeeded in relieving me of my stomach pains; but Dr Morell has done the trick.'

Hitler was a bit of a pill addict and was always taking pills of some sort or another after each meal, and gradually increasing the doses. One day he became seriously ill, however, and for the first time in his life he took to his bed and stayed there for three days.

Morell told me that he displayed all the cramp symptoms associated generally with a case of poisoning. In the meanwhile, Professor Brandt had sent some of these pills that had been prescribed by Morell's predecessor, for analysis, and they were found to contain a minute quantity of strychnine; taken as prescribed and for short periods at a time, the pills were harmless. But in Hitler's case, he had been taking the things in large quantities for months on end, and the poison had got to work on his system.

Brandt made his report to Hitler; but his further reproach that it was Morell's duty to have warned the Führer of the dangerous nature of his habits was not at all well received.

Shortly afterwards, Professor Brandt paid us a visit at our place near Altoetting and with very downcast mien told me the final upshot of the 'Anti-Gas Pills' affair.

'A few days ago,' he said, 'Hitler sent for me and informed me in frigid tones that my services were no longer required at Headquarters. My wife and child could continue to come to Obersalzberg, but he did not wish to see me ever again! And that is the thanks I get for seven years of devoted service!'

Bormann's amiable intentions towards me were only too clear, but academic deduction would serve no purpose at the moment; I had to act, and act quickly.

My first step was to go straight to 12 Wassenburgerstrasse, a few minutes' walk, where, in a small house, Eva Braun was living with her younger sister, Gretl.

'Come in, Herr Hoffmann. Good heavens, man! What on earth has happened?'

Before ever I could begin to reply, Eva swiftly fetched a bottle of cognac and poured out a glass for each of us. I took a deep gulp and then told her the story of my telephone conversation with Führer-Headquarters.

'Now – calm yourself – there's nothing at all to worry about! In the first place it's perfectly obvious that there's nothing whatever the matter with you, and in the second place, I shall be telephoning as usual at ten o'clock tonight to the Führer and I'll talk to him about it. Obviously, there's been some silly mistake. On the other hand, Master Bormann is quite capable of any dirty intrigue that suits his book!'

'When you speak to the Führer, do please explain the whole thing to him and tell him that I am going to Vienna tonight to see my wife, who is expecting me. Please make a point of that – otherwise it will look as if I had fled!'

'Don't get so worked up about it! I'll explain everything, and you can phone to me tomorrow morning from Vienna, by which time I expect to be able to tell you that all is well again. And now, let's drink a little bottle of champagne to our next merry meeting! Good health, Herr Hoffmann!'

The next morning my wife was waiting for me at the Imperial Hotel in a state of great excitement.

'Everybody at home seems to be completely mad!' she said. 'Yesterday when I rang up to ask when you were coming, the answer I got was that you were seriously ill, but that orders had come "from above" that the strictest silence was to be observed and that no telephone message was to be sent to me! I was just about to rush off to Munich, when a message arrived to say that you had left for Vienna! Is everybody mad – or am I?'

'They're trying to say that I've got paratyphus, and I've been forbidden to go to Führer-Headquarters!' Swiftly I told my wife what had happened.

'Bormann!' said my wife emphatically. 'He's at the bottom of it!' And went straight to the telephone and rang up a doctor friend of ours, Dr Demmer, and asked him to come round at once.

When Demmer heard what was afoot, he tapped himself significantly on the forehead. 'Can't you see, my good man, that they want to get rid of you? Nevertheless, I'll have you examined by Frau Professor Cortini of the bacteriological section of our Lainz Hospital, who is an authority on these matters; and to ease your mind, I tell you here and now that there's nothing whatever the matter with you.'

In the meanwhile my wife had put through an urgent call to Munich. The bell rang, and I seized the receiver. 'Eva? ... Were you able to have a talk with him yesterday?'

'Yes, Herr Hoffmann; but it was terrible! Hitler is completely convinced that you have typhus, and he raved like a madman when I told him that you had been to see me before leaving for Vienna. It was utterly irresponsible on your part, he shouted, to refuse to be isolated – your family, your son-in-law and every-body else with whom you come in contact in Vienna would catch it from you! It seemed to me that Bormann had cast a veritable spell over him, and I told him so! "We'll see," was his retort, "but, by God, I'll get to the bottom of this affair!" I'm awfully sorry, Herr Hoffmann, that I haven't better news for you,' she concluded.

'Thank you very much, Eva! I'm sorry to have put you to so much unpleasant inconvenience.'

Next we telephoned to our own house in Munich. 'Two gentlemen from the Public Health Department were here only a little while ago and said they had come to fetch the Herr Professor,' was the news we received.

That done, I went straight to the bacteriological section of the hospital to be examined, and within a week, as I had confidently expected, I had no less than three certificates: 'Result negative – no trace of paratyphus.' But I was still not quite satisfied. I worried intensely over the possibilities. Perhaps, after all, they would find some germ, or perhaps the disease might come upon me suddenly – and in either case, I was lost. And what if, after all, I turned out to be a germ-carrier, one of those people, who …! This latter thought caused me such acute anxiety that it became an obsession, and nothing my wife or my doctors could say made any difference.

Eventually my wife summed it up in a sentence. 'You haven't got paratyphus,' she said, decisively. 'What you're suffering from is a hyper-mania fixation!'

I could not bear to wait and wanted to send the photographic results of my examination at once to Führer-Headquarters.

'For goodness' sake, have a little patience,' counselled my wife. 'Wait for a month or so and let things settle down; if you rush at it like this, they'll only start some new intrigue!'

But I would not have it. 'Here's proof enough!' I cried, waving the photographs, and I wrote at once to Morell, telling him there must be some mistake and asking him to submit the photos at once to Hitler.

For weeks I waited in vain for any answer. Then at last an answer arrived – in the person of Commissioner Högl of the CID, from Führer-Headquarters, Hitler's most trusted man. 'Herr Professor, I have a very painful duty to perform. I have been instructed to interrogate everyone who has been in contact with you and, if necessary, to arrest them!'

Now what had happened? The photographs I had sent to Headquarters had been marked: 'Heinrich Hoffmann, Grenadier, twenty-six years of age.' As the Lainz Hospital had for the duration of the war become a purely military hospital, Dr Demmer had thought that would simplify matters; and even more important, as it seemed to him, he would in this way prevent the dissemination of any rumours that paratyphus had broken out at Führer-Headquarters.

The CID Commissioner conscientiously carried out his duties, in the course of which it came out by chance that my son Heinrich was exactly twenty-six years old, and that it had been assumed that the tests referred to him.

Bormann next turned his attack against the Health Authorities in Vienna, and it was thanks only to the categorical attitude adopted by these latter that no arrests occurred.

From then on, I was compelled to submit to extremely painful research in two official institutions, under the supervision of a pair of SS guards; and this continued until at last the Director of SS Medical Services refused any longer to continue with the operation. During these long weeks, I amassed a heap of medical documents, one and all certifying that I was in perfect health in every way. I, too, had become completely fed up with the continual examinations, and the bacteriologists, who were unaware of the orders 'from above', thought I was completely mad.

At long last, after an absence of more than six months from Führer-Headquarters, during which I received no message from the Führer, I was quite convinced, not only of my own clean bill of health but also of Bormann's infamous treachery; and I decided that I would go myself to Hitler and lay my proofs before him.

During these months, the Wolfsschanze Headquarters had been transferred to the Chancellery in Berlin, and at the beginning of April 1945, to Berlin I went. Although the air raids had already caused great damage to the Chancellery, there was no noticeable change in the routine, and I was greeted by the same two SS men, who had always controlled the entrance and who had of course no idea of the cause of my long absence. The Kaiserhof Hotel, in which for twelve years I had always stayed when in Berlin, had been completely destroyed by bombs, and I was therefore given a room on the first floor of the Chancellery itself.

It was just about midday when I arrived, and to a warm welcome from everybody. 'Where have you been all this time?' they asked. I took my accustomed place at table beside Keitel and Jodl. They told me that this room, which used to be Hindenburg's sitting-room, was the only one left undamaged in the whole building. At table, only Hitler's place was vacant.

Everybody regarded it as quite natural that I should once more have joined the circle. 'Thank God you're back, Hoffmann; perhaps you'll be able to cheer the Führer up a bit!' and like remarks greeted my arrival.

Suddenly the door opened, and an ADC announced: 'The Führer is about to come to inspect a new architect's model. You will all please remain seated, gentlemen!'

Hitler was coming, and I thought it right that I should report my arrival to him. As I advanced towards him, he stretched out both his arms in a defensive gesture and stepped back a pace. 'How have you got here, Hoffmann? You're ill – desperately ill, and you'll infect us all!'

I could no longer contain myself. 'Herr Hitler,' I cried. 'I am not ill, and I never have been ill! Here are the proofs of it. I have been the victim of an infamous intrigue, and I have come to tell you the truth!'

But Hitler without a word went swiftly past me and out of the room, and I resumed my seat. Bormann came in and made towards Hitler's usual seat; but when he caught sight of me he stopped short, glaring as if he meant to strike me. At that moment the sirens howled the alarm.

Bormann rushed at me like a madman. 'Who the hell told you to come here,' he roared. 'You'd have been much better employed if you'd invented some ray to bring down these aircraft!'

'This place is like a bloody lunatic asylum,' I cried, and flinging down my knife and fork, I left the table.

On my way to my room I thought to myself: Out of this just as quickly as possible! While I was rather frantically throwing my few things back into my bag, in came Johanna Wolf, who had been Hitler's secretary for many years.

'Take it easy,' she said, quietly. 'The alarm's gone, and you must come down into the shelter. In any case, you simply cannot leave without saying goodbye to the Führer. As soon as the all-clear sounds, I'll have a word with him. He has been constantly asking about you and how you were, you know.'

Later on, towards evening, Fraulein Wolf told me that Hitler would receive me that same night – but on one condition, the subject of my illness would not be mentioned.

By midnight the air attacks for the day had ceased, and I made my way to Hitler's dug-out.

'Hoffmann, my dear fellow,' he said, almost in the same breath as he greeted me, 'please do me a favour – not a word about your illness!'

In silence, I offered him the papers I was carrying in my hand.

'No – no,' he said. 'Give those to Morell.' For a long time he gazed at me in silence.

'When I see you sitting there, the picture of health,' he said at last, 'even I must believe that you've been victimised! And now – not another word about it!'

He was alone with Eva in the dug-out. He rang the bell, and when his servant appeared I ordered tea.

'Why tea?' enquired Hitler, wonderingly.

'Fraulein Wolf has told me, Herr Hitler, that you had directed Bormann to give me a hint to avoid alcohol!'

'You drink what you like! You've always liked your glass of wine and now, when everybody is being forced by events to turn to the solace of alcohol, why should you, of all people, suddenly become a teetotaler!'

I ordered a glass of hot, spiced wine.

'You haven't got a cold, have you? No – no; bring the Herr Professor a bottle of champagne!'

'What a very long time it is,' he sighed, 'since we three were sitting peacefully together!'

When Eva and I raised our glasses to him, he became a little more cheerful, and soon we were on the good old subject of art. Shortly afterwards, Eva left us, and I was alone with Hitler.

'How long are you staying?' he asked.

'I'm leaving again tomorrow, Herr Hitler.'

'Won't you stay one more day? There are a lot of things I want to talk to you about.'

'Of course. I have a certain number of important business and personal affairs to attend to – among other things, to make my will; but I intend to be back here, in any case, for your birthday on 20th April.'

'Your will? There's plenty of time before you need worry about that!'

Does he still believe in the possibility of victory? I wondered.

As the war drew inexorably to its inevitable and catastrophic conclusion, Hitler had become less and less communicative. Light conversation, the anecdotes in which we formerly delighted were wholly out of place, and in any case we had not the heart to try and indulge in them. Very occasionally some chance remark on art would strike a spark of interest, but it would quickly die out, and Hitler would relapse into brooding silence.

The tremendous strain of twenty-five years of ceaseless and most strenuous endeavour, the destruction of all that he had accomplished, the death of every dream and ambition for the future and the after-effects of the July bomb explosion had all combined to take grim toll of the man; sick at heart, mentally stunned to the point of derangement and physically exhausted beyond redemption, he was but a shivering shadow of his former self, a charred hulk, from which all life, fire and flame had long since departed.

Only once, when the latest reports from the armies of Schoerner and Wenck, on whom our last, forlorn hopes rested, brought home to us the hopelessness of the situation in all its stark and glaring reality, did he burst forth and expose the fury of rage, fear, despair and frustration that the nightmare of Russian domination aroused in him.

'My enemies are mad!' he cried, and there was a note of hysteria in his voice. 'God has forsaken and blinded the Western Powers! Yes – they'll enjoy, briefly, the fruits of victory – perhaps! But can't they see, will nothing convince them that each forward step taken by the Russian hordes is yet another nail in their own coffin! If only they would let me withdraw my armies from the West, I could still save Germany, them – and the whole of Europe!'

But of that and of Hitler's sincerity none of the German negotiators, not even Himmler himself, could convince the Allies.

The next night, too, Hitler was lying as usual on the sofa. The ravages of many sleepless nights and intolerable burdens were plainly visible on his haggard face. His left hand was trembling, his movements were slow and apathetic. It distressed me deeply to see him thus.

'Hoffmann, I have a favour to ask of you,' he said, when we were alone.

'Of course, Herr Hitler – if it's in my power to do it.'

'About Eva! Hoffmann, you must do your very best to persuade her to leave here with you, when you go. I can't put any official car at her disposal – that, in the present circumstances, would be too dangerous. How are you yourself proposing to get to Munich?'

'I've been offered a seat in the Postmaster General's car. There's plenty of room, as the car is going almost empty. I promise you, Herr Hitler, I'll do my utmost to persuade Eva to come with me.'

Although she had repeatedly declared that in no circumstances would she leave Berlin, I made one more attempt to make her change her mind.

'You know better than anyone, Hoffmann, what close ties bind me to Hitler. What would people say, if I deserted him now, in his hour of greatest need? No, my friend! Where the Führer is concerned, I stand fast to the very end!'

The next day I told Hitler of my failure. In silence he listened to what I had to say. Then the alarm went.

'You can't go for the time being,' he said. That was obvious, and so we sat together in the dug-out, listening to the bombs whistling down all around us. Even so, it was essential that I should get away as quickly as possible. At any moment Bormann might have come in; and if he did, well, then I should never leave the Chancellery at all.

These disquieting thoughts were still in my mind when the all-clear sounded. I hastily bade farewell to Hitler, Eva and the others, seized my bag, which was already packed, and prepared to leave the Chancellery. At all costs, I had to avoid running into Bormann.

When I saw the devastation in the Wilhelmsstrasse, I realised that this was no ordinary departure; it would be a flight! But I was not fleeing either from Hitler or from the chaos, but from Bormann!

I gladly accepted the risks that a journey along an Autobahn entailed, even though low flying attacks never ceased, and every mile or so we passed burnt-out vehicles, some of them with their occupants dead inside them. The attacks were so ubiquitous and continuous that we did not reach our destination until the next morning.

In spite of everything, I was quite determined to return to Berlin for the Führer's birthday on 20th April. But it was not to be. Military developments rendered any journey to Berlin impossible.

When the final collapse came, I heard it on the radio. Fate had at least spared me from the obligation of recording these last fateful events with my camera.

A question, which even to this day I am frequently asked, is: 'What happened to Bormann? Is he really dead?' He is dead, and for the following authentic, eye-witness account of the manner of his dying I am indebted to Axmann, who was Reichs Youth Leader at the end of the war.

After Hitler's death, and as the Russians advanced ever nearer to the Chancellery, a small handful of men, including Bormann, Doctor Stumpfegger, who had succeeded Professor Morell as Hitler's physician, Kempka, Hitler's chauffeur, who had supervised the burning of the Führer's body, and Axmann himself, decided to make a dash for freedom in the wake of a German tank.

They found, however, that the Russians had already crossed the Spree and that little or no hope remained. The party decided to split up, Bormann and Stumpfegger going left along the river and the others going to the right. Axmann and his party, finding very quickly that their further progress was barred, retraced their steps and followed the direction taken by Bormann and Stump-fegger. They had not gone very far when they reached one of the bridges over the Spree, at the near end of which two bodies were lying spread-eagled on their backs.

Axmann crept forward to investigate and found, as he expected, that the corpses were those of Bormann and Stumpfegger. Neither body showed any signs of a wound, but Axmann satisfied himself that they were indeed dead, and he assumed that, seeing the complete hopelessness of their situation, the two men had taken poison tablets rather than fall into the hands of the Russians. Clasped under Bormann's arm was a briefcase, and, thinking it might well contain important documents, Axmann tried to recover it. But at that moment the Russians spotted him and opened fire with a machine-gun, and he was compelled to abandon the attempt. He succeeded in crawling away unharmed, hid himself in a shell hole in the midst of some neighbouring ruins and finally made his way to safety.

Epilogue

DURING THE FINAL DAYS of the German collapse I was at our little country house, 'Heinrichshof', in the vicinity of Altoetting, the scene of many devout pilgrimages in Upper Bavaria. On the advice of neighbours, my wife had left the house a week before my arrival and had gone off in the direction of the Tyrol.

No sooner had I arrived than a body of some two hundred German Officers and men marched in and took up their quarters in the village; some of them immediately set about obtaining civilian clothing, in the hope that they would thus evade capture.

As I had played no part in either the political or the military events of the past, I was quite sure that nothing would happen to me, and I therefore had no intention of quitting my home. But one of the many people, who had taken asylum as refugees in the house, begged me to leave. My presence, it was declared, would only further enhance the grave dangers to which the employees on my property and their families were already exposed. This special pleading proved later to be by no means disinterested; it was hoped to get rid of me and to lay claim to part of the property, before, as would inevitably happen sooner or later, it was confiscated and requisitioned.

At the time, however, impressed with the urgency of her arguments, I agreed to go, and on 28th April, the same day upon which Hitler and Eva Braun ended their lives, I set forth. Through the streams of retreating troops I made my way to friends in Oberwoessen, a small village between Marquartstein and Reit-im-Winkel, some 50 kilometres to the west of 'Heinrichshof.'

Just beyond the village of Reit-im-Winkel, the road passes into a narrow gorge, surrounded on each side by high, precipitous mountains. Here a large body of SS had built a defensive locality, where they were determined to make a last stand. When the American forces arrived a few days later, white flags were flying on all the houses of both Oberwoessen and Reit-im-Winkel; but the SS refused absolutely to give up the strong position they held and to surrender the abundant stores of food that they had amassed there. It was only after much parley and the promise of a safe conduct that they agreed to depart and thus put an end to hostilities in this part of Bavaria. And for a fortnight or so all was peace.

Early on the morning of 15th May, however, two Americans arrived, accompanied by an old German-American friend of mine, whose activities in the Security Branch of the German Secret Service were well known to me. Great was my scornful indignation, when I found that I had been denounced to the Americans and my arrest demanded! There was nothing for it; grabbing hastily a few of my belongings, I got into the jeep and was taken to the C.I.C. in Munich for interrogation.

My initial reception by the C.I.C. was a pleasant surprise. I was given a nice room and was most hospitably entertained with good food, wine and cigarettes in profusion. There were no uniformed armed guards to be seen – only a few Germans in civilian clothing – members, apparently, of the so-called German underground resistance group.

Inquisitively I strolled about the building unhindered, and it was only when I was stopped by an American soldier at the main entrance and was politely told that I could not leave the premises that any suggestion of forcible detention became apparent.

Shortly after I had returned to my room, there was a knock on the door, and an American officer entered.

'Have you everything you want, Herr Hoffmann?' he asked. 'If not – do please say so.' He smiled in a friendly fashion. 'We know a good deal about your habits, you know; tell me – would you prefer to be interrogated by day or by night?' The habits of Hitler's intimate circle, when we were usually invited to take an 'evening' drink at about 3 a.m. were evidently well known to the Allies.

The first interrogation followed about a week later. It was short, formal and by no means unfriendly.

'Herr Hoffmann,' said the presiding officer, 'I must tell you that your name is on Priority List No. 1, given to us by the Russians, of the people they wish us to hand over to them.' He paused significantly for a moment. 'In Vienna,' he continued quietly, 'the Russians are hanging every SS-man they catch and stringing them up in the shop windows.'

He stopped and offered me a cigarette.

'I have just three questions to ask you, Herr Hoffmann, and if you will answer them truthfully, you won't need to worry about the Russians.'

I waited somewhat apprehensively.

'Do you know Professor Hahn?'

'I know several Professor Hahns; do you mean the famous Professor in New York who ......'

'I do not.'

'Then there's my old friend, Hahn, the eminent professor of anatomy at Munich, but he died.'

'Listen, Hoffmann. I don't want to know about the dead Hahns. What do you know about the living Professor Hahn, who spent so much time at Hitler's Headquarters?'

For a moment I was completely nonplussed; then I remembered. True enough there had been a fellow named Hahn, a scientist of some sort, but that's all I knew about him, and I said so.

'Right! Now – do you know anything about the atom bomb?'

This, be it remembered, was in May 1945, long before the ordinary man in the street had ever heard of such a thing.

'I'm sorry,' I answered. 'I've never even heard of it.'

'What about other secret weapons?'

'I did once see the technical check-up preview of a film of the performance of a one-man submarine, prior to its being shown to Hitler.'

'And now, thirdly – do you know Engineer Kurz?'

'Kurz? Yes – of course, the eminent physicist – whatever that may be! But all I know about him is that recently he offered to sell Hitler a very large and very valuable porcelain vase and that Hitler refused, because, as he told me, he didn't see much point in spending a lot of money for something that was bound to be blown to hell in next to no time!'

The American officer grinned. 'O.K., Herr Hoffmann. I guess I've had my turn. Now – is there anything on your mind – anything you'd like to talk about?'

Emboldened by the friendly and pre-eminently fair reception, I had no hesitation in speaking up.

'I should be most grateful for your help in one thing, Sir,' I said. 'My house in Munich has, I regret to say, been looted; all my pictures, my own personal property, among them water-colours by my friend, Hitler, which I value grea ......'

I got no further. One of the Germans present had seized a large glass fruit bowl standing on the table, and with a resounding crash, he brought it down on my head!

'Stop that!' intervened the American officer, sharply. 'I'll have none of that sort of thing here! If you can't behave – get out!'

And that was the end of my interrogation; but a little sequel was to follow.

Some days later, about midnight, there was a timid knock at my door. A man entered with somewhat furtive haste, placed bread and butter, a bottle of Niersteiner and a packet of cigarettes on the table. 'A little peace offering – I'm damn sorry,' he muttered and withdrew as hastily as he had come. It was my fruit-discus throwing pal!

I hadn't had a smoke or a drink for quite a time – and I had no corkscrew! Only those who know me well can picture the impatient patience with which I picked at the cork with my finger nail, until I managed to push the darn thing down the neck of the bottle! The next day I was transferred to the notorious Stadlheim prison in Munich.

Here I was told that I was suspected of having stolen a number of masterpieces from the various galleries and museums of Europe on behalf of Göring and Hitler; and three weeks later I was transferred for further interrogation to Altausee in Austria, in the disused mines of which the treasures of the German galleries and private collections had been placed for protection against air raids.

I had been so weakened by the rigours and the starvation diet of the weeks in Stadlheim prison, that I was hardly able to walk without help. Thanks to the assiduous and most kind attentions of a coloured American soldier I recovered to a certain extent; even so, it was a full week before I was fit enough to be interrogated.

Captain Rossow, of the Metropolitan Museum in New York was in charge of the interrogation and he showed much understanding of the difficult position in which I found myself. There was little I could say in my defence beyond a complete denial of the charge against me. But Rossow made exhaustive enquiries from the authorities of a number of galleries whose treasures had been looted, and with local art dealers he confirmed my assertion that I had certainly acted as Hitler's expert adviser and had acquired many pictures for him; but I had always paid for them in the ordinary way. In this way, the kindly Rossow was very soon convinced of my complete innocence and he dismissed the charge against me.

In the middle of July 1945, I was transferred to the camp in Augsburg, in which all the prominent Nazi personalities were being held. There I caught sight of Göring and my son-in-law, Baldur von Schirach; but we were not allowed to join them, and all we could do was to exchange a wave of the hand when we were taken out for exercise. Here we remained only for a few weeks and were then taken to Seckenheim, in the vicinity of Heidelberg.

In Seckenheim we were quartered in three massive old buildings – probably former army barracks. I myself was in Block A, and we were comfortably installed and well-fed on American Army ration scale. Among other well-known people in my block were a number of scientists and industrialists like Messerschmitt and Thiessen, the steel king, general officers such as Guderian, von Leeb, von Blomberg, and Schmidt, the Chief Interpreter of the German Foreign Office. Many of them I was to meet again later in the Witnesses' Quarters of the Military Prison in Nuremberg. This time, however, I remained only a few days in Seckenheim and was then sent to the Witnesses' Quarters in the American zone of the Nuremberg suburb, Erlenstegen.

After all the discomfort and fatigue of many moves into various camps and prisons, the small villa in Erlenstegen, with its pretty little garden, seemed like paradise. I was asked for, and gave my parole that I would not leave Nuremberg, but was otherwise to wander at will round the town. The Americans had seized my very considerable archives in Munich, but in the process the card index had been lost or destroyed, and I was ordered to sort everything out and make a new list. Although the Munich office had contained only a fraction of my archives, there were never- theless many thousands of photographs, taken over a period of thirty years and more, all in hopeless disarray, and the sorting and listing was a long and wearisome business. Each morning I was fetched by a jeep and had to report to the International Military Tribunal, which had set up its headquarters in the

Ministry for Justice, and once this formality was over, I was free to do what I liked.

The trial before the International Military Tribunal lasted for a whole year, during which a very great number of witnesses were called. These, of course, had to be provided with quarters for the period of the stay in Nuremberg, and for this purpose two large villas had been requisitioned by the Allies in Erlenstegen, a suburb on the north side of the city.

From October 1945, onwards the comings and goings round these villas were reminiscent of the busy activities of a beehive, as an endless stream of witnesses, mostly for the prosecution, came and, having said their piece, again departed; and here for the first time I came in contact with people who had for many years been opponents and enemies of Hitler – diplomats, Generals, members of the July 1944 conspiracy and so on, some of whom I had already met before, without having had the least idea of their political convictions or activities.

Early in 1946 my wife succeeded in slipping illegally (no private travelling being at the time allowed) from the Tyrol into Bavaria. Once she had arrived, the Bavarian authorities allowed her to stay, in order that she might look after her ailing father in Epfach, Upper Bavaria. From there she seized every opportunity of paying me a quick visit, wherever I happened to be for the time being; at last she succeeded in renting a tiny room in Munich itself, and from then onwards the whole aspect of my life changed.

She was allowed to visit me as she liked in Munich and, when the second bed in my room was not required for one of the many witnesses who were constantly coming and going, she was even allowed to spend the night with me. Her courage and loyalty, her sense of proportion and, perhaps most important of all, of humour were of immense help to me, both then and much more so later, when I was handed over for 'de-nazification' to the far less considerate Bavarian authorities. All I could do at the time in return was to give her a goodly share of my American rations and thus solve some of her material preoccupations; but I shall never forget how deeply indebted I am to her, and my gratitude will remain with me as long as I live.

We all messed together and after the evening meal we would foregather in the ante-room for a cup of coffee and to listen to the broadcast commentary of the day's proceedings in the court, given over the German radio by Gaston Ulman, who had been appointed as sole commentator by the occupation authorities. In contrast to the independent foreign broadcasts, and particularly that of the Swiss radio network, Ulman's commentary was always much less objective and caused a great deal of controversy; it was, too, a strange feeling to sit there and listen to the recording of the evidence given earlier in the day by some of those who were now quietly sipping their coffee among us.

Some of the witnesses remained only a day or two, while others were required to stay for weeks and even months on end. Almost every grade of intelligence, every station of social life and every shade of political opinion found its representatives among them, and though we lived a completely communal existence, one subject by tacit consent was absolutely taboo, and politics were never, under any circumstances, discussed among us. For three weeks, for instance, I sat almost daily next to Severing, the well-known Social Democrat Minister for the Interior, but the word '*politik*' was not once mentioned by either of us.

The longer the trial lasted, the more colourful and variegated became the company of witnesses. Galician Jews in kaftan and strange robes, wild swarthy Bohemian and Hungarian gipsies mingled with such prominent ex-prisoners from the Concentration Camps as Dr Eugen Kogon, the author of *The SS State,* Dr Hans Luther, the former Chancellor of the Reich, Dr Pelzer, the famous Olympic runner, Colonel Friedrich Ahrens, who was accused by the Russians of having perpetrated the terrible murders of Polish officers at Katyn Camp, and General Erich von Lahousen, one of Admiral Canaris' principal officers and many others whom it would be tedious to enumerate.

General Lahousen was particularly vehement in his accusations against Göring and was again and again subjected to examination and cross-examination. He gave the impression of living under great nervous strain, particularly on the last day when he appeared, under escort, for his last cross-examination. In the evening, with the General among us, we all heard this cross-examination, which was given verbatim on the radio, and this did lead to a lively discussion on the whole trial.

The long and involuntary intimacy in which we were compelled to live gave rise to a considerable measure of friendly companionship among us. There were many who were greatly interested in art and music, and for those fortunate ones the time passed quickly in lively and entertaining discussion. Dr Michael Skubl, the Chief of the Vienna Police before the Anschluss, and a most charming and cultivated old gentleman, frequently read some of his own very excellent poems to us and organised poetry competitions among us. When he left, my wife was particularly sad, for to have been able to talk of Vienna, the scene of her happy childhood and young womanhood, had been like a breath of fragrant and fresh air to her.

Other witnesses were destined to meet with tragic fates. Professor Karl Haushofer, the eminent geographist, was a great personal friend of Rudolf Hess and was the only man who was allowed to visit Hess in his cell – a privilege he owed to the high esteem, as a man and a scientist, in which the Americans held him. His description of his visits to Hess given with the stark, almost macabre precision of the scientist, made a deep and horrifying impression on us. Hess had not recognised his friend and former teacher, but had presented a wild and terrifying picture of insanity. Only for one brief instant did he appear sane, when Haushofer pulled from his pocket a photograph of Hess's son and showed it to him. His long imprisonment, the nerve-racking cross-examinations, the confiscation of his property were loads too heavy for Professor Haushofer to bear; he took a fatal dose of poison, and his wife hanged herself.

One day Nikolaus Horthy, junior, arrived, looking very well and smart in rough tweed coat and a brightly-coloured silk scarf. He had come from Rome to give evidence on Hungarian affairs and was a most animated conversationalist and always most gallant to all the ladies. His father, the Hungarian Regent, was at that time in the witnesses' wing of the Nuremberg prison, where all the more senior officers, diplomats and officials in captivity had been housed.

There were also many women among the witnesses. Among them was Frau Elizabeth Strünk, whose husband had been hanged by the Gestapo for his share in the July 1944 plot. A slightly-built, quiet woman of middle age, dressed always in sombre clothes, Frau Strünk was the only woman to whom the details of the July plot had been at the time confided and on her face the traces of the Gestapo hospitality she had enjoyed were grimly and indelibly marked.

One mysterious woman who was brought in by the Americans at dead of night was an intriguing puzzle to us all. Day after day, week after week, she sat silent and apart, reading or knitting the whole time. At first we thought she must be a spy, planted rather clumsily in our midst; but her obvious distress at the surroundings in which she found herself and the constant expression of grief and bewilderment on her face seemed – unless she were a consumate actress – to refute the idea. Suddenly she disappeared as quietly as she had come; and later we found out that she had been the victim of mistaken identity, arrested in the place of someone of a like name.

On another occasion a young man arrived, dressed in a shabby suit and carrying a down-at-heel little suitcase. 'Streicher junior,' he introduced himself. He had come for but one night in order to take farewell the next morning from his father, before he was executed.

Very few were the witnesses who appeared for the defence. Among them was the Swedish industrialist, Birger Dahlerus, who bore witness on Göring's behalf. This cultured and kindly

Swede objected very strongly to being placed under guard, but when it was explained to him that the guard had been furnished for security reasons and as an escort for a neutral witness, he rather grudgingly withdrew his objection. Göring, he said in a long and detailed statement, had come to his country house in August, 1939, in order to meet six British politicians and had then said that he would do everything in his power to save the peace, and particularly to ensure that there was no war between Germany and Britain.

Witnesses, as I have said, came and went, but Hoffmann stayed on. For a year and more I was involuntarily in the very midst of the events that immediately followed the collapse of Germany. The charming young Hungarian refugee countess, who had been appointed as housekeeper by the Americans, used to call me the senior of her resident guests, and to me it is a pleasing thought that many of the important men, when taking leave of me, were good enough to thank me for the unfailing good humour I had always displayed and to say that, all political opinions apart, Hoffmann and his jokes would remain as a happy interlude in an otherwise grim and tragic duty.

There is one dramatic episode that I shall never forget. That was when, on the 20th October 1946, I sat with my daughter in front of the radio in my room, awaiting the broadcast of the sentences passed by the Nuremberg Court. Never, in the long course of historic and dramatic scenes of which I had been a witness, have I ever experienced such minutes of intense drama and anxiety. Tensely my daughter and I sat, motionless and silent before the softly crackling set.

'The court is now re-assembling,' said the announcer, 'for the President to read out the findings and sentences of the court.'

'... Guilty ... sentenced to death by hanging ...' as one after the other, the fateful verdicts were read in measured, emotionless and solemn tones, our nervous tension became all but unbearable.

'Baldur von Schirach' – for an almost intolerable few seconds, as if his attention had been distracted by some movement in the court, the President paused; then –

'Baldur von Schirach,' he repeated, 'Imprisonment for twenty years!'

'Thank God,' gasped my daughter, at the end of her tether. 'Thank God! at least he lives!'

Nor was the final episode of my year's stay in the Witness House a very pleasant one. One evening a new arrival joined us at table, introducing himself as Dr Schmidt. Over coffee, I exchanged a few inconsequential words with him, as was customary with a newcomer. Immediately afterwards this rather silent man dressed in sombre black left us, giving an evasive answer to the question as to whether he would be coming back. The next day my wife paid me a visit.

'This,' she said, pointing to a photograph in a newspaper she had brought with her, 'is said to be the famous Dr Schmidt. Do you know him?' Then we all recognised him. 'Dr Schmidt' was none other than the then Prime Minister of Bavaria, Dr Wilhelm Högner, who had been required to be present as the representative of the Bavarian Government to witness the execution of the war criminals, which had taken place the very night before.

The next day I reported, as usual, to the American authorities. A most unpleasant surprise awaited me. The Premier of Bavaria, I was told, had repeatedly demanded that I be handed over for trial by the Bavarian De-nazification Court; now that I had completed my task on my archives, the Americans felt that they could neither retain me in custody nor offer me any longer the asylum of the Witnesses' Quarters. I was released by them and immediately re-arrested by the Bavarian Government and it was then that my real sufferings in captivity began. Injustice at the hands of an enemy is easier to bear than injustice at the hands of one's own kith and kin; of the former I had experienced but little; under the latter I am suffering still to this day.

As soon as I was released by the Americans, I had, of course, to relinquish my room in the Witnesses' Quarters, and although a good friend in Munich offered to put me up, the Bavarian authorities refused to allow me to accept the offer and flung me instead into the local prison. For the first few nights I shivered in an icy cell, and then thanks to the efforts of a kindly disposed warder, I was transferred to a smaller cell, but one that had, at least, a stove in it. By sheer force of character my wife succeeded in getting permission to pay me a brief occasional visit, and then, just before Christmas I was transferred to Munich. In the eyes of the authorities I was, apparently, regarded as a desperate character, and I was taken from the prison to the station heavily manacled, by tram, much to the indignation of many of the other passengers, who expressed their opinion of this bit of unnecessary barbarism in no uncertain terms. The journey to Munich was undertaken in a special prison carriage attached to the train, in which I travelled alone with my two warders. In Munich I was put into the remand section of the notorious Neudeck prison, where I remained for several weeks, sharing a cell with two others, accused of very different crimes to my own alleged misdemeanours.

The Bavarian authorities decided to make a *cause celèbre,* a real showpiece and example, of my case. Herf, the Government attorney and prosecutor in the case, refused to give my wife any information whatsoever. She knew I had been moved from Nuremberg, but where I had been taken, when and where the case against me would be heard, what steps she could take to assist in my defence, they refused to tell her. At last, through the good offices of a fellow prisoner who was released, I was able to let her know where I was, and forthwith to Munich she followed me. In spite of the strictest measure to ensure my isolation, my wife managed with her customary skill and courage to get in touch with me and bid me be of good cheer. More than that even her forthright energy could not accomplish. 'Even the greatest criminal has a right to prepare his defence,' she declared, and she demanded that the lawyer whom she had enlisted on my behalf should forthwith be allowed to see me. But it was of no avail; the authorities turned a deaf ear to her repeated efforts, and it was only two days before the case against me was heard – far little time in which to produce witnesses or documentary evidence – that my lawyer was allowed to see me. But as the result was a foregone conclusion, before even the case came on, it didn't really make much difference.

The farcical proceedings lasted for three hours. There were no witnesses either for the prosecution or the defence. Most of the period was occupied by a long accusation, interspersed with assumptions, annotations, hints and presumptions by the prosecuting counsel. My own lawyer's demand for time to gather material and witnesses for the refutation of the charges brought against me was curtly refused, and on 31st January 1947, sentence was passed upon me: 'Ten years in a prison labour camp, confiscation of all property, withdrawal of all civic rights and prohibition to practise any profession on release.'

I remained in Neudeck prison until the beginning of March and was then sent to the camp in Moosburg.

There were about ten thousand of us in Moosburg camp, where we lived in large, barrack-like huts. The food was just about as bad as it could be. Once a month we were allowed three-quarters of an hour's conversation with visitors; but the visitors' room was one large barrack, down the entire length of which ran a table. From the centre of the table, up to the ceiling and along its whole length was stretched dividing wire-netting, and we prisoners sat cheek by jowl on one side and our visitors on the other. In the clatter and clamour of voices it was almost impossible to carry on any conversation; and when my wife sat on the table in order to come a little closer, she was at once told it was not allowed.

I must digress for a moment and pay tribute to the utter un-selfishness of the women who visited their imprisoned menfolk. Even though they as often as not had nothing for themselves and their children to eat, they invariably brought something as a gift – even if it were only potato peelings.

Many of the prisoners spent their time making toys and shoes out of any old remnants they could find; these they handed over to their dependants in the hope that they could sell them and buy food for themselves.

While these visits were a godsend for us, they often entailed great hardship for our devoted visitors. The trains on visitors day were absolutely crammed, the walk from the station to the camp was a long and wearisome one, and then the visitors had to queue for hours while permits were scrutinised and parcels examined, before they were allowed to enter the Visitors' Barrack. All this on top of the sorrowful nature of the pilgrimage made great demands on our faithful womenfolk.

Later on, conditions improved a little, and the visits were no longer restricted to the precise three-quarters of an hour prescribed. The population around the camp, too, were very kind and did all they could to help the prisoners, bringing them such food as they could spare and even sometimes a drop to drink. I know what I'm talking about; and believe me there is no finer Schnapps in the world than the drop that is unexpectedly smuggled in to you! So life continued for a whole year, during which my wife was a tower of strength to me in every way. Only much later, after I was finally released did I get any glimmering of all the difficulties that beset her; but during my imprisonment not a word of complaint ever passed her lips.

My mainstay during this time as a pastime was sketching and drawing caricature, many of which I 'sold' to the subjects thereof for a cigarette or two. But best of all I liked to sit and write long letters to my wife – a luxury I had never had time to enjoy during the Nazi régime, when most of my correspondence was restricted to a card with a few cryptic letters: D E! L a K! H. (which meant Dear Erna, Love and a Kiss! Heini).

At the end of a year I was transferred to Dachau of evil memory, where I earned promotion in the criminal hierarchy: I was set to work in the X-ray department of the camp laboratory, and as my health was pretty poor, I was allowed also to live in the laboratory. I managed to get hold of an electric stove, and many were the cups of coffee (!) my wife and I brewed and enjoyed together.

For six months, during which time most of the other prisoners were released, all went – in the circumstances – well; then, at the end of June 1948, the camp was taken over and reconstructed as a refugee camp, and I was transferred to a building in Munich that had previously been a detention prison for coloured American defaulters. Here the accommodation was primitive in the extreme, and our quarters consisted of barracks with a triple tier of wooden bunks and some rather musty old straw mattresses. But there were great compensations; our families could visit us every afternoon and stay until it became dark, and we were allowed to sit in the courtyard in the open air – a wonderful feeling, even though we were behind barbed wire! And very soon not only relatives but also a limited number of friends were occasionally allowed to come and see us. It all seemed too good to last.

It was. Shortly before Christmas, without warning we were loaded into lorries and taken to Langwasser camp, near Nuremberg. The constant moves and the separation from my wife had left a serious mark on me, and this was the last straw. I had a nervous breakdown when told to pack, I tried to gash open a vein with a razor blade, and struggled desperately against being put into the lorry. As a result I was sent, not to Langwasser, but to the observation ward of a psychiatric hospital. The same day my devoted wife was there and managed to pacify me. But the idea of spending the night in this lunatic asylum was more depressing to me even than the thought of Langwasser camp, and very soon I was released from observation and sent to Langwasser.

The few short weeks I spent in Langwasser camp, in which I was put in the hospital ward, were by no means as disagreeable as I feared. My good wife faithfully followed me to Nuremberg, whence she frequently visited me, bringing food, books and flowers and did much to help me over the barbed-wire fixation that had gripped me.

And so to my next and last prison, the internment quarters in Eichstätt. Although we were now internees and not prisoners, and we consequently enjoyed many more privileges, we could not get away from the prison atmosphere, for the building in which we were housed was in fact the Eichstätt prison. And although our cell doors remained permanently open, although we could foregather when and where we liked, the tiny windows high up in the cell walls allowed neither a ray of sunshine to enter or a glimpse of the world outside; and this, I found, was even more depressing than my dreaded barbed-wire.

During all this period of my imprisonment and internment, I had been fighting my case on appeal. In the first instance the original sentence was confirmed; but on further appeal it was reduced to four years labour camp, confiscation of eighty per cent of property and restitution of civic rights. To this a special rider was added that the titles of Official Photographer, Professor, Town Councillor, Holder of the Party Insignia in Gold, were not regarded as incriminating in any way in the assessment of my case. At this second appeal thirty-five witnesses were called in my defence and over a hundred documents were produced, sworn statements mostly from people who had been persecuted on political or racial grounds by the Third Reich and whose lives I had saved or whose liberation from concentration camps had been thanks to my intervention.

Christmas, 1949, and the New Year passed, thanks to the forethought of my dear wife, who brought me a tiny, decorated Christmas tree, as an almost happy interlude, and then, at long last, on 4th February 1950, I was released and was once more a free man.

For a long time after my release I desired nothing more than to remain static, in full enjoyment of the sole, all-important fact that I was once more a free man. The tremendous pace at which I had lived for twenty years and more, the fears and anxieties, the hardships and deprivations, both physical and moral of captivity, the shock not only of losing by confiscation all that I had possessed, but also of being precluded from any activity in which, even at my age, I might hope to make a fresh start to earn my modest daily bread – all these things have combined to take a heavy toll of me. But here, the sturdy Bavarian peasant stock from which I spring, has stood me in good stead; for a considerable time I suffered from violent headaches and insomnia, and my heart was not as sound as it might have been. Gradually, with the assiduous devotion of my wife, I have regained at least a good measure of my former physical robustness, until now, I think, I am as well and as fit as a man of my age has a right to expect. Mentally, I confess, I have had enough; I want no new experiences, I need no new impulses; I am content to sit back in peace.

Although on second appeal the court ruled that twenty per cent of my possessions and fortune were to be restored to me, the authorities are still considering to what, exactly, that twenty per cent amounts; one day – soon, I hope – a decision will be reached and the amount, whatever it is, will be paid to me. Meanwhile, the Bavarian Government has made me a provisional advance, which suffices for our modest needs until the financial case is finally settled.

In these circumstances a goodly measure of philosophical retrospection is inevitable. One thing that has struck me most forcibly is the profound truth of the old proverb and tag: 'A friend in need is a friend indeed.' It was only after my release that I extracted, bit by bit, the full story of the sacrifices and hardships endured by my dear wife on my behalf – the selling of her modest collection of jewellery, her furs, her clothes and anything else of value she possessed in the ceaseless struggle to obtain money – money for the endless journeys she made in order to visit me in all the various camps and prisons; money with which to buy, often at the most cruelly exorbitant prices of the black market, a few cigarettes and gifts with which to comfort me; and money to keep at least a roof over her own head and provide herself with the barest minimum essentials for herself to keep body and soul together. And on the other side there are the many 'friends,' who in former times had had good reason to be grateful to us and had always been only too eager to keep in our good graces. But in the hour of need not one came forward voluntarily with an offer of material help or even with a word of encouragement to my wife, but passed, like the Pharisee, on the other side of the road; and my wife, I am glad to know, was too proud to beg from those, who felt no sense of compunction or obligation.

Looking back, I see a full and interesting life behind me. I rose steadily and prosperously in my profession during the zenith of my country's greatest days; I lived through her eclipse in the first war, her resurgence between wars, and at the storm centre of the events that led to her final collapse and disintegration. I amassed great wealth in my time and lived well and free from all care; and I have lost all I possessed. My profession has taken me all over Europe – to England, France and the Netherlands, to Italy, Greece and Russia, and through every corner of Germany and the old Austro-Hungarian Empire; in the course of thirty-odd years, by plane, train and car, I have covered well over a million miles; many of the most famous monarchs, princes and commoners of my times have posed before my camera, and the total number of photographs taken by myself and my assistants in my various branches all over Europe must be in the region of two to two and a half million. In short, I have lived and lived well and have survived with but little hurt.

There is, too, much to be thankful for. Ten years have now passed. My son, Heinrich, is well on the way to following in father's footsteps and is making a success both as a press photographer and as a publisher; my daughter, who has divorced her husband, Baldur von Schirach, is now happily occupied in the film industry, and her children are completing their courses of study in the professions they have chosen.

And I myself? I have no plans. I am more than content to sit at modest peace and rest with my wife in the circle of my artist friends, with a glass of good wine to warm our hearts.

I have long since ceased to practise photography, and the last of my cameras was traded in the immediate post-war years with some peasant or other in exchange for a few articles of food. The man from whose side I scarcely stirred for nearly a quarter of a century lives on in my memory. History, of which I was permitted to perpetuate a few fragments on my films and plates, has marched on along its predestined path, oblivious of the fate that overtook him.

But later, when a few pictures are pulled out, to be shown as documentary evidence of this buried piece of European history to those future generations that were not there to live through it, then among them will be some truly historical photographs, ghostly transfixed fragments of history, perpetuated by a man named Heinrich Hoffmann.

Index

for sweetmeats, 46; physical and mental condition (April, 1945), 227–8; plans art gallery, 182–3; 'pilgrims' visits, 192–3; predicts Roosevelt's death, 135–6; prepares 9th November putsch, 54–5; prepares 'Operation Sealion,' 123–5; rages of, 216, 227–8; reactions at news of Churchill's Cairo visit, 210–11; reactions to talks on separate peace, 215; rebuilds Nazi Party, 61 ff.; receives foreign ambassadors, 89; rejects astrology, 135–6; released from prison, 60–1; re-models Chancellery, 198–9; respect for British statesmen, 88–9; shows emotion at French capitulation, 121; sixth sense of, 137–9, 152; speaks on radio, 69; speaking tour of (1923), 53 ff.; supports Church against Bormann, 131; supports Zabel-System, 190; teetotaller, 201, 202–3; underground quarters of, 207; vegetarian, 72, 186, 199; veneration for Geli Raubal's memory, 155–9; visited by foreign statesmen, 77–8; visits Exhibition of Degenerate Art, 173–4; visits Munich Art galleries, 170 ff.; visits Venice (1934), 88

Hitler, Alois, 146, 147
Hitler, Paula, 146, 147
Hitler Youth, *passim*
Hoepner, 208
Hoffmann, Erna, 73–5, 97–8, 100–1, 115, 150–1, 190, 219, 221–23, 231, 237, 243–4, 245, 247
Hoffmann, Heinrich, *passim;* appeals against sentence, 247; arrested by Americans, 232; as Hitler's companion, 41 *passim;* as Hitler's photographer, 41 *passim;* as photographer, *passim;* as photographer in London, 27–8; at Nuremberg Trials, 236–42,

early life of, 16–41; friendship with Hitler, 41 *passim;* gives parole (1945), 236; imprisoned at Seckenheim, 236; imprisoned at Eichstätt, 247; in Augsburg camp, 236; in Dachau, 245–6; in England, 27–8; in Langwasser camp, 246; in Moosburg camp, 244–5; in Neudeck Prison, 243–4; in Stadheirn Prison, 235; interrogated by American Intelligence, 232–4; joins Nazi Party, 41; on Russian Priority List, 233; on trial in Bavaria, 243–5; released from prison, 247; sentenced, 244; travels with Hitler, *passim*

Hoffmann, Heinrich, Jun., 50, 223, 249
Hoffmann, Henriette, 34, 50, 130, 190, 191, 241–2
Hoffmann, Lelly, 28–9, 33, 49, 50–1
Högl, Commissioner, 223
Högner, Dr Wilhelm, 242
Homburg, 22–5
Hoppé, E. O., 26–7
Horthy, Nikolaus, 240
House of German Art, Munich, 171 ff.

Innitzer, Cardinal, 132

Jodl, General, 209, 224

Kahr, Herr, 55, 56
Kannenberg, 102
Kathyn camp, murders at, 238
Kaulbach, F. August, 198
Keitel, Field-Marshal, 121, 124
Kempka (Hitler's chauffeur), 229–30
Knirr, Professor, 25, 30–1, 47
Koestring, General, 105–6
Kogon, Dr Eugen, 238
Kurz, Dr, 125